CYBERLAW

CYBERLAW
Legal Principles of Emerging Technologies

Jeffrey A. Helewitz, JD, LLM, MBA

Consulting Editor
Athena Group, Inc.

PEARSON
Prentice
Hall

Upper Saddle River, New Jersey 07458

Library of Congress Cataloging-in-Publication Data

Cyberlaw : legal principles of emerging technologies / Jeffrey A. Helewitz
    p. cm.
  Includes index.
  ISBN 0-13-114287-9
  1. Computers—Law and legislation—United States. 2. Computer networks—Law and legislation—United States. 3. Internet—Law and legislation—United States. I. Title: Cyber law. II. Helewitz , Jeffrey A.
KF390.5.C6.C927 2004
343.7309'944—dc22

2003064759

Editor-in-Chief: Steve Helba
Director of Production and Manufacturing: Bruce Johnson
Executive Editor: Elizabeth Sugg
Managing Editor—Editorial: Judy Casillo
Consulting Editor/Composition: Athena Group, Inc.
Editorial Assistant: Cyrenne Bolt de Freitas
Marketing Manager: Leigh Ann Sims
Managing Editor—Production: Mary Carnis
Manufacturing Buyer: Ilene Sanford
Production Editor: Denise Brown
Design Director: Cheryl Asherman
Design Coordinator/Cover Design: Chris Weigand
Cover Image: Bek Shakirov/Stock Illustration Source
Cover Printer: Phoenix Color
Printer/Binder: Banta Book Group/Harrisonburg, VA

Pearson Education LTD.
Pearson Education Singapore, Pte. Ltd
Pearson Education, Canada, Ltd
Pearson Education–Japan
Pearson Education Australia PTY, Limited
Pearson Education North Asia Ltd
Pearson Educaçion de Mexico, S.A. de C.V.
Pearson Education Malaysia, Pte. Ltd

10 9 8 7 6 5 4 3 2 1

ISBN 0-13-114287-9

CONTENTS

Chapter One

INTRODUCTION TO CYBERLAW

Chapter Overview

Exactly what is meant by the term "cyberlaw?" As a general working definition **cyberlaw** can be viewed as the legal doctrines and principles that apply to the operation and development of computer technology and the Internet. Because of the rapid advance of technology during the twentieth century, what once had been viewed as science fiction has become a circumstance of everyday life. The proliferation of the new technology has demanded rapid legislative and judicial responses to resolve legal problems of the emerging technology.

Historically, new law has been created by applying arcane legal principles to new situations as problems arose. For example, when air transportation first became commercially feasible and injuries occurred due to this new form of transport, there was no readily available body of air and space law. To resolve these new problems the judiciary applied existing legal doctrines dealing with maritime law to the air, thereby forming the basis of modern air law concepts. As this body of law grew, specific laws, both legislatively and judicially created, were developed to address these new legal issues. In this same manner, modern jurists are expanding traditional legal concepts to the new computer technology and the legislatures are proposing specific statutes designed for cyberspace legal problems.

Because cyberlaw, at this point in time, is a continually developing area that is attempting to keep pace with the expanding technology, this text can only provide an overview of the legal *principles* that form the current body of cyberlaw. As the twenty-first century opened, a survey was conducted among the legal community to arrive at a consensus as to what are the most important unresolved legal issues facing the cyberlaw practitioner. Their responses form the basis of this text:

1. *Jurisdiction*—because the Internet and each website has worldwide impact, the problem of jurisdiction and choice of law becomes paramount in determining how cyberspace can be regulated. Is a website operating in the United States subject to legal process and potential censure in a country on the other side of the world because one of that country's citizens has been legally injured? If so, how could the website operator be able to meet the legal standards of every country, and how could any judgment be enforced?

2. *Constitutional issues*—the United States Constitution, either directly or by judicial interpretation, affords persons subject to U.S. jurisdiction certain rights with respect to privacy, free speech and property. However, these guarantees are not universally afforded by all nations. How can the United States preserve and implement these Constitutional protections for its citizens when a problem involves other nations where such rights do not exist?

3. *E-business*—simply, an **e-business** is a commercial enterprise that operates primarily or exclusively on the Internet as its "place of business." In this context problems arise with respect to cash and credit payments for purchases made over the web, creation of contracts requiring signatures and writings, security issues with regard to supplying personal information, as well as security fraud issues dealing with financing the enterprise. What is the legal obligation of the e-merchant to customers?

4. *Property rights*—because almost all activities on the Internet involve copying information, problems arise with respect to protecting the rights of an intellectual property right holder. What are the rights and protections granted the holder of a copyright, patent or trademark with such online activities as framing, acquiring domain names, downloading literature and so forth?

5. *Criminal activities*—the term **cybercrime** has garnered a vast amount of media attention. It concerns the use of computers and computer technology to injure others by violating societal norms of behavior. Can laws and enforcement policies be developed to protect persons from criminal injury caused by computer use?

Each of these identified topics will be discussed in turn in the remainder of this text. However, this chapter is designed to provide a general overview of the technology and the existing regulation of cyberspace that establishes the parameters of this emerging area of law.

Development of Cyber Technology

The **Internet** refers to computer interaction. The term **network** refers to the various functions that are available to an Internet user such as e-mail, chat rooms, and the World Wide Web that can be used to connect information and business from user to user. Originally, the Internet started as **Arpanet**, a United States government program developed in 1969 that was designed to enable records maintained by the Defense Department to connect with and share information with researchers and agencies around the world. Some of the Arpanet **sites**, or information locations, were designed to provide nondefense specific information. Arpanet eventually became the Internet, and Arpanet itself ended in 1990. The following year the World Wide Web was developed to add commercial centers to what was originally a governmentally restricted program.

The specific technology associated with the Internet is beyond the scope of this text, and probably beyond the specific interest of the reader. However, a few basic concepts should be analyzed to provide a background for the legal doctrines that form the body of law called cyberlaw.

Information system is the term generally given to all methods of storing, maintaining, and retrieving information. More specifically, it has come to mean the use of computers to store, process, and retrieve data. There are three main types of computers in general use—the microcomputer, the minicomputer, and the mainframe.

Microcomputer

The microcomputer is commonly referred to as a notebook or laptop. It is the smallest type of computer. The microcomputer either operates on its own or may be connected to other computers to share information and peripheral devices such as printers and modems. Computers that are connected together become a **network**. A network of microcomputers is known as a **local area network (LAN).** The computers in the LAN are called nodes or workstations. In a peer-to-peer LAN, a workstation can access information stored on any of the other workstations in the LAN. In a client-server LAN, each workstation has access to the information stored on the computer controlling the LAN, called the file server.

Minicomputer

A **minicomputer** is a mid-size computer either used as a stand-alone unit, a file server for a microcomputer LAN, or as the main computer in a network that consists of the minicomputer and display terminals. A minicomputer is usually referred to as a personal computer or P.C. A display terminal has only a **keyboard** and a **monitor**. Display terminals are completely dependent on the computer controlling the network and cannot function or store information independently. Minicomputers are generally capable of performing functions faster than microcomputers, but a minicomputer network with display terminals is more vulnerable than a microcomputer LAN. In the event of a failure of the main computer, a minicomputer network ceases to function. In the case of a microcomputer LAN, however, a failure of the main computer still leaves each workstation with a fully functioning stand-alone computer.

Mainframe

A mainframe is the largest type of computer, typically able to store large amounts of data. It is organized in a network configuration with display terminals or microcomputers at each workstation. Access is usually controlled by the use of **passwords**, specific words or symbols that permit the user to enter the computer or specific information areas.

Computer Hardware

Computer hardware is the term used to describe the physical components of the computer system. Hardware can be divided into three main categories:
1. hardware used to process and store information
2. hardware used to input information into the computer, and
3. hardware used to receive information from the computer.

The system unit is the physical unit that houses the majority of the computer's hardware. It contains the computer's main memory, its processor(s), its secondary memory storage devices such as hard disks and drives for diskettes, magnetic tapes, CDs, and DVDs, and its communication devices such as a modem.

Main Memory

Main memory in the computer consists of **ROM** and **RAM**. ROM and RAM are located on chips in the system unit. ROM—"read-only memory"—is the memory that stores instructions for the computer that have been placed on the chips by the manufacturer. It is read by the computer and cannot be written to.RAM—"random access memory"—is the workspace that is available to hold programs while they are being used and documents that are being created. RAM is temporary memory and is erased when the computer is turned off. To save documents and data, they must be stored on some type of secondary memory device such as a **magnetic disk**. The amount of RAM contained within the computer determines how many programs and documents that may be opened simultaneously.

Secondary Memory

Secondary memory is where information is stored. Most of the computer's information will be stored on an internal magnetic disk. This magnetic disk is often called the "hard drive" and will store the programs that are used on the computer and any documents that are created using the computer. Portable magnetic disks are used to store documents and software files outside of the computer. These portable magnetic disks can be removable hard disks or CDs. These devices are inserted into a drive in the system unit being used.

Input Devices

Input devices are items of computer hardware that are used to place information into the computer. The original input device was the **punched card**. Holes were punched into the cards to represent the instructions to the computer. The cards were then stacked and run through a card reader to input the information. The most common input devices used today are the **keyboard** and the **mouse**. The keyboard consists of alphabetic and numeric keys, cursor movement keys, special command keys, and function keys. The function keys are used with software programs to activate the programs' features. A mouse consists of a roller bail that moves the position of an arrow or other indicator on the screen. As the user moves the mouse, buttons on the top of the mouse can be pressed to activate features. Other devices that are similar to the mouse are the **trackball**, **touchpad**, and the **integrated pointing device**. These devices are mainly found on notebook computers. A trackball looks like an upside-down mouse. The user moves the ball with the fingers and selects items with the trackball's buttons. A touchpad is a pad that is sensitive to a person's touch. Moving a finger across the touchpad will move the pointer on the screen. Tapping the touchpad or pressing a button will select items. An integrated pointing device looks like the head of a pencil eraser. It is moved like a joystick to move the pointer on the screen. Buttons are then used to select the items pointed to.

Other input devices in common use are scanners, bar code readers, touch screens, and devices capable of recognizing speech and handwriting. **Scanners** are used to scan documents into a word-processing program for editing or to capture the image of a document onto an optical disk. **Bar code readers** are used to scan bar codes that are used with a bar coding system. **Touch screens** are special monitors that recognize the touch of a finger or an electronic pen.

Output Devices

Output devices are pieces of hardware that are used to communicate the results of the computer's processing to the user. The most common output devices are monitors. Monitors resemble a television screen and are sometimes referred to as "cathode ray tubes" (CRTs) and "video display terminals" (VDTs).

If the user wishes to have the accessed information written on paper—what is known as a "hard copy"—a printer may be used to print the document. There are two categories of printers in current use. The first are impact printers in which the characters appearing on the screen are "typed" onto a piece of paper in a manner similar to a typewriter, with some part of the printer impacting the paper. Impact printers include dot matrix and daisy wheel printers. The second are nonimpact printers. With nonimpact printers, the printer's hardware does not physically impact the paper. Nonimpact printers include laser and inkjet printers. Nonimpact printers are faster than impact printers.

Communication Devices

Communication devices are used to contact a computer from a remote location, access electronic mail (e-mail), and access online services and databases. The most common of these devices is the modem. The modem translates the digital signals of the computer into analog signals that can travel through the telephone lines. The modem in the receiving computer translates the incoming analog signals back into digital signals.

Online services have greatly increased the amount of information that is readily available to computer users by giving them access to the Internet and worldwide databases. Online capability means that the user can be connected to an increasing network of websites and individuals. However, linking to some networks may create a problem with unwarranted access to files, resulting in breaches of confidentiality and other ethical concerns. (See Chapters Three and Six)

Computer Software

Computer software consists of the instruction codes that run the computer's hardware. Computer software can be divided into four categories:
1. computer languages
2. operating systems
3. utility programs
4. applications.

Computer languages are the language codes used to write the other three categories of programs. Operating systems manage the storage, utilization, and movement of files on the computer system. An operating system is necessary in adding computer programs to a computer. Operating systems include Unix, DOS, Windows 95, 98, or 2000, OS/2 Warp, and System 7 for the Macintosh. Utility programs are pieces of software that enhance your computer system. Utility programs include screen savers, virus scanners, and undelete and unformat programs. Applications are software programs graphs, and colors. This use of the computer is more effluent and cost-effective than paying an outside printing service.

Database Management Software

Database management software is used to manage large amounts of data. A **database** is an organized collection of related information. There are two main types of databases: summary databases and full-text databases. A **summary database** is one that utilizes a digest or abstract of the information stored. An example of a summary database would be a local telephone directory. A **full-text database** stores the complete text of a particular document. **Imaging databases** can fall into either category of databases. Imaging databases are used to store an image of a document or photograph on an optical disk. When the image is scanned onto the optical disk, a summary database can be used to record the document number, title, date, and other specifics about the document. If a full-text database program is available, the full text of the scanned documents can be stored on a separate disk.

In order for a person to access information on the Internet, he or she must have a computer that has a **modem** connection to a telephone line, either landed or cellular. Modem is simply the term for the physical device that provides such access. To connect with Internet, the user must use the services of an **Internet service provider** such as America on Line (AOL) that acts as the middleman between the user and the Internet.

Example: *A student wants to find out which texts his school library has on a subject that he is researching. He uses his computer to sign on, or access, his service provider that will then connect him, by means of his telephone line that is connected to the computer by means of the modem, to the Internet. Once on the Internet, the student can then access his school's website.*

Each computer that is linked to the Internet is provided with a unique address, called an **Internet protocol**. This Internet protocol identifies the user in the same fashion that a unique corporate name identifies a particular company, and is used to communicate with that company. In this fashion the computer user, once linked to the Internet, can simply type in the domain name of the website he or she wishes to access, and the connection between the user and the site is automatically made. A **domain name** is a word or group of words that identifies a particular website. A **website** is a location on the Internet.

Example: *A student wants to purchase a book by using her computer. She uses the computer to connect with the website of Pearson Prentice Hall to view its titles. To connect with this website, she types in the Pearson domain name prenhall.com.*

Every domain name also includes a sub-level domain name as a suffix, the letters that appear after a dot (.). The sublevel domain names used in the United States are:
1.   com, for commercial sites
2.   gov, for government sites
3.   net, for networks
4.   org, for organizations
5.   edu, for educational sites

Further, each country is assigned its own sub-level domain name, such as US for the United States, which is used to **link**, or connect, with sites originating in countries other than the one in which the user is located.

In order to ensure that a network was compatible with other networks it was necessary to develop a standardized format so that every computer would be able to retrieve desired data. This can be analogized to having one universal form of electrical outlet so that an electrical appliance can be plugged in anywhere in the country. To generate such universal access to information by means of the computer, **hypertext markup language (HTML)** was created as a universal document format, and **hypertext transfer protocol (HTTP)** was developed as the method whereby such documents could be transferred over the World Wide Web. Older readers may remember having to type the letters "http" at the beginning of domain names addresses to connect with sites; nowadays all computer programs automatically include these letters when the world wide web is accessed by typing the letters www. Many domain names now no longer require typing "www" because it is the universal access code.

Example: *Originally, to access a website, the user had to type in the following protocol: http.//www.prenhall.com. Today simply typing "prenhall.com" may access such site.*

Very simply, to access the Internet and the World Wide Web, a computer user just follows these steps:
1.   Turn on the computer.
2.   Move the **cursor** (arrow appearing on the screen) to the user's Internet provider.

3. When the Internet provider's name is highlighted, the user clicks on the **mouse** (presses down on the device used to move the cursor around the computer screen) which starts the process of connecting the provider to the Internet by means of the modem.
4. The Internet provider's logo appears on the screen and the user types in the information that the provider requires to identify the user and to provide services.
5. The user is then connected to the Internet.
6. In the designated space the user types in the desired website and presses the "enter" key on the keyboard, and the site is accessed.

This overly simplified scenario has now provided the background for the legal problems whose resolutions form the remainder of this text:

1. How are the user and the technology protected from unauthorized and unwelcome intrusions?
2. Which authority has the jurisdiction to adjudicate and regulate such intrusions?

Regulation of Cyberspace

As will be discussed in detail in the next chapter, regulation of cyberspace is one of the most complex and challenging problems facing the cyberlaw professional. **Cyberspace** is the term generally employed to refer to the transmission of information over the Internet. Because no one person, organization or entity "owns" cyberspace, its regulation is, at present, subject to myriad conflicting regulations enacted by individual states, by statutes passed by separate sovereign countries, and international treaties entered into by the international community.

The Internet was arguably designed as a means whereby academics and scientists could interact all over the world to provide a free exchange of information. However, with the growth of the commercial private use of the Internet, certain problems have been identified with respect to security and use.

In order to regulate cyberspace, the regulatory authority must be able to enforce its policies against those persons or institutions that violate its dictates. However, since jurisdiction is typically geographically limited, and cyberspace is worldwide, it is virtually impossible for one entity or state to regulate cyberspace unless the violator has some nexus, either personal or property based, with the regulator.

To overcome such jurisdictional problems, over the past decade many countries have entered into treaties to provide both uniformity and jurisdictional authority over the regulation of cyberspace. Such treaties deal with jurisdiction, intellectual property rights, security, privacy and criminal activities, and will be discussed in turn throughout the text. However, at this point in time such regulation of cyberspace is virtually nonexistent.

Chapter Review

The advent of the Internet, coupled with the proliferation of private computer use, has created an emerging area of law referred to as cyberlaw. Cyberlaw principles and doctrines address the problems associated with the use and dissemination of computer technology. Because such technology is so new, traditional legal principles must be adopted to new uses until legislators create statutes that are specifically designed to deal with this emerging area of legal endeavor.

The term "Internet" refers to the method whereby computer users can exchange information by means of computer technology all over the world. Information appears in what is referred to as a site, and the computer user accesses the site by means of an Internet provider. Once accessed, all information stored on the site is accessible.

The Internet originally was developed as part of a United States Department of Defense program designed to provide bureaucrats and academics with access to defense and nondefense information. However, with the continued growth of the commercial use of the Internet, numerous legal problems associated with such use have been identified. These identified problems concern the usurpation of property rights by means of using a computer, the operation of business over the World Wide Web, the application of constitutional principles to Internet use, and the potential for criminal activity to be effectuated by means of computer technology.

In order to address these problems, various states and countries have attempted to formulate some regulatory legislation. However, because the Internet is universal, the effectiveness of such regulation is dependent upon the regulatory authority's ability to gain jurisdiction over the presumptive offenders. Further, it becomes necessary in order to regulate such a universal medium that all governments agree to apply the same regulations.

The remainder of this text will discuss each of these problems as jurists, legislators and practitioners alike attempt to formulate legal policies to deal with cyberspace legal problems.

Key Terms

Arpanet—Original version of the Internet developed by the Department of Defense

Bar Code—Method of reading information

CD-Rom—Compact disk read-only memory

Cursor—Arrow appearing on a computer screen

Cybercrime—Crimes committed by means of computer technology

Cyberlaw—Legal principles dealing with cyberspace regulation

Cyberspace—Transmitting information by means of computer technology and the Internet

Database—Organized collection of information

Disk—External method of storing information

Domain Name—Unique identifier for a particular website

E-business—Commercial activity operated over the Internet

Full-text Database—Device that stores the complete text of a document

Hardware—The physical components of a computer

Hypertext Markup Language (html)—Universal language so that all information input into a computer can be shared with other computers

Hypertext Transfer Protocol (http)—Universal method of effectuating communication between computers by means of the Internet

Imaging Database—Device used to store images

Impact Printer—Output device that prints data onto paper like a typewriter

Input Device—Method of placing information into the computer

Integrated Pointing Device—Input device that resembles a pen

Internet—Method of transmitting information by using computer technology

Internet Protocol—Method of linking computers for information transmission

Internet Service Provider—Entity that provides the link between an individual computer and the Internet

Link—Access

Keyboard—Input device that resembles a typewriter

Local Area Network (LAN)—A network of computers

Mainframe—Largest type of computer

Microcomputer—Smallest type of computer

Minicomputer—Personal computer

Modem—Device to link a computer with a telephone line to provide Internet access

Mouse—Input device

Network—Group of linked computers

Nonimpact Printer—Type of printer that does not physically impact the paper

Output Device—Device used to communicate the results of the computer's processing

Password—Code used to access a computer's databases

Personal Computer—Minicomputer

Punched Card—Original input device

RAM—Random access memory

ROM—Read only memory

Scanner—Input device for documents and images

Secondary Memory—Place in computer where information is stored

Summary Database—Database that uses an abstract of the information stored

Site—Where information data is stored on the Internet

System Unit—Physical unit that houses the computer's memory

Touch Screen—Input device activated by human touch

Touchpad—Notebook computer input device

Trackball—Notebook computer input device

Website—Internet information location

Edited Cases

The following cases are presented to highlight some of the issues facing legal professionals in the area of cyberlaw. The first case, *Island Online, Inc. v. Network Solutions, Inc.,* concerns weighing constitutional rights of free speech against permitting allegedly obscene domain names being registered. The second case, *Marobie-Fl, Inc. v. National Association of Fire, Fire Equipment Distributors and Northwest Nexus*, discusses various aspects of becoming an expert in the new Internet technology.

Island Online, Inc. v. Network Solutions, Inc.
119 F. Supp. 2d 289 (E.D.N.Y. 2000)

In October of 1999, plaintiff Island Online ("IOL") brought this suit, styled as a sec. 1983 action, against defendants Network Solutions, Inc. ("NSI") and the National Science Foundation ("the NSF") for damages, declaratory judgment and injunctive relief arising out of NSI's refusal to register three Internet domain names desired by IOL. IOL contends that NSI's policy of filtering out certain obscene domain names, coupled with NSI's affiliation with the NSF, a government entity, constitutes a violation of IOL's First and Fifth Amendment rights under the United States Constitution and IOL's rights to freedom of speech and due process of law guaranteed by Article 1, sec. 8 and Article 1, sec. 6 of the New York State Constitution respectively. NSI now moves for dismissal of IOL's complaint and/or summary judgment, and the NSF has moved for dismissal, or, in the alternative, for a more definite statement. Both defendants argue that, even accepting all of IOL's allegations as fact, IOL has no standing to bring suit, and NSI is not a state actor and, consequently, cannot be liable for alleged violations of IOL's constitutional rights. IOL opposes summary judgment and has made a cross-motion to amend its complaint to assert a cause of action under Bivens and to add individual employees of NSI and the NSF as defendants. NSI and the NSF oppose the motion to amend, maintaining that any amendment would be futile.

Background

1. The Internet and the Cooperative Agreement

The "Internet" is a worldwide system of computer networks and individual computers that are interconnected by communications facilities. See Decl. George Strawn P4 [hereinafter "Strawn Decl."]. The antecedents of the Internet were systems for two relatively small groups of research-oriented governmental, academic and corporate entities—ARPANET and NSFNET. *See id.* P5. ARPANET received its principal support from the Department of Defense and related agencies, while NSFNET's support came from numerous sources, including the NSF and other federal agencies, academic institutions and corporate sponsors. *See id.*

Under a system first implemented on the ARPANET, each entity connected to the Internet is assigned one or more unique numeric "addresses" which permit other connected entities to send it communications. *See id.* P11. These addresses, known as "IP addresses," are similar in function to telephone numbers and are written as a series of no more than 12 digits separated by periods (e.g. "204.146.46.8"). *See id.* During the early days of the Internet, IP addresses were maintained and assigned by one individual, Dr. Jon Postel at the University of Southern California's Information Sciences Institute, who performed this task as part of the ARPANET experiment. *See id.* P12.

Later, Dr. Postel's project came to be known as the Internet Assigned Numbers Authority ("IANA"). *See id.* The IANA oversaw the allocation of IP addresses until November 1998, when the Internet Corporation for Assigned Names and Numbers ("ICANN"), a private, nonprofit corporation, was formed and designated as the governing body responsible for IP address space allocation, as well as other Internet-maintenance responsibilities. *See id.*

Because IP addresses could be difficult to remember, network users informally assigned alphabetic names to their own computers, and these names were tracked and associated with their corresponding IP numbers in a file maintained by Dr. Postel and downloaded to the host computers at all Internet sites. *See id.* P13. In 1987, this practice evolved into what is known as the Domain Name System ("DNS") for associating names with IP numbers on the Internet. *See id.* P14. The DNS makes it possible for users to address messages to other users and to Internet-attached computers by name rather than number. *See id.* P15.

The sequences of alphanumeric characters that make up domain names are segmented by periods (*e.g.,* "ibm.com" or "nsf.gov"). *See id.* P16. The segments are hierarchically related to one another. *See id.* The far right segment is called the top-level domain ("TLD"), the next is called the second level domain ("SLD"), and so on. *See id.* In the above examples, ".com" and ".gov" are TLDs; "ibm" and "nsf" are SLDs. *See id.* Each domain name must be unique; it is impossible for more than one entity to register for any given domain name. *See id.* P21.

Whereas TLDs are generic, SLD names are typically expressive of the content and interfaces that one would expect to find on the particular site designated by the domain name. *See Pl.* Island Online, Inc.'s Opp. Mem. at 3 [hereinafter Pl.'s Opp. Mem.]. They are marketing tools designed to appeal to the public at large and a key marketing strategy for many new businesses. *See id.* Many businesses now even trademark their "dot.com" names and use those names to express a message to consumers and to the public. *See id*. The TLD ".com" in particular is intended for use by private, commercial businesses such as IOL. *See id*. at 2.

Since the need for DNS name resolution (conversion of domain names into IP numbers) is constant, it is necessary to maintain and update the DNS database continuously. *See Strawn Decl. P22*. The new domain name information is obtained and disseminated through a process called DNS registration. *See id*. An Internet user who wishes to register a domain name first obtains an IP address to be associated with the desired domain name from an Internet Service Provider or from an IP address registry. *See id*. If the desired domain name has not already been registered in the TLD of the user's choice, it can generally be registered on a first-come, first-served basis. *See id*.

The TLD zone files are replicated at 13 different locations (including NSI) known as the "root server system," but the master root server is maintained by NSI in Herndon, Virginia, pursuant to the Cooperative Agreement detailed below. *See id*. PP24-25. The other 12 root servers obtain the daily updated domain name information by copying from the master root server. *See id*. P25. These other root server operators have no contractual or other legal relationship with the master root server. *See id*. Rather, they have a purely voluntary association with it because of their common interests in a universally resolvable DNS. *See id*.

On January 1, 1993, NSI and the NSF, an agency of the United States Government, entered into Cooperative Agreement No. NCR-9218742 (the "Cooperative Agreement" or "Agreement"). *See id*. P26. Pursuant to the terms of that Agreement, NSI undertook the task of registering SLD names within the generic TLDs of ".com," ".org," ".net," ".edu" and ".gov." *See id*. P27. The NSF's role was not to regulate the administration of the Internet but to provide support for domain name registration. *See id*. P28. The NSF engaged in general oversight of NSI's performance of its responsibilities under the Agreement but not NSI's day-to-day managerial activities. *See id*. Specifically, the Agreement includes the following provisions:

[NSI] has primary responsibility for ensuring the quality, timeliness and effective management of the registration services provided under this Agreement. To the extent that NSF does not reserve specific responsibility for accomplishing the purposes of this Agreement, by either special condition or general condition of this Agreement, all such responsibilities remain with [NSI] . . .

NSF has responsibility for registration services support, support planning, oversight, monitoring, and evaluation. NSF will make approvals required under the General Conditions and, where necessary and appropriate, NSF will contact and negotiate with Federal agencies and other national and International [sic] members of the Internet community to further the efforts of this project.

App. Exs. Supp. Mot. Dismiss by Def. Network Solutions, Inc., Ex. G at 7. In September 1998, responsibility for the Agreement was transferred to the National Telecommunications & Information Administration ("NTIA") of the Department of Commerce. See Strawn Decl. P30. NTIA is now the federal agency that oversees the administration of the Cooperative Agreement, which was due to expire on September 30, 2000. *See id*. PP29-30.

In November 1998, in response to President Clinton's initiative to increase competition in and promote international participation in the DNS, NTIA entered into a Memorandum of Understanding with ICANN to collaborate on the design, development and implementation of the mechanisms that need to be in place to privatize management of the DNS. *See id*. P31. Under the Memorandum of Understanding, ICANN also undertook the responsibility of working with the Department of Commerce to establish the rules for and accrediting of competing registrars to use NSI's Shared Registration System ("SRS") to register domain names in ".com," ".net," and ".org" domains. *See id*. P32. Through the SRS, there is no limit on the number of registrars that may register domain names. *See id*.

On April 21, 1999, ICANN introduced this competition by naming five entities which would compete with NSI in the registration of domain names. *See id*. P33. As of March 16, 2000, NSI was already only one of approximately 35 competitive SLD name registrars (soon to be over 100). See Decl. David M. Graves Supp. Mot. by Network Solutions, Inc. P17 [hereinafter Graves Decl.].

2.   NSI's Registration Process and the Obscenity Policy

NSI is a profit-making Delaware corporation with its principal place of business in Virginia. *See id*. P2. NSI's board of directors and executive officers do not include, nor have they ever included, any members of the NSF or any other governmental agency. *See id*. P3. Nor does the NSF have the right to appoint, approve or confirm any of the directors or officers of NSI. *See id*.

In 1992, NSI responded to a solicitation issued by the NSF for one or more privately-owned and operated "Network Information Service Managers." *See id*. P4. As a result, the company won a competitively awarded Cooperative Agreement to provide, among other things, SLD name registration services in the Internet TLDs of .com, .org, .net, .edu and .gov. *See id*. In connection with these domain name registration services, NSI enters into private, commercial contracts with registrants of domain names. *See id*. P6.

During the initial period of performance under the Cooperative Agreement, NSI received funding from the U.S. government. Beginning September 14, 1995, however, the government funding was replaced with fees, charged to the customers for the provision of registration services, and NSI does not now receive any funding or subsidies for its domain name registration from the federal government. *See id*. P8. NSI presently charges registrants an initial two-year registration fee of $70 and a subsequent one-year registration fee of $35. *See id*. P7. No portion of this fee is presently shared with the NSF or any other agent of the federal government, *see id*., nor has any federal or state government ever acted as either a registry or a registrar of domain names in the .com, .org, .net and .edu TLDs. *See id*. P18.

As a registrar, NSI accepts applications for new SLD names and generally registers them on a first-come, first-served basis. *See id*. P19. If a domain name registration agreement should expire for any reason, such as the registrant's failure to pay for the registration or failure to re-register under the terms of the agreement, NSI deletes the domain name and cancels the contract, at which point the next applicant who creates and applies for the name becomes the new domain name registrant. *See id*. P19. Currently, new SLD names are registered with NSI at a rate of over 500,000 a month, a new one every five seconds, and NSI has registered eight million SLD names to date. *See id*. P20.

As dictated by the volume of registrations, the registration process is completely automated, taking a matter of minutes by computer without any action by anyone other than the prospective registrant. *See id*. P22. Since the registration process is fully computerized, NSI generally has no knowledge of individual registrations, including the circumstances surrounding the registration or even that a particular domain name has been registered. *See id*. P22. Likewise, NSI has no information as to the particular use made of a domain name, and it is entirely at the discretion of the registrant whether the domain name is associated with a website, e-mail, etc. or just reserved for later use. *See id*. P23.

While the registration of domain names is done automatically, NSI restricts the registration of domain names that contain six of the seven obscenities similarly prohibited for broadcast by the FCC and major television networks. *See id*. P31. This practice is implemented through an automatically triggered filter in the domain name registration process. *See id*. P34. The filter blocks the registration of SLD names containing the exact letter strings contained in the restricted words. *See id*.

NSI implemented this policy as a corporate business decision in the summer of 1996. *See id*. P32. Although NSI offered no further explanation of what specific "corporate business" considerations led them to adopt the policy, NSI's vice-president, General Counsel for the NSF and the NSF's program official responsible for oversight of the Cooperative Agreement with NSI all declare that the NSF had no involvement with the formulation and implementation of NSI's obscenity policy beyond knowing of its existence. *See id*. P32, Decl. of Lawrence Rudolph P3, Decl. of Donald Mitchell PP3-4.

Because NSI's policy was not adopted until mid-1996, approximately 42 domain names had been previously registered which contained the restricted words. *See Graves Decl. P35*. NSI did not cancel or otherwise breach the registration contracts with those domain name registrants but rather allowed them to continue. *See id*. However, as these registrations expired or were canceled by the registrants, NSI has declined to register them to a new registrant. *See id*. There are approximately 23 such SLD names remaining in the master database, which were registered by NSI. *See id*. In addition, because NSI's policy has not always been error-free, at times, prospective registrants have been able to obtain an otherwise "filtered" domain name despite the "filter." *See id*. P37. When NSI has been made aware of these violations of its practice within a reasonable time after the registration, the offending registrations have been deleted. *See id*. At the present time, a significant number of the registrars that appeared in the wake of ICANN's introduction of competing registrars on April 21, 1999, do permit registration of the character strings restricted by NSI. *See id*. P36.

3. NSI's Rejection of IOL's Domain Names

IOL, a New York corporation headquartered in Richmond County in the Borough of Staten Island, is in the business of providing adult content to consumers on websites on the Internet. Pl's Opp. Mem. at 1-2. Like most Internet companies, IOL uses the development of websites and the registration of domain names to increase its outreach to the public. *See id*. at 2.

On or around April 3, 1999, IOL attempted to register the following domain names: "fuckme.com," "fuckyou.com," and "cocksuckers.com." *See id*. at 3. At this time, NSI was still the sole registrar of SLD names for nongovernmental individuals and businesses such as IOL. See Decl. of Nicole Watts P5. Before April 1999, there had been 15 prior attempts by unrelated third parties to register the domain name "fuckme.com," 15 prior attempts by unrelated third parties to register the domain name "fuckyou.com" and 14 prior attempts by unrelated third parties to register the domain name "cocksuckers.com." See Graves Decl. PP40-43. Pursuant to NSI's policy of registering domain names on a first-come, first-served basis, the domain names would have been registered to any of these earlier applicants prior to plaintiff's applications if NSI had not exercised the obscenity policy that is the subject of this litigation. *See id*. P44.

In order to register a domain name, Nicole Watts, the Chief Operating Officer of IOL, would follow the same procedure each time: She would log on to the NSI Internet website located at www.networksolutions.com, type in the domain name she sought to register as prompted by the instructions and, if that domain name was not already registered to another entity, execute the online "Network Solutions Domain Name Registration Agreement" and send this agreement via e-mail to NSI. *See id*. P6. On or around April 5, 1999, Watts sent checks on behalf of IOL to NSI via Federal Express in payment for each of the domain names she had sought to register. *See id*. P9. On or around April 8, 1999, each of the checks dated April 5, 1999, was debited from IOL's checking account. *See id*. P12.

On or around April 14, 1999, NSI notified IOL via e-mail correspondences that NSI had declined to register each of the three domain names that are the subject of this litigation. *See id*. P13. Each e-mail offered the following paragraphs as an explanation for such denials:

> Network Solutions has a right founded in the First Amendment to the Constitution to refuse to register, and thereby publish, on the Internet registry of domain names words that it deems to be inappropriate.

> Additionally, Network Solutions' outside counsel has advised us that the Supreme Court of the United States has held that no corporation can be compelled to engage in publication which that corporation finds to be inappropriate. *See id*. After contacting NSI, Watts secured credits for IOL's cashed checks several weeks after having sent them to NSI. *See id*. P17. IOL contacted NSI numerous times via e-mail to request an explanation as to why NSI determined the Domain Names to be "inappropriate" but received no further elucidation. *See id*. PP18-19.

On October 22, 1999, IOL brought suit against NSI and NSF, alleging numerous violations of the United States Constitution and the New York State Constitution and seeking damages, as well as a declaration that NSI's obscenity policy is unconstitutional and injunctive relief awarding the contested domain names to IOL. At the present time, the contested domain names have been registered to third parties unrelated to the litigation through registrars other than NSI that do not have a policy of filtering out the obscenities that appear in the contested domain names. *See Graves Decl. PP46-48*.

Discussion

1. Standing [omitted]

2. State Action

   a. IOL's sec. 1983 Claims

Plaintiff's claims are framed as a suit under 42 U.S.C. sec. 1983, and "sec. 1983, enacted pursuant to the authority of Congress to enforce the Fourteenth Amendment, prohibits interference with federal rights under color of state law." *Rendell-Baker v. Kohn*, 457 U.S. 830, 838, 102 S. Ct. 2764, 2769, 73 L. Ed. 2d 418 (1982). In suits brought under sec. 1983, "'under color' of law has consistently been treated as the same thing as the 'state action' required under the Fourteenth Amendment." 102 S. Ct. at 2769-70.

To support its assertion that NSI is a state actor, IOL relies on a bevy of claimed connections between NSI and the NSF, a federal agency. But, as a threshold matter, sec. 1983 requires action by the state, not by the federal government. See *District of Columbia v. Carter*, 409 U.S. 418, 424-25, 93 S. Ct. 602, 606, 34 L. Ed. 2d 613 (1973), rehearing denied, 410 U.S. 959, 93 S. Ct. 1411, 35 L. Ed. 2d 694 (1973). The proposition that federal actors do not act under color of state law is a well-established one.

John's Insulation is particularly instructive here because the plaintiff there, like IOL here, relied on a government contract between a private defendant and a U.S. agency, the Army in that case, in order to assert state action under sec. 1983. *John's Insulation*, 774 F. Supp. at 158. The Court dismissed the plaintiff's claim because "actions of the federal government or its officers are exempt from the proscriptions of sec. 1983." *Id.* at 161.

But IOL, at best, can claim that NSI is a federal actor, and so it is left without a foothold in sec. 1983. Summary judgment is, therefore, granted with respect to IOL's sec. 1983 claims, and the inquiry as to all of IOL's federal claims would end here but for IOL's proposed amendment of its complaint to include a Bivens action.

b. IOL's Proposed Bivens Claim

Bivens actions are typically analyzed under the same methodology as sec. 1983 claims:

A Bivens action is a nonstatutory counterpart of a suit brought pursuant to 42 U.S.C. Section 1983, and is aimed at federal rather than state officials. By direct analogy to Section 1983, a Bivens action has two principal elements: first, a claimant must show he has been deprived of a right secured by the Constitution and the laws of the United States; second, he must show that in depriving him of that right the defendant acted under color of federal law. For this purpose, the statutory "under color of law" requirement is equivalent to the constitutional doctrine of state action. *Lugar v. Edmondson Oil Co.*, 457 U.S. 922, 929-30, 102 S. Ct. 2744, 2749-50, 73 L. Ed. 2d 482 (1982). Thus, where there has been no state action, a Bivens claim must fail at the outset. *Mahoney v. Nat'l. Org. for Women*, 681 F. Supp. 129, 132 (D. Conn. 1987) (citations omitted); *see also Bordeaux v. Lynch*, 958 F. Supp. 77, 84 (N.D.N.Y. 1997) (dismissing plaintiff's sec. 1983 claims against federal Drug Enforcement Administration officers and proceeding to analyze whether defendants acted under "color of federal law" under Bivens). Because of the analogous state action standards under Bivens and sec. 1983, we can proceed to apply the same state action tests that we would have applied had there been a colorable sec. 1983 claim.

There are four commonly utilized state action tests:

Courts will find state action despite the presence of a private party in four discernible situations. First, state action exists given a "symbiotic relationship" between the private actor and the state. Second, the "nexus test" finds state action when the state commands or encourages the private discriminatory action. A third situation sufficient to support a finding of state action occurs when a private party carries on a traditional public function. Finally, state action is present when the involvement of governmental authority aggravates or contributes to the unlawful conduct. *Air Line Pilots Ass'n v. Dep't of Aviation of the City of Chicago*, 45 F.3d 1144, 1149 (7th Cir. 1995) (citations omitted). The four tests are not absolutely orthogonal to one another, but among them, they thoroughly cover the relevant jurisprudential territory. Since IOL tacitly invokes all four, the Court will go systematically through each, one by one.

The "public function" test is more accurately described as an "exclusive public function" test. *See Rendell-Baker*, 457 U.S. at 842, 102 S. Ct. at 2772. It has been "limited strictly, and covers only private actors performing functions 'traditionally the exclusive prerogative of the State.'" *National Broad. Co., Inc. v. Communications Workers of America*, AFL-CIO, 860 F.2d 1022, 1026 (2d Cir. 1988) (citations omitted). The Supreme Court stressed the limited nature of the public function test in *Jackson v. Metropolitan Edison Co.*, 419 U.S. 345, 95 S. Ct. 449, 42 L. Ed. 2d 477 (1974), where a customer tried to sue a utility company for termination of her electrical service without prior notice or hearing. *Id.* at 346-348, 95 S. Ct. at 451-452. The company, private though it was, held a certificate of public convenience issued by the Pennsylvania Utility Commission, which empowered it to deliver electricity to a service area wherein the plaintiff resided. *Id.* at 346, 95 S. Ct. at 451. The Court wrote:

Petitioner . . . urges that state action is present because respondent provides an essential public service required to be supplied on a reasonably continuous basis by [a Pennsylvania state statute], and hence performs a "public function." If we were dealing with the exercise by [respondent] of some power delegated to it by the State which is traditionally associated with sovereignty, such as eminent domain, our case would be quite a different one . . . . Doctors, optometrists, lawyers, [respondent], and Nebbia's upstate New York grocery selling a quart of milk are all in regulated businesses, providing arguably essential goods and services, "affected with a public interest." We do not believe that such a status converts their every action, absent more, into that of the State.

In fact, the range of activities where private actors were found to be performing traditional public functions is prohibitively constricted, including operating a company town, *see Marsh v. Alabama*, 326 U.S. 501. No traditional public function was found, however, in cases that involved providing workers' compensation benefits or medical treatment to injured workers, *see American Mfrs. Mut. Ins. Co. v. Sullivan*, 526 U.S. 40, 119 S. Ct. 977, 143 L. Ed. 2d 130 (1999), providing nursing home services to Medicaid patients, *see Blum v. Yaretsky*, 457 U.S. 991, 102 S. Ct. 2777, 73 L. Ed. 2d 534, running a private school, *see Rendell-Baker*, 457 U.S. 830, 102 S. Ct. 2764, 73 L. Ed. 2d 418, or operating a utility company, as in Jackson itself. As the Court has said: "The range of government activities is broad and varied, and the fact that government has engaged in a particular activity does not necessarily mean that an individual entrepreneur or manager of the same kind of undertaking suffers the same constitutional inhibitions." *Evans*, 382 U.S. at 300; 86 S. Ct. at 489.

IOL contends that "registration of business names, assumed names, and trademarks, and the granting of a property right are functions that are traditionally the role of the States." Pl.'s Opp. Mem. at 20. "NSI is a state actor acting under color of state law because NSI performs a function that is a traditional role of the State—registration of business names." *Id.* IOL's contentions in this regard are unsupported by the record.

Although the U.S. Department of Defense was indeed an instrumental agent in the Internet's origins, the Internet is, by no stretch of the imagination, a traditional and exclusive public function. For most of its history, its growth and development have been nurtured by and realized through private action. *See American Civil Liberties Union v. Reno*, 929 F. Supp. 824, 832 (E.D. Pa. 1996), aff'd, 521 U.S. 844, 117 S. Ct. 2329, 138 L. Ed. 2d 874 (1997) ("no single entity—academic, corporate, governmental, or nonprofit—administers the Internet."); also *see Cyber Promotions, Inc. v. American Online, Inc.*, 948 F. Supp. 436 (E.D. Pa. 1996) ("no single entity, including the State, administers the Internet").

Moreover, registration of Internet domain names, the focal point of this case, has never been a public function at all. As the D.C. Circuit wrote recently, Congress chose not to require NSF or any other agency of the federal government to register domain names. Simply because NSF might have been able to perform the function does not transform this activity into a government service or thing of value. A recent and novel function such as domain name registration hardly strikes us as a "quintessential" government service, as registrants suppose. Indeed, it was not the government but the Internet Assigned Numbers Authority—headed by the late Dr. Postel at USC . . . that originally maintained host computer name lists. *Thomas v. Network Solutions, Inc.*, 336 U.S. App. D.C. 74, 176 F.3d 500, 511 (D.C. Cir. 1999), cert. denied, 528 U.S. 1115, 120 S. Ct. 934, 145 L. Ed. 2d 813 (2000). "The mass scale registration of commercial domain names has never, never been a Government function, ever." App. Exs. Supp. Mot. Dismiss by Def. Network Solutions, Inc., Ex. J. In light of the facts and the relevant case law, IOL's claim that NSI's registration of domain names is an exclusive public function cannot be maintained.

The "symbiotic relationship" test finds its origins in *Burton v. Wilmington Parking Authority*, 365 U.S. 715, 81 S. Ct. 856, 6 L. Ed. 2d 45 (1961), where a private restaurateur leased space from a state parking authority in a publicly owned building and engaged in racial discrimination in his restaurant. On those facts, the Court held that the state had so far insinuated itself into a position of interdependence with the restaurant that it had become a joint participant in the restaurateur's business enterprise. *Id.*, at 725, 81 S. Ct. at 861. However, the holding of *Burton* was subsequently limited to cases involving leases of public property, *see Jackson*, 419 U.S. at 358, 95 S. Ct. at 457, and "privately owned enterprises providing services that the State would not necessarily provide, even though they are extensively regulated, do not fall within the ambit of *Burton.*" *Blum*, 457 U.S. at 1011, 102 S. Ct. at 2789. The Supreme Court has also confined the Burton fact pattern to cases where the State benefits financially from a private entity's discriminatory conduct. *Rendell-Baker*, 457 U.S. at 843, 102 S. Ct. at 2772. NSI's relationship with the NSF does not come close to satisfying these requirements.

The "close nexus" test requires that "the challenged action of the regulated entity . . . may be fairly treated as that of the State itself." *Blum*, 457 U.S. at 1004, 102 S. Ct. at 2786. The State must have exercised such "coercive power" or have provided "such significant encouragement, either overt or covert, that the choice must in law be deemed to be that of the State." Id. "Action taken by private entities with the mere approval or acquiescence of the State is not state action." *American Mfrs.*, 526 U.S. at 52, 119 S. Ct. at 986. But the NSF did no more than acquiesce—and very tacitly at that—in the NSI obscenity policy challenged by IOL. Moreover, as soon as the domain name registration field was opened to competition by the government, multiple registrars with no obscenity policy entered the market without a word of protest on the government's part. This state of affairs amounts to a level of involvement that is easily insufficient to meet the Supreme Court's formulation of the close nexus test.

IOL attempts to close the gap by citing decisions holding NSI to be a federal instrumentality immune from antitrust liability under the Sherman Act. *See Pl.'s Opp. Mem.* at 14-15. IOL can offer no authority to support its claim that these decisions, some involving glaringly inapposite fact patterns, are in any way related to the requirements of the close nexus test. Furthermore, the Jackson Court has stated explicitly that monopoly status is not dispositive on the close nexus issue:

It may well be that acts of a heavily regulated utility with at least something of a governmentally protected monopoly will more readily be found to be 'state' acts than will the acts of an entity lacking these characteristics. But the inquiry must be whether there is a sufficiently close nexus between the State and the challenged action of the regulated entity. . . . *Jackson*, 419 U.S. at 350-51, 95 S. Ct. at 453. Here there is no such nexus, and so the close nexus test remains unsatisfied. Beyond knowing of its existence, the NSF had absolutely no involvement with NSI's obscenity policy.

Finally, a court could find state action when government involvement in some way contributes to or aggravates the private entity's challenged action, as when a state regulation compels or influences the private actor's alleged Constitutional violation. *See Rendell-Baker*, 457 U.S. at 841, 102 S. Ct. at 2771. It is not altogether apparent that this test is wholly independent from the close nexus inquiry, and the Supreme Court has, at times, treated the two as fungible. *See Jackson*, 419 U.S. at 351, 95 S. Ct. at 453. In any event, where, as here, the challenged action is in no way undertaken at the behest of, under the influence of or for the financial benefit of the State, state action will not be found, even if an "extensive" and "detailed" substratum of state regulation is in place. *Rendell-Baker*, 457 U.S. at 841-42, 102 S. Ct. 2771-72.

Thus, IOL's complaint fails to assert a cognizable basis for finding state action. NSI's obscenity policy is purely private conduct in which the NSF and the relationship between the two entities play no role. Summary judgment for defendants is granted with respect to all of IOL's federal claims.

    c.   IOL's Claims Under the New York State Constitution [omitted]

3.   IOL's Request for Further Discovery [omitted]

4.   IOL's Proposed Amendments [omitted]

Conclusion

For the foregoing reasons, NSI and the NSF's motions for summary judgment are granted. IOL's motion for leave to amend the complaint is denied as futile.

Case Questions

1. According to the court's analysis, how are domain names registered?

2. How does the petitioner argue that state action is involved? Why is that important?

Marobie-Fl, Inc. v. National Association of Fire,
Fire Equipment Distributors and Northwest Nexus
2001 U.S. Dist. LEXIS 4042 (N.D. Ill. 2001)

Plaintiff moves to exclude the testimony of defendant's proposed expert Jerry Saperstein ("Saperstein"). Plaintiff first argues that Saperstein proposes to give opinion testimony as to no less than 29 separate items. Indeed, Saperstein's report seems to support this accusation. In his report, Saperstein opines, among other things, as to:

- The Hyper Text Transmission Protocol and its use in the World Wide Web,

- How computers communicate on the World Wide Web,

- The rated speeds of communication devices in the World Wide Web in comparison to actual speeds,

- The speed with which a file is downloaded,

- The likely behavior of users of such communication devices,

- Internet access provider server logs,

- The nature, use and number of automated agents (robots) on the World Wide Web,

- The frequency of disconnections likely to be experienced while downloading files,

- The number of people who were equipped to access the World Wide Web during the relevant time period,

- The attitude of persons who try to download files from NAFED's web page—the likelihood that such persons actually viewed any downloaded files,

- An analysis of Galactic Firehouse Clip Art as a product,

- An analysis of Galactic's marketing strategy,

- The preferences of the fire protection industry for art,

- The originality of the Firehouse Clip Art,

- An economic analysis of the plaintiff's sales figures and of the price elasticity of plaintiff's product.

The list goes on and on. The above opinions cover such broad and diverse areas of expertise as technical electronic software and hardware issues, the behavior patterns of Internet consumers, Internet marketing strategies and, even, the particular qualities of plaintiff's clip art as a consumer product. Mr. Saperstein has also attempted to give opinions as to copyright infringement and validity issues. Mr. Saperstein appears to have no formal technical training or education to qualify him to give expert opinion testimony regarding any of these topics. His formal education extends to three years of college courses and a high school diploma. He claims relevant experience through his company, FontBank, which publishes fonts or typefaces and as a result of having used a variety of analog clip art collections in the course of completing numerous graphic design projects. He also claims experience as a result of establishing an online electronics store called "Jerry's World, the Electronics Superstore." During the course of this project he claims involvement in investigating the markets for clip art, reviewing dozens of clip art vendors and their wares, negotiating reseller agreements and licenses with them, preparing the visual catalogs of these wares and presenting them for sale in an online venue. He claims to have amassed more than 40,000 clip art images to be distributed electronically through Jerry's World. He is, however, not a trained economist or financial analyst nor does he have any direct experience or training with regard to the fire protection industry. Saperstein claims a significant degree of experience with respect to a variety of computer technology disciplines. In addition, he claims as a result of his activities to be "conversant and familiar with the licensing terms and conditions sought by such entities to protect themselves against allegations of copyright and trademark infringement when licensing such materials from third parties." (Affidavit of Jerry Saperstein, paragraph 6.) This is the type of statement one might expect from a legal expert. However, he does not possess formal education in either computer hardware or software, business or economics, accounting (with the exception of a few lower level college courses) or the practice of law.

The most troublesome aspect of Mr. Saperstein's report is his apparent inability to appreciate and understand his own limitations. He fails, for example, to appreciate that experience in negotiating reseller agreements with clip art vendors does not in and of itself qualify him as an expert in the field. Mr. Saperstein appears to be of the opinion that if he has had experience in the course of his business with any issue involved in the case at bar, he is qualified, by virtue of that experience, to give expert testimony. He is mistaken. Similarly, the fact that Mr. Saperstein has experience in selling and supporting products through online venues including the World Wide Web does not make him an expert on such topics as Hyper Text Transmission Protocol, how computers communicate on the World Wide Web, and the rated speeds of communication devices in the World Wide Web in comparison to actual speeds. Anecdotal experience is not a substitute for training and education—especially in technical fields. Nor is reading computer magazine literature a sufficient basis for testifying as to such technical fields. Mr. Saperstein is not trained in electronics. There is no indication that he understands the technical scientific bases upon which Internet communications function. There is no indication that he has any scientific basis for the technical testimony he intends to present. Indeed, Mr. Saperstein may have seen and experienced much that is relevant to the issues before us, and, he may, with the proper foundation, be allowed to testify as to his own first-hand experiences. However, it is another thing altogether to cloak him with the authority of an expert in such diverse fields, as he seems to claim and allow him, before the trier of fact, to extrapolate general principles and opinions from those experiences without the benefit of formal training and education.

For example, in paragraphs 9 through 14 of his report Mr. Saperstein gives what appears to be a lucid and informative explanation of how sites on the World Wide Web are hosted. He explains and opines on the use and function of the Hyper Text Transmission Protocol, HTTP servers, Internet Presence Providers, and even about the log function in and extent of use of the Apache HTTP server. The problem is that we have no idea upon what basis of knowledge this proposed testimony is founded. There is no indication that Mr. Saperstein has gained this knowledge in a reliable manner and from reliable sources. It was certainly not part of his formal education or training. He has not received a technical education regarding the functioning of the Internet. He is not educated in the scientific principles upon which Internet communications rely. He is not a trained programmer. As far as we know he was not the creator of the Apache Web server. There is no indication as to how he knows what he purports to explain about net servers in general. While it is possible that he has learned a great deal based upon his apparent experience in conducting business matters on the Internet, this is not sufficient for technical testimony. It is one thing to allow a witness to be qualified as an expert on a single narrow topic based purely upon his experience with that topic, it is quite another to allow a businessman, albeit one with substantial experience, to testify as an expert on a wide variety of technical topics including purely technical general software/hardware concepts to specific technical topics about specific programs and Web servers to the number of particular types of Web servers in use today. This court is perfectly capable of reading a magazine article which states that the most popular HTTP server in use today is the Apache server and that it is in use in more than one million installations around the world. This does not, however, provide a sufficient basis for the court to qualify as an expert witness and testify to this as a fact. Yet, when Mr. Saperstein makes the same assertion in his report we are given no source for this knowledge other than his declarations of the vast amounts of business experience he has had in establishing websites and conducting business on the Internet. The problem with evaluating this type of testimony is that it is almost impossible to discern which of Mr. Saperstein's opinions are based on sufficient experience to qualify him as an expert, which are based on no more than the type of shallow and incomplete experience that a businessmen might have with many aspects of the business world with which he deals only in certain limited capacities, and which of his opinions are based on sheer speculation.

It appears that with only three years of college and no further scientific or technical education Saperstein lacks training in and fails to employ the type of rigorous scientific methodology and or academic requirements which would force him to recognize and therefore to limit his testimony and opinions to those areas and facts as to which he has true in-depth expert knowledge. Instead, Saperstein seems to believe that all of his opinions regarding all aspects of clip art on the Internet, the technical workings of the Internet, consumer habits on the Internet and more, qualify as expert opinions. He is mistaken.

This type of testimony is particularly dangerous because it has a great capacity to confuse the trier of fact. Just as Mr. Saperstein seems unable to separate his own areas of true expertise from those in which he is not an expert, so will the trier of fact listening to his testimony have similar difficulties. The result may very well be that the trier of fact will give undue weight to testimony which does not merit the "expert" designation. For example, in his deposition testimony it is clear that Mr. Saperstein has undertaken to analyze and evaluate the merchandising and marketing of Galactic Software, including the media in which they advertised, the method of advertising, the size and content of their ads, their promotional policies and even a comparison to competitors. He even undertook, by conducting his own review of websites, to evaluate the use and scope of clip art products by entities in the fire protection industry. This is quite an undertaking for a person who lacks a degree in marketing or statistics. It is also quite an undertaking for a person who has no knowledge that we are aware of as to the fire protection industry. Mr. Saperstein describes his review of the use of clip art products by the fire protection industry as "visiting a number of websites that were put up by fire departments, both government-owned if you will and volunteer; by fire fighting fans; by fire fighting or fighter-related equipment manufacturers trying to see what the use and scope of use of the clip art products were." But, how can we be sure that this "visiting a number of websites" constitutes a valid survey which would yield reliable results? The answer is, of course, that we cannot. In fact the record does not establish that Mr. Saperstein knows what statistically significant results would be, or that he employed any scientific methodology whatsoever in doing his survey; or even, for that matter, that he realizes the need to do so when conducting a survey upon which an expert opinion will be based. Insofar as we know Saperstein has no training whatsoever in constructing surveys. Nor, apparently, did he consult with experts in the fire protection industry prior to undertaking this survey and analysis, as a true expert witness would likely have done. He apparently did not consult or even include in his survey any professional associations in the field. He did not send out questionnaires to fire departments around the country. Why would local fire departments not be a prime source of information regarding the demand for this type of clip art? Indeed, there is no indication that he has the technical expertise to construct a representative sample of such departments to survey. In fact, he employed no questionnaires at all. Clearly his review of websites does not qualify as a survey of a representative sample of potential consumers of plaintiff's product. He employed no protocol and gives no scientifically defensible basis for limiting his source of information to a review of websites and or magazines. Yet, based upon this research he purports to give an expert opinion.

In his deposition testimony of January 11, 1999, at pages 379-380 when being questioned about the scientific basis for one of his opinions, Mr. Saperstein states, "Again, I believe that based on my forty years' experience in marketing that I can confidently make that statement; and that few people with even a shred of common sense and a reasonable degree of intelligence would argue it." From this testimony it is impossible to determine whether his "statement" is based upon specialized knowledge he has gained from forty years of experience, or from his own common sense and intelligence. While opinions based upon common sense and intelligence may be admissible, they would be admissible as lay opinions, not as expert opinions, which should be based upon specialized knowledge beyond that of the ordinary common sense and intelligence that the average trier of fact possesses. This testimony highlights the difficulties that allowing Mr. Saperstein's testimony would present. He clearly fails to differentiate between his opinions which are based upon any specialized knowledge he may have which is beyond the average person, and his own common sense personal observations which do not qualify as expert testimony. And so will the trier of fact face similar problems in evaluating his testimony as Mr. Saperstein slips back and forth between expert opinions and his own personal "common sense" opinions. The ultimate result will be that the record will be contaminated with lay opinions cloaked with the heightened weight and prestige of expert testimony—with opinions which may truly be based upon specialized knowledge born of experience side by side with [*13] those that have no sufficient scientific or other reliable basis—no basis at all other than Mr. Saperstein's common sense.

At page 373 of the same deposition when queried about the scientific methodology he used in obtaining information from which to arrive at a conclusion Mr. Saperstein states, "In the course of learning, which is something I do every day, I talk to a number of people, particularly people in my business; and we compare notes on how we're achieving market penetration of our products. And over the course of a number of years I had spoken to people who also operate small software publishing companies faced with a lack of capital, a lack of personnel, a lack of time; and we have discussed various methods that we've used to promote sales and their effectiveness . . . ." He goes on at page 379 to explain, "If you asked me today to go out and build a bibliography of articles and books that say the same thing or to compile a list of marketers who agree with me, fine. You pay me. I will do it just for you. However, this conclusion is based on my experience of forty years in marketing . . . ." A true expert witness, one schooled in rigorous academic and scientific methodology, would have compiled and thoroughly studied such a list of articles and books authored by and published in reliable sources before venturing an opinion. Instead, Mr. Saperstein relies upon a series of anecdotal conversations with other businessmen. We have no idea whether such associates were involved in undertakings sufficiently related to the fire protection industry to form an appropriate basis for reaching conclusions which would be relevant to the case at bar. Nor do we know whether they were involved with products sufficiently related to the product at issue to warrant considering their experiences and conclusions. Nor, do we know, without the requisite research of articles and books and surveys which Mr. Sapperstein appears to regard as an afterthought, whether such a group of associates forms a representative sample from which a reliable conclusion may be drawn. Mr. Saperstein obviously believes strongly in the correctness of his conclusions. And, indeed, his conclusions may be correct; but so too might a wild guess. We cannot allow wild guesses to come in as expert testimony on the chance that they may be correct. Nor can we allow Mr. Saperstein's years of experience as an excuse or substitute for an appropriately reliable and verifiable basis for his proposed expert opinions.

For the reasons given above plaintiff's motion to exclude the testimony of Jerry Saperstein is granted.

Case Questions

1. How does the court address the question of the qualifications to give expert testimony?

2. Why was Mr. Saperstein not permitted to give his opinion as an expert?

Exercises

1. Determine whether your own state has enacted statutes specifically designed to regulate cyberspace.

2. Use the Internet to access your state governments' website.

3. Briefly discuss what you believe to be the area of greatest concern with respect to cyberlaw.

4. List the websites that you personally use the most frequently.

5. Briefly discuss some cyberlaw problems that you think may be faced by a law office's use of a computer and the Internet.

6. What restrictions, if any, do you believe should be placed on the use of Internet?

7. Which political subdivision do you feel is best equipped to regulate the Internet? Why?

8. Briefly outline the history of the development of the World Wide Web.

9. What training do you think would be necessary to make a law office "computer literate?"

10. Which types of property rights do you see being affected by the Internet?

Related Websites

Thomas.loc.gov
Findlaw.com
Lawyertool.com

Chapter Two

JURISDICTION

Chapter Overview

The rapid growth of technology and the Internet has demanded that legal professionals re-examine and re-evaluate traditional legal principles with respect to their application to jurisdictional problems associated with cyberspace. Briefly stated, **jurisdiction** refers to a court's (or other legal entity's) ability to adjudicate a particular matter and have its decision enforced against the party who is found liable. Traditionally, jurisdiction has been based primarily on geographic boundaries, those boundaries establishing the extent to which a law may be imposed and the ability of a tribunal to enforce its decision. However, because the Internet may be considered physically present anywhere in the world where a computer user can access a site, new rules and applications have had to be developed to keep pace with modern realities.

The Internet created a global jurisdiction because each website may be accessed anywhere in the world. Because of this borderless impact, the law must determine whether an action that takes place on the Internet is controlled by the law of the country in which the site is located, where the Internet provider is situated, where the user is resident, or whether an entirely new jurisdictional base should be created exclusively for cyberspace.

This chapter will examine the traditional concepts of legal jurisdiction and how these doctrines have been applied, both domestically and internationally, to cyberspace.

Jurisdiction Defined

A particular court may only consider a legal problem if the court has the authority to adjudicate that type of matter. This authority is referred to as jurisdiction. The concept of jurisdiction includes two separate legal questions: whether the court has the ability to hear the type of problem brought before it, known as **subject matter jurisdiction**, and whether the court has the ability to enforce its decision over the parties to the lawsuit, known as **personal jurisdiction**.

Subject Matter Jurisdiction. This type of jurisdiction addresses the court's ability to grant the type of relief sought by the allegedly injured party. Each court's jurisdiction is established by statute (or treaty on an international level, to be discussed below) and, as a basic tenet, neither the court nor the parties may **waive**, or decide to overlook, a court's subject matter jurisdiction. Pursuant to American law, questions relating to the subject matter jurisdiction of a particular court may be raised at any time during the judicial process, even for the first time at the appellate level.

Example: The Constitution of the United States grants exclusive jurisdiction to the federal courts to determine matters regarding patents. A lawsuit based on a patent infringement was filed in a state court and the plaintiff prevailed. On appeal, for the first time, the defendant questioned the state court's ability to hear the matter. The appellate court agreed that the state court lacked subject matter jurisdiction to determine patent disputes, and the case was dismissed.

The threshold question involved in instituting any lawsuit is the determination of which court has the appropriate authority to hear the matter. If the initial forum in which the lawsuit was instituted lacks subject matter jurisdiction, the lawsuit may either be dismissed by the court or removed to the appropriate court by motion of the parties. A **motion** is a request to the court that the court take a particular action. If the court that adjudicated the matter lacked the authority to hear that type of case, its decision may be declared null and void.

Example: A company has copyrighted and marked its logo (see Chapter Five) with the federal government in Washington, D.C. The company uses the logo as the opening page of its website. Recently, another company has started using a logo that is confusingly similar to the copyrighted and marked one for its own web page, and the company files suit in the state court in which the alleged wrongdoer maintains its business. Because the subject matter of the lawsuit involves a federally regulated issue, the state court may lack the authority to entertain the problem.

However, even if the court does have the legal ability to hear the type of dispute brought before it, it may still lack the ability to enforce its decision unless it has jurisdiction over the parties.

Jurisdiction Over the Parties. **Personal jurisdiction** refers to a court's ability to have its judgment enforced against the parties to the lawsuit. This type of jurisdiction is usually only applied to the **defendant** in the lawsuit, the person or institution that has been alleged to have committed a wrongdoing. Because the **plaintiff**, the person who institutes the lawsuit, has voluntarily requested the court to intervene, it is presumed that the plaintiff has accepted the court's jurisdiction over it. Unlike subject matter jurisdiction which can never be waived, personal jurisdiction may always be waived by the parties.

In order to acquire jurisdiction over the parties, three separate bases may be applied by the court:

1. **in personam jurisdiction**: this type of jurisdiction over the parties refers to the court's authority over the actual person of the defendant. Generally, most courts are empowered to exercise in personam jurisdiction if the defendant meets any of the following criteria:

   a) the defendant is physically present in the geographic boundaries of the courts' jurisdiction. Be aware, however, that most courts will refuse to apply this basis of authority over the defendant if the defendant was **fraudulently induced** to enter the state by the plaintiff just so the plaintiff could acquire jurisdiction, or if the defendant is only in the state voluntarily to appear as a witness in another judicial or quasi-judicial proceeding.

Example: To acquire jurisdiction over a defendant, a potential plaintiff calls the defendant who lives in a neighboring state and tells him that his wife has been in an accident in the plaintiff's state. The defendant rushes to the hospital where the plaintiff has told him his wife was taken, and in the emergency room the plaintiff has the defendant served with papers. Because the defendant was fraudulently induced to enter the plaintiff's state, the court lacks in personam jurisdiction over the defendant.

   b) if the defendant is **domiciled**, which means that he or she is permanently resident in the state, that court automatically has jurisdiction.

Example: A corporation is incorporated and has its principal place of business in Ohio. Even if it has offices around the world it can be sued in Ohio, which is where it is deemed to be domiciled.

    c)   if the defendant is doing business in the area of the court's jurisdiction on a regular and continual basis, the court may be able to exercise jurisdiction over it. This method of acquiring personal jurisdiction raises a host of questions with respect to Internet uses. As stated in the Chapter Overview, Internet use is global, meaning that a website owner may be considered to be "doing business" everywhere in which the site may be accessed. It is this method of obtaining personal jurisdiction over a defendant that has caused the greatest concern with respect to applying traditional jurisdictional principles to cyberlaw.

    d)   most courts have what it referred to as **long-arm jurisdiction** over a defendant if the defendant transacts any business within the court's geographical area of authority, or commits any tortious act that has an effect in such area. This basis of jurisdiction may be used even if such act has only occurred once, unlike the requirements for acquiring jurisdiction by doing business as discussed above, which must be of a continuing nature.

Example: A website owner publishes a defamatory statement about a resident of Missouri. A couple in St. Louis accesses the website and sees the defamatory statement. This isolated incident may be sufficient to permit the Missouri courts to exercise long-arm jurisdiction over the website owner.

    e)   the defendant, by contract, may agree to the jurisdiction of a particular court.

Example: In its encryption contract, a business based in Los Angeles agrees to submit any dispute to the jurisdiction of the courts in Delaware where the encryption company is incorporated. The California company has expressly agreed to be subject to the jurisdiction of the Delaware courts.

    f)   if the defendant uses the courts of a given state, it is considered that the defendant has agreed to submit to that state's jurisdiction. This theory is based on the assumption that if one seeks an advantage, he or she may be subject to obligations as well.

    g)   if the defendant actually answers the allegations appearing in the complaint without challenging the court's personal jurisdiction over him or her, he or she is considered to have waived any objection to the court's jurisdiction.

2. **in rem jurisdiction**: this refers to a court's ability to adjudicate disputes over property physically located within the geographic boundaries of its authority. Although the basis of acquiring this jurisdiction is usually limited to physical property, it may be possible to assert that cyberspace is physically present within such boundaries, especially if the issue is coupled with some property located within the state.

Example: Two people are disputing the ownership of a domain name. Because the title to the domain name is in question and the name may appear in cyberspace within a given jurisdiction, it is conceivable that it might be able to be litigated in any state.

3. **quasi-in-rem jurisdiction**: this type of jurisdiction grants a court authority to hear a dispute if the defendant has property in the state, even if it is not the property that is the subject of the lawsuit, which may be used to satisfy the plaintiff's claim. Quasi-in-rem jurisdiction is rarely asserted.

Example: A U.S. retailer has purchased computers from a German manufacturer, and the contract has been breached. The German manufacturer maintains a bank account in Chicago. The retailer may be able to sue the German manufacturer in Chicago based on the bank account which can be used to satisfy the claim.

Once it is determined that the court has jurisdiction, the person must be served with the initial pleading to commence the lawsuit. This notification to a person that he or she is being sued is referred to as **service of process**. Each jurisdiction, as well as the federal courts, has its own rules with respect to the appropriate method of serving a party to a lawsuit. In order to meet these requirements, the person who initiates the lawsuit must follow the statutory requirements of the court where the matter will be heard. This is true even if the subject matter of the litigation involves a question of cyberlaw. Therefore, the rules followed by the particular court must be analyzed to determine the correct method of service.

It should be noted that more and more courts are permitting parties to file court papers, including the initial pleadings on-line rather than in person. At the present time, the bankruptcy courts are requiring on-line filings, and many government agencies, such as the Securities and Exchange Commission, also require or permit electronic filing to reduce paperwork and promote efficiency.

The foregoing represents the traditional theories of jurisdiction that apply to adjudicating a matter in the courts. It is these theories that are now required to be applied to the problems emanating from the increased use of cyberspace.

Domestic Jurisdiction

The determination of a court's jurisdiction under American law is dependent upon the application of the due process clause of the United States Constitution. **Due process** requires, in jurisdictional terms, that persons be protected from being forced to be a litigant in a lawsuit unless it can be determined that the person at least had some connection with the forum so that the application of the court's jurisdiction will not offend traditional concepts of substantial justice and fair play. Consequently, the traditional principles discussed above with respect to obtaining jurisdiction must be shown to meet this due process standard when applied to problems involving cyberspace. All individuals who are engaged in electronic business, generally referred to as **e-business**, are entitled to these constitutional guarantees, as well as any other particular safeguards that the company enjoys under the law of the place in which the company is physically located.

Civil Jurisdiction

Civil law refers to those matters in which a private individual, or group of individuals, has been injured by another person's actions. The concept is based on preventing injury to particular persons. In contrast, **criminal law**, which will be discussed in the next section, involves injuries to society at large.

As discussed above, the primary area of jurisdictional concern with respect to cyberlaw involves a court's ability to acquire jurisdiction over a defendant who transacts business within the geographic boundaries of the court's authority. In this context, a website may be divided into two distinct categories: passive and interactive. A **passive website** is one that only transmits information and does not sell a product or service online. An example would be a web page that may be accessed without paying a fee that is created by a bar association to provide general information to the public regarding new laws. An **interactive website**, by contrast, is one that actively solicits business such as a clothing company that creates a website to sell its products. Theoretically, it might be considered a due process violation if the owner of a passive website is sued in a court in a location in which it is not actually physically present except for the fact that its web page has been accessed by a resident of that state. To distinguish between active and passive websites, several cases have established basic criteria to be examined to determine whether a court can constitutionally obtain jurisdiction over a website owner:

- Some courts have held that the operation of a website in conjunction with a toll-free telephone number that appears on the web page may be sufficient for a court to assert its long-arm jurisdiction over the e-business. However, be aware that this method of determining long-arm jurisdiction is not universally applied, and some courts have reached a contrary conclusion, stating that simply posting an 800 number on a web page is insufficient to establish a business transaction within the state.

- If an e-business does solicit business but limits its solicitation to a particular geographic location where the business is physically located, the use of its telephone number may not necessarily be considered sufficient business contact to grant a court jurisdiction over the company. In this instance the mere fact that a consumer may be able to access information about a product on the Internet does not mean that such business is being actively solicited.

- Whenever a website is established to conduct a business, it is considered that the business is merely putting its products in the stream of commerce. To establish long-arm jurisdiction, something more must be demonstrated to form the basis of a court's jurisdiction:

  1) to meet the standards of due process, it must be shown that the e-business conducted a present business in a manner that has some actual contact with the forum state, and

  2) the method by which such jurisdiction is obtained does not violate constitutional concepts of fair play. To avoid violating this concept, it must be shown that there is a statutory basis for the court's exercise of jurisdiction.

Example: *A Delaware travel agent working for a New York client accessed a Florida company's database for information regarding local car rentals. In an ensuing dispute over payments, the Florida company attempted to have the Florida court assert jurisdiction over the Delaware travel agent. The court could refuse because, based on these facts, exerting such jurisdiction might offend traditional notions of fair play.*

In this context, the determination of jurisdiction may be based on the contract between the e-business and the consumer. If the contract can be totally executed over the Internet, it may be considered that the e-company transacted business in the forum state. Conversely, if the contract must be signed off at the physical location of the e-business, jurisdiction may be more questionable. Therefore, the ultimate determination of a particular state's jurisdiction over an e-business usually devolves to a factual question analyzed on a case-by-case basis.

Criminal Jurisdiction

Criminal law involves acts that injure society as a whole, not just an individual citizen. A detailed discussion of **cyber crime**, crimes committed by means of the Internet and/or computer technology, appears in Chapter Six. This section of the text will only examine the jurisdictional bases that may be used by a court to punish a cyber criminal.

The concept of cyber crime jurisdiction first gained interest in 1996 when a California couple was convicted in a Tennessee court on an obscenity charge. The case, *United States v. Thomas*, 74 F. 3d 702 (6th Cir. 1996) concerned a website created and published in California that provided a database of questionably pornographic materials. Under judicial doctrines, whether or not a particular item is obscene must be determined by the standards of the community in which the material is shown or distributed. Under California law according to community standards, the material on the database was not considered to be obscene.

A family in Tennessee accessed the web page, viewed the material, and found it offensive. They subsequently filed an obscenity complaint in Tennessee. The Tennessee court held that even though the California court had not found the items pornographic, and it conceded that under California standards the material was not obscene, the appropriate standard in this instance should be that of Tennessee where the material did offend community standards. The jurisdiction of the court was based on the end-use, not where the material was created. The access and ability to print out the material in Tennessee gave Tennessee the ability to assert long-arm jurisdiction as well as the ability to apply Tennessee law.

Recently several states have enacted specific statutes to address the question of cyberspace jurisdiction in criminal actions. In these jurisdictions the State Attorney-General's Office provides warnings on the official state web page regarding which crimes may be subject to state criminal law jurisdiction if engaged in on the Internet. To avoid potential jurisdictional questions, these states have created statutes that specifically exert long-arm jurisdiction to activities accessed in cyberspace that have an effect within its borders. This legislative approach to jurisdictional problems may be viewed as the wave of the future with respect to cyber jurisdiction.

International Jurisdiction

Special legal problems are encountered whenever jurisdiction is attempted to be asserted over foreign nationals. Not only must the procedures of the forum state be met, but the legalities of the foreign defendant's own country must also be addressed. To resolve these issues, many nations have entered into specific treaties to determine jurisdiction and applications of legal doctrines. The most recent of these treaties, the **Convention on Cybercrime**, was enacted on November 23, 2001, and its text appears as Appendix A. These treaties attempt to create a consensus among its signatory nations to provide a unified doctrine regarding cyber jurisdiction.

Generally, American courts, when attempting to exert jurisdiction over foreign nationals absent a specific treaty on point, use a three-pronged test to ascertain whether jurisdiction may be asserted:

1. whether the foreign national knowingly and purposefully directed its activities to an American market or availed itself of the protection of American law. If so, the first test has been met.

Example: *A European company knowingly disparaged an American corporation's products on its website. The American company wants to sue the European company in an American court. If the court finds that the statement was geared to the American market and that the European company was hoping to obtain contracts with American consumer, the court may decide to assert jurisdiction over the European defendant.*

2. whether the foreign national actually has a presence in the forum country. This can be met if the defendant was soliciting business in the forum state.

3. whether the assertion of jurisdiction meets the constitutional standards of fair play and substantial justice. To answer this question, several factors must be analyzed:

   a) the extent of the defendant's activity in the forum state

   b) the cost to the defendant to defend the action

   c) the conflict that may exist with the law of the defendants' own country

   d) the forum's interest in deciding the merits

   e) the most practical manner to settle the dispute

   f) the availability of an alternative forum.

The question of a particular court's jurisdiction in the international arena is far more problematic than it is locally. Because the Internet has global application, a plaintiff may forum shop to locate a court whose law would provide the relief sought so as to adjudicate a problem that might not be able to be asserted in either party's home country. Because of these potentially conflicting applications of legal principles, the most reasonable approach might be to create an international tribunal for the adjudication of Internet problems. However, it is important to note that to date the American courts have not been required to address this problem directly.

Chapter Review

Jurisdiction refers to a particular court's ability to adjudicate a legal dispute. Jurisdiction is based both on the court's ability to hear the particular matter placed before it and, most importantly for cyberlaw, the court's ability to enforce its decision against the particular parties. To this end, the courts and the legislatures have been forced to apply traditional jurisdictional doctrines to the new technology of the Internet.

In order for a given court to assert personal jurisdiction over a defendant and meet the constitutional guarantees of due process, it must be shown that the grant of jurisdiction over the defendant does not offend traditional notions of fair play or violates substantial justice. To meet these requirements, most jurisdictions have determined that some connection exists between the website and the user in whose forum jurisdiction is asserted. However, to meet this standard, the website owner must be conversant with the local laws of the potential user to make sure that it does not infringe on that user's legal rights, which may be nearly impossible considering the global reach of the Internet.

Recently, various legislatures have attempted to create statutes to deal with the question of jurisdiction in cyberspace. This approach in addressing the specific problems of the new technology will probably be the most practical answer to these questions for the legal professional of the future.

Key Terms

Civil Law—Laws addressing the rights of private individuals

Convention on Cybercrime—International meeting to discuss problems of crimes committed by means of the computer and computer technology

Criminal Law—Laws to protect society at large

Cybercrime—Crimes committed by means of a computer or computer technology

Defendant—Alleged wrongdoer in a lawsuit

Domicile—Permanent home

Due Process—Constitutional guarantee

E-business—Commercial enterprise conducted on the Internet

Fraudulently Induced—Tricking someone to enter the state to acquire jurisdiction over the person

In Personam Jurisdiction—Jurisdiction over a party to a lawsuit

In Rem Jurisdiction—Jurisdiction based on property that is the subject of a lawsuit

Interactive Website—Internet site in which the user communicates with the site

Jurisdiction—The ability to hear and adjudicate a matter

Long-arm Jurisdiction—Method of obtaining jurisdiction over an out-of-state defendant

Motion—Request to the court

Passive Website—Internet site that only provides information without communication with the user

Personal Jurisdiction—Jurisdiction over an individual

Plaintiff—Person who institutes a civil lawsuit

Quasi-in-rem Jurisdiction—Jurisdiction based on property that can be user to satisfy the claim

Subject Matter Jurisdiction—Ability to adjudicate a particular kind of dispute

Waive—Forgo a right

Edited Cases

The following cases are presented to highlight some of the issues introduced in this chapter. *Zippo Manufacturing v. Zippo Dot Com, Inc.* underscores the problem of acquiring jurisdiction over a defendant, and *VP Intellectual Properties, LLC v. Imtec Corp.* distinguishes between jurisdiction and venue.

Zippo Manufacturing Company v. Zippo Dot Com, Inc.
952 F. Supp. 1119 W.D. Pa. 1997

This is an Internet domain name dispute. At this stage of the controversy, we must decide the Constitutionally permissible reach of Pennsylvania's Long Arm Statute, 42 Pa.C.S.A.

sec. 5322, through cyberspace. Plaintiff Zippo Manufacturing Corporation ("Manufacturing") has filed a five-count complaint against *Zippo Dot Com, Inc.* ("Dot Com") alleging trademark dilution, infringement, and false designation under the Federal Trademark Act, 15 U.S.C. sec. 1051-1127. In addition, the Complaint alleges causes of action based on state law trademark dilution under 54 Pa.C.S.A. sec. 1124, and seeks equitable accounting and imposition of a constructive trust. Dot Com has moved to dismiss for lack of personal jurisdiction and improper venue pursuant to Fed.R.Civ.P 12(b)(2) and (3) or, in the alternative, to transfer the case pursuant to 28 U.S.C. sec. 1406(a). For the reasons set forth below, Defendant's motion is denied.

Background

The facts relevant to this motion are as follows. Manufacturing is a Pennsylvania corporation with its principal place of business in Bradford, Pennsylvania. Manufacturing makes, among other things, well known "Zippo" tobacco lighters. Dot Com is a California corporation with its principal place of business in Sunnyvale, California. Dot Com operates an Internet website and an Internet news service and has obtained the exclusive right to use the domain names "zippo.com," "zippo.net" and "zipponews.com" on the Internet.

Dot Com's website contains information about the company, advertisements and an application for its Internet news service. The news service itself consists of three levels of membership—public/free, "Original" and "Super." Each successive level offers access to a greater number of Internet newsgroups. A customer who wants to subscribe to either the "Original" or "Super" level of service fills out an on-line application that asks for a variety of information including the person's name and address. Payment is made by credit card over the Internet or the telephone. The application is then processed and the subscriber is assigned a password which permits the subscriber to view and/or download Internet newsgroup messages that are stored on the Defendant's server in California.

Dot Com's contacts with Pennsylvania have occurred almost exclusively over the Internet. Dot Com's offices, employees and Internet servers are located in California. Dot Com maintains no offices, employees or agents in Pennsylvania. Dot Com's advertising for its service to Pennsylvania residents involves posting information about its service on its Web page, which is accessible to Pennsylvania residents via the Internet. Defendant has approximately 140,000 paying subscribers worldwide. Approximately two percent (3,000) of those subscribers are Pennsylvania residents. These subscribers have contracted to receive Dot Com's service by visiting its website and filling out the application. Additionally, Dot Com has entered into agreements with seven Internet access providers in Pennsylvania to permit their subscribers to access Dot Com's news service. Two of these providers are located in the Western District of Pennsylvania.

The basis of the trademark claims is Dot Com's use of the word "Zippo" in the domain names it holds, in numerous locations in its website and in the heading of Internet newsgroup messages that have been posted by Dot Com subscribers. When an Internet user views or downloads a newsgroup message posted by a Dot Com subscriber, the word "Zippo" appears in the "Message-Id" and "Organization" sections of the heading. The news message itself, containing text and/or pictures, follows. Manufacturing points out that some of the messages contain adult oriented, sexually explicit subject matter.

Standard of Review

When a defendant raises the defense of the court's lack of personal jurisdiction, the burden falls upon the plaintiff to come forward with sufficient facts to establish that jurisdiction is proper. *Mellon Bank (East) PSFS, N.A. v Farino*, 960 F.2d 1217, 1223 (3d Cir. 1992) (citing *Carteret Savings Bank v. Shushan*, 954 F.2d 141 (3d Cir. 1992), cert. denied 506 U.S. 817, 121 L. Ed. 2d 29, 113 S. Ct. 61 (1992)). The plaintiff meets this burden by making a prima facie showing of "sufficient contacts between the defendant and the forum state." *Mellon East*, 960 F.2d at 1223 (citing *Provident Nat. Bank v. California Fed. Sav. & Loan Assoc.*, 819 F.2d 434 (3d Cir. 1987)).

Discussion

A Personal Jurisdiction

1. The Traditional Framework

Our authority to exercise personal jurisdiction in this case is conferred by state law. Fed.R.Civ.P. 4(e); *Mellon*, 960 F.2d at 1221. The extent to which we may exercise that authority is governed by the Due Process Clause of the Fourteenth Amendment to the Federal Constitution. *Kulko v. California Supreme Court*, 436 U.S. 84, 91, 56 L. Ed. 2d 132, 98 S. Ct. 1690 (1978).

Pennsylvania's long arm jurisdiction statute is codified at 42 Pa.C.S.A. sec. 5322(a). The portion of the statute authorizing us to exercise jurisdiction here permits the exercise of jurisdiction over non-resident defendants upon:

2) Contracting to supply services or things in this Commonwealth.

42 Pa.C.S.A. sec. 5322(a). It is undisputed that Dot Com contracted to supply Internet news services to approximately 3,000 Pennsylvania residents and also entered into agreements with seven Internet access providers in Pennsylvania. Moreover, even if Dot Com's conduct did not satisfy a specific provision of the statute, we would nevertheless be authorized to exercise jurisdiction to the "fullest extent allowed under the Constitution of the United States." 42 Pa.C.S.A. sec. 5322(b).

The Constitutional limitations on the exercise of personal jurisdiction differ depending upon whether a court seeks to exercise general or specific jurisdiction over a nonresident defendant. *Mellon*, 960 F.2d at 1221. General jurisdiction permits a court to exercise personal jurisdiction over a nonresident defendant for nonforum related activities when the defendant has engaged in "systematic and continuous" activities[**8] in the forum state. *Helicopteros Nacionales de Colombia, S.A. v. Hall*, 466 U.S. 408, 414-16, 80 L. Ed. 2d 404, 104 S. Ct. 1868 (1984). In the absence of general jurisdiction, specific jurisdiction permits a court to exercise personal jurisdiction over a nonresident defendant for forum-related activities where the "relationship between the defendant and the forum falls within the 'minimum contacts' framework" of *International Shoe Co. v. Washington*, 326 U.S. 310, 90 L. Ed. 95, 66 S. Ct. 154 (1945) and its progeny. *Mellon*, 960 F.2d at 1221. Manufacturing does not contend that we should exercise general personal jurisdiction over Dot Com. Manufacturing concedes that if personal jurisdiction exists in this case, it must be specific.

A three-pronged test has emerged for determining whether the exercise of specific personal jurisdiction over a nonresident defendant is appropriate: (1) the defendant must have sufficient "minimum contacts" with the forum state, (2) the claim asserted against the defendant must arise out of those contacts, and (3) the exercise of jurisdiction must be reasonable. *Id*. The "Constitutional touchstone" of the minimum contacts analysis is embodied in the first prong, "whether the defendant purposefully established" contacts with the forum state. *Burger King Corp. v. Rudzewicz*, 471 U.S. 462, 475, 85 L. Ed. 2d

528, 105 S. Ct. 2174 (1985) (citing *International Shoe Co. v. Washington*, 326 U.S. 310, 319, 90 L. Ed. 95, 66 S. Ct. 154 (1945)). Defendants who "'reach out beyond one state' and create continuing relationships and obligations with the citizens of another state are subject to regulation and sanctions in the other State for consequences of their actions." *Id.* (citing *Travelers Health Assn. v. Virginia*, 339 U.S. 643, 647, 94 L. Ed. 1154, 70 S. Ct. 927 (1950)). "The foreseeability that is critical to the due process analysis is . . . that the defendant's conduct and connection with the forum State are such that he should reasonably expect to be haled into court there." *World Wide Volkswagen Corp. v. Woodson*, 444 U.S. 286, 295, 62 L. Ed. 2d 490, 100 S. Ct. 559 (1980). This protects defendants from being forced to answer for their actions in a foreign jurisdiction based on "random, fortuitous or attenuated" contacts. *Keeton v. Hustler Magazine, Inc.*, 465 U.S. 770, 774, 79 L. Ed. 2d 790, 104 S. Ct. 1473 (1984). "Jurisdiction is proper, however, where contacts proximately result from actions by the defendant himself that create a 'substantial connection' with the forum State." Burger King, 471 U.S. at 475 (citing *McGee v. International Life Insurance Co.*, 355 U.S. 220, 223, 2 L. Ed. 2d 223, 78 S. Ct. 199 (1957)).

The "reasonableness" prong exists to protect defendants against unfairly inconvenient litigation. *World Wide Volkswagen*, 444 U.S. at 292. Under this prong, the exercise of jurisdiction will be reasonable if it does not offend "traditional notions of fair play and substantial justice." *International Shoe*, 326 U.S. at 316. When determining the reasonableness of a particular forum, the court must consider the burden on the defendant in light of other factors including: "the forum state's interest in adjudicating the dispute; the plaintiff's interest in obtaining convenient and effective relief, at least when that interest is not adequately protected by the plaintiff's right to choose the forum; the interstate judicial system's interest in obtaining the most efficient resolution of controversies; and the shared interest of the several states in furthering fundamental substantive social policies." *World Wide Volkswagen*, 444 U.S. at 292 (internal citations omitted).

2.   The Internet and Jurisdiction

In *Hanson v. Denckla*, the Supreme Court noted that "as technological progress has increased the flow of commerce between States, the need for jurisdiction has undergone a similar increase." *Hanson v. Denckla*, 357 U.S. 235, 250-51, 2 L. Ed. 2d 1283, 78 S. Ct. 1228 (1958). Twenty-seven years later, the Court observed that jurisdiction could not be avoided "merely because the defendant did not physically enter the forum state. *Burger King*, 471 U.S. at 476. The Court observed that:

> It is an inescapable fact of modern commercial life that a substantial amount of commercial business is transacted solely by mail and wire communications across state lines, thus obviating the need for physical presence within a State in which business is conducted.

Enter the Internet, a global "'super-network' of over 15,000 computer networks used by over 30 million individuals, corporations, organizations, and educational institutions worldwide." *Panavision Intern., L.P. v. Toeppen*, 938 F. Supp. 616 (S.D.Cal. 1996) (citing *American Civil Liberties Union v. Reno*, 929 F. Supp. 824, 830-48 (E.D.Pa. 1996). "In recent years, businesses have begun to use the Internet to provide information and products to consumers and other businesses." *Id.* The Internet makes it possible to conduct business throughout the world entirely from a desktop. With this global revolution looming on the horizon, the development of the law concerning the permissible scope of personal jurisdiction based on Internet use is in its infant stages. The cases are scant. Nevertheless, our review of the available cases and materials reveals that the likelihood that personal jurisdiction can be constitutionally exercised is directly proportionate to the nature and quality of commercial activity that an entity conducts over the Internet. This sliding scale is consistent with well-developed personal jurisdiction principles. At one end of the spectrum are situations where a defendant clearly does business over the Internet. If the defendant enters into contracts with residents of a foreign jurisdiction that involve the knowing and repeated transmission of computer files over the Internet, personal jurisdiction is proper. *E.g. Compuserve, Inc. v. Patterson*, 89 F.3d 1257 (6th Cir. 1996). At the opposite end are situations where a defendant has simply posted information on an Internet website which is accessible to users in foreign jurisdictions. A passive website that does little more than make information available to those who are interested in it is not grounds for the exercise personal jurisdiction. *E.g. Bensusan Restaurant Corp. v. King*, 937 F. Supp. 295 (S.D.N.Y. 1996). The middle ground is occupied by interactive websites where a user can exchange information with the host computer. In these cases, the exercise of jurisdiction is determined by examining the level of interactivity and commercial nature of the exchange of information that occurs on the website. *E.g. Maritz, Inc. v. Cybergold, Inc.*, 940 F. Supp. 96, 1996 U.S. Dist. LEXIS 14976 (E.D.Mo. 1996).

Traditionally, when an entity intentionally reaches beyond its boundaries to conduct business with foreign residents, the exercise of specific jurisdiction is proper. *Burger King*, 471 U.S. at 475. Different results should not be reached simply because business is conducted over the Internet. In *Compuserve, Inc. v. Patterson*, 89 F.3d 1257 (6th Cir. 1996), the Sixth Circuit addressed the significance of doing business over the Internet. In that case, Patterson, a Texas resident, entered into a contract to distribute shareware through Compuserve's Internet server located in Ohio. *Compuserve*, 89 F.3d at 1260. From Texas, Patterson electronically uploaded thirty-two master software files to Compuserve's server in Ohio via the Internet. *Id.* at 1261. One of Patterson's software products was designed to help people navigate the Internet. *Id.* When Compuserve later began to market a product that Patterson believed to be similar to his own, he threatened to sue. *Id.* Compuserve brought an action in the Southern District of Ohio, seeking a declaratory judgment. *Id.* The District Court granted Patterson's motion to dismiss for lack of personal jurisdiction and Compuserve appealed. *Id.* The Sixth Circuit reversed, reasoning that Patterson had purposefully directed his business activities toward Ohio by knowingly entering into a contract with an Ohio resident and then "deliberately and repeatedly" transmitted files to Ohio. *Id.* at 1264-66.

In *Maritz, Inc. v. Cybergold*, Inc., 947 F. Supp. 1328, 1996 U.S. Dist. LEXIS 14978 (E.D. Mo. 1996), the defendant had put up a website as a promotion for its upcoming Internet service. The service consisted of assigning users an electronic mailbox and then forwarding advertisements for products and services that matched the users' interests to those electronic mailboxes. *Maritz*, 947 F. Supp. 1328, 1996 U.S. Dist. LEXIS 14978 at *7. The defendant planned to charge advertisers and provide users with incentives to view the advertisements. *Id.* Although the service was not yet operational, users were encouraged to add their address to a mailing list to receive updates about the service. *Id.* The court rejected the defendant's contention that it operated a "passive website." *Id.* at *16. The court reasoned that the defendant's conduct amounted to "active solicitations" and "promotional activities" designed to "develop a mailing list of Internet users" and that the defendant "indiscriminately responded to every user" who accessed the site. *Id.* at *14-17.

Inset Systems, Inc. v. Instruction Set, 937 F. Supp. 161 (D. Conn. 1996) represents the outer limits of the exercise of personal jurisdiction based on the Internet. In *Inset Systems*, a Connecticut corporation sued a Massachusetts corporation in the District of Connecticut for trademark infringement based on the use of an Internet domain name.

Inset Systems, 937 F. Supp. at 162. The defendant's contacts with Connecticut consisted of posting a website that was accessible to approximately 10,000 Connecticut residents and maintaining a toll free number. *Id.* at 165. The court exercised personal jurisdiction, reasoning that advertising on the Internet constituted the purposeful doing of business in Connecticut because "unlike television and radio advertising, the advertisement is available continuously to any Internet user." *Id.* at 165.

Bensusan Restaurant Corp. v. King, 937 F. Supp. 295 (S.D. N.Y. 1996) reached a different conclusion based on a similar website. In *Bensusan*, the operator of a New York jazz club sued the operator of a Missouri jazz club for trademark infringement. *Bensusan*, 937 F. Supp. at 297. The Internet website at issue contained general information about the defendant's club, a calendar of events and ticket information. *Id.* However, the site was not interactive. *Id.* If a user wanted to go to the club, she would have to call or visit a ticket outlet and then pick up tickets at the club on the night of the show. *Id.* The court refused to exercise jurisdiction based on the website alone, reasoning that it did not rise to the level of purposeful availment of that jurisdiction's laws. The court distinguished the case from *Compuserve, supra*, where the user had "'reached out' from Texas to Ohio and 'originated and maintained' contacts with Ohio." *Id.* at 301.

Pres-Kap, Inc. v. System One Direct Access, Inc., 636 So. 2d 1351 (Fla. App. 1994), review denied, 645 So. 2d 455 (Fla. 1994) is not inconsistent with the above cases. In *Pres-Kap*, a majority of a three-judge intermediate state appeals court refused to exercise jurisdiction over a consumer of an on-line airline ticketing service. *Pres-Kap* involved a suit on a contract dispute in a Florida court by a Delaware corporation against its New York customer. *Pres-Kap*, 636 So. 2d at 1351-52. The defendant had leased computer equipment which it used to access an airline ticketing computer located in Florida. *Id.* The contract was solicited, negotiated, executed and serviced in New York. *Id.* at 1352. The defendant's only contact with Florida consisted of logging onto the computer located in Florida and mailing payments for the leased equipment to Florida. *Id.* at 1353. *Pres-Kap* is distinguishable from the above cases and the case at bar because it addressed the exercise of jurisdiction over a consumer of on-line services as opposed to a provider. When a consumer logs onto a server in a foreign jurisdiction he is engaging in a fundamentally different type of contact than an entity that is using the Internet to sell or market products or services to residents of foreign jurisdictions. The *Pres-Kap* court specifically expressed concern over the implications of subjecting users of "on-line" services with contracts with out-of-state networks to suit in foreign jurisdictions. *Id.* at 1353.

3. Application to This Case

First, we note that this is not an Internet advertising case in the line of *Inset Systems* and *Bensusan, supra*. Dot Com has not just posted information on a website that is accessible to Pennsylvania residents who are connected to the Internet. This is not even an interactivity case in the line of *Maritz, supra*. Dot Com has done more than create an interactive website through which it exchanges information with Pennsylvania residents in hopes of using that information for commercial gain later. We are not being asked to determine whether Dot Com's website alone constitutes the purposeful availment of doing business in Pennsylvania. This is a "doing business over the Internet" case in the line of *Compuserve, supra*. We are being asked to determine whether Dot Com's conducting of electronic commerce with Pennsylvania residents constitutes the purposeful availment of doing business in Pennsylvania. We conclude that it does. Dot Com has contracted with approximately 3,000 individuals and seven Internet access providers in Pennsylvania. The intended object of these transactions has been the downloading of the electronic messages that form the basis of this suit in Pennsylvania.

We find Dot Com's efforts to characterize its conduct as falling short of purposeful availment of doing business in Pennsylvania wholly unpersuasive. At oral argument, Defendant repeatedly characterized its actions as merely "operating a website" or "advertising." Dot Com also cites to a number of cases from this Circuit which, it claims, stand for the proposition that merely advertising in a forum, without more, is not a sufficient minimal contact. This argument is misplaced. Dot Com has done more than advertise on the Internet in Pennsylvania. Defendant has sold passwords to approximately 3,000 subscribers in Pennsylvania and entered into seven contracts with Internet access providers to furnish its services to their customers in Pennsylvania.

Dot Com also contends that its contacts with Pennsylvania residents are "fortuitous" within the meaning of *World Wide Volkswagen*, 444 U.S. 286, 62 L. Ed. 2d 490, 100 S. Ct. 559 (1980). Defendant argues that it has not 'actively' solicited business in Pennsylvania and that any business it conducts with Pennsylvania residents has resulted from contacts that were initiated by Pennsylvanians who visited the Defendant's website. The fact that Dot Com's services have been consumed in Pennsylvania is not "fortuitous" within the meaning of World Wide Volkswagen. In *World Wide Volkswagen*, a couple that had purchased a vehicle in New York, while they were New York residents, were injured while driving that vehicle through Oklahoma and brought suit in an Oklahoma state court. *World Wide Volkswagen*, 444 U.S. at 288. The manufacturer did not sell its vehicles in Oklahoma and had not made an effort to establish business relationships in Oklahoma. *Id.* at 295. The Supreme Court characterized the manufacturer's ties with Oklahoma as fortuitous because they resulted entirely out of the fact that the plaintiffs had driven their car into that state. *Id.*

Here, Dot Com argues that its contacts with Pennsylvania residents are fortuitous because Pennsylvanians happened to find its website or heard about its news service elsewhere and decided to subscribe. This argument misconstrues the concept of fortuitous contacts embodied in *World Wide Volkswagen*. Dot Com's contacts with Pennsylvania would be fortuitous within the meaning of *World Wide Volkswagen* if it had no Pennsylvania subscribers and an Ohio subscriber forwarded a copy of a file he obtained from Dot Com to a friend in Pennsylvania or an Ohio subscriber brought his computer along on a trip to Pennsylvania and used it to access Dot Com's service. That is not the situation here. Dot Com repeatedly and consciously chose to process Pennsylvania residents' applications and to assign them passwords. Dot Com knew that the result of these contracts would be the transmission of electronic messages into Pennsylvania. The transmission of these files was entirely within its control. Dot Com cannot maintain that these contracts are "fortuitous" or "coincidental" within the meaning of World Wide Volkswagen. When a defendant makes a conscious choice to conduct business with the residents of a forum state, "it has clear notice that it is subject to suit there." *World Wide Volkswagen*, 444 U.S. at 297. Dot Com was under no obligation to sell its services to Pennsylvania residents. It freely chose to do so, presumably in order to profit from those transactions. If a corporation determines that the risk of being subject to personal jurisdiction in a particular forum is too great, it can choose to sever its connection to the state. *Id.* If Dot Com had not wanted to be amenable to jurisdiction in Pennsylvania, the solution would have been simple—it could have chosen not to sell its services to Pennsylvania residents.

Next, Dot Com argues that its forum-related activities are not numerous or significant enough to create a "substantial connection" with Pennsylvania. Defendant points to the fact that only two percent of its subscribers are Pennsylvania residents. However, the Supreme Court has made clear that even a single contact can be sufficient. *McGee*, 355 U.S. at 223. The test has always focused on the "nature and quality" of the contacts with the forum and not the quantity of those contacts. *International Shoe*, 326 U.S. at 320. The

Sixth Circuit also rejected a similar argument in *Compuserve* when it wrote that the contacts were "deliberate and repeated even if they yielded little revenue." *Compuserve*, 89 F.3d at 1265.

We also conclude that the cause of action arises out of Dot Com's forum-related conduct in this case. The Third Circuit has stated that "a cause of action for trademark infringement occurs where the passing off occurs." *Cottman Transmission Systems Inc. v. Martino*, 36 F.3d 291, 294 (citing *Tefal, S.A. v. Products Int'l Co.*, 529 F.2d 495, 496 n.1 (3d Cir. 1976); *Indianapolis Colts v. Metro. Baltimore Football*, 34 F.3d 410 (7th Cir. 1994)). In Tefal, the maker and distributor of T-Fal cookware sued a partnership of California corporations in the District of New Jersey for trademark infringement. *Tefal*, 529 F.2d at 496. The defendants objected to venue in New Jersey, arguing that the contested trademark accounted for only about five percent of national sales. *Id*. On appeal, the Third Circuit concluded that since substantial sales of the product bearing the allegedly infringing mark took place in New Jersey, the cause of action arose in New Jersey and venue was proper. *Tefal*, 529 F.2d at 496-97.

In *Indianapolis Colts*, also case cited by the Third Circuit in *Cottman*, an Indiana National Football League franchise sued a Maryland Canadian Football League franchise in the Southern District of Indiana, alleging trademark infringement. *Indianapolis Colts*, 34 F.3d at 411. On appeal, the Seventh Circuit held that personal jurisdiction was appropriate in Indiana because trademark infringement is a tort-like injury and a substantial amount of the injury from the alleged infringement was likely to occur in Indiana. *Id*. at 412.

In the instant case, both a significant amount of the alleged infringement and dilution, and resulting injury have occurred in Pennsylvania. The object of Dot Com's contracts with Pennsylvania residents is the transmission of the messages that Plaintiff claims dilute and infringe upon its trademark. When these messages are transmitted into Pennsylvania and viewed by Pennsylvania residents on their computers, there can be no question that the alleged infringement and dilution occur in Pennsylvania. Moreover, since Manufacturing is a Pennsylvania corporation, a substantial amount of the injury from the alleged wrongdoing is likely to occur in Pennsylvania. Thus, we conclude that the cause of action arises out of Dot Com's forum-related activities under the authority of both *Tefal* and *Indianapolis Colts*, supra.

Finally, Dot Com argues that the exercise of jurisdiction would be unreasonable in this case. We disagree. There can be no question that Pennsylvania has a strong interest in adjudicating disputes involving the alleged infringement of trademarks owned by resident corporations. We must also give due regard to the Plaintiff's choice to seek relief in Pennsylvania. *Kulko*, 436 U.S. at 92. These concerns outweigh the burden created by forcing the Defendant to defend the suit in Pennsylvania, especially when Dot Com consciously chose to conduct business in Pennsylvania, pursuing profits from the actions that are now in question. The Due Process Clause is not a "territorial shield to interstate obligations that have been voluntarily assumed." *Burger King*, 471 U.S. at 474.

B   Venue Under 28 U.S.C sec. 1391

Defendant argues that, under the law of this Circuit, venue is only proper in trademark cases in the judicial district in which "a substantial part of the events or omissions giving rise to the claim occurred." In support of this proposition, Defendant cites *Cottman Transmission Systems, Inc. v. Martino*, 36 F.3d 291 (3d Cir. 1994). We cannot agree.

Venue in this case is governed by 28 U.S.C. sec. 1391(b), the relevant portion of which provides:

(b) A civil action wherein jurisdiction is not founded solely on diversity of citizenship may, except as otherwise provided by law, be brought only in (1) a judicial district where any defendant resides, if all defendants reside in the same State, (2) a judicial district in which a substantial part of the events or omissions giving rise to the claim occurred, or a substantial part of the property that is the subject of the action is situated, or (3) a judicial district in which the defendant may be found if there is no district in which the action may otherwise be brought.

28 U.S.C. sec. 1391(b), Subsection (c) further provides that a corporate defendant is "deemed to reside in any judicial district in which it is subject to personal jurisdiction at the time the action is commenced." 28 U.S.C. sec. 1391(c). Dot Com is the only defendant in this case and it is a corporation. Thus, under the plain language of 28 U.S.C. sec. 1391(b)(1), our previous discussion of personal jurisdiction is dispositive of the venue issue. Contrary to Dot Com's contention, *Cottman* does not command a different result.

Cottman involved a suit by a Pennsylvania corporation against a former Michigan franchisee and his wholly owned corporation for trademark infringement arising out of the continued use of the plaintiff's trademark after termination of the franchise agreement. The suit was brought in the Eastern District of Pennsylvania. Both defendants were Michigan residents and the corporation did business exclusively in Michigan. In the district court, the plaintiff relied exclusively on 28 U.S.C. sec. 1391(b)(2) to establish venue. The district court found venue proper, reasoning that a "substantial part of the events or omissions giving rise to the claim occurred" in Pennsylvania. *Cottman Transmission v. Metro Distributing*, 796 F. Supp. 838, 844 (E.D. Pa. 1992). Thus, on appeal, the only issue before the Third Circuit was the propriety of venue under sec. 1391(b)(2). In fact, the Third Circuit expressly stated that it was analyzing the case under sec. 1391(b)(2). *Cottman*, 36 F.3d at 294. The Third Circuit read the record as only capable of supporting the contention that the defendants attempted to pass off the trademarks at issue in the Eastern District of Michigan. *Id*. at 296. Thus, the Third Circuit reversed, because a "substantial part of the events or omissions giving rise to the claim" had not occurred in the Eastern District of Pennsylvania. *Id*.

The fact that the Third Circuit analyzed *Cottman* under the standard in sec. 1391(b)(2) does not mean that it applies to every trademark case. In fact, at oral argument, Dot Com conceded that if its reading of *Cottman* were the law, it would effectively render sec. 1391(b)(1) inapplicable to trademark cases and require the plaintiff to always satisfy sec. 1391(b)(2) in order to lay venue. If the Third Circuit had intended to create such a radical departure from the plain language of sec. 1391, it would have said so.

Since venue has been properly laid in this District, we cannot dismiss the action under 28 U.S.C sec. 1406(a). *Jumara v. State Farm Inc. Co.*, 55 F.3d 873, 877 (3d Cir. 1995). We are also not permitted to compel the Plaintiff to accept a transfer against its wishes. *Carteret v. Shushan*, 919 F.2d 225, 232 (3d Cir. 1990).

Conclusion

We conclude that this Court may appropriately exercise personal jurisdiction over the Defendant and that venue is proper in this judicial district. An appropriate order follows.

Case Questions

1. According to the court, who has the burden of proof when a challenge to jurisdiction is raised?

2. How does the court determine that it has jurisdiction over the defendant?

VP Intellectual Properties, LLC v. Imtec Corporation
1999 U.S. Dist. LEXIS 19700 (D. N.J. 1999)

Defendant Imtec Corporation ("Imtec") moves to dismiss plaintiff VP Intellectual Properties' ("VP") complaint for lack of personal jurisdiction and improper venue. In the alternative, Imtec requests severance and the transfer of this case to the District of Oklahoma. Imtec's motion to dismiss for lack of jurisdiction and improper venue is granted in part; its request to sever is placed before the magistrate judge for consideration.

Facts

Defendant Imtec is an Oklahoma corporation with its principal place of business in Ardmore, Oklahoma. VP is a limited liability company with its headquarters at Fort Lee, New Jersey. VP filed the present complaint against four defendants, including Imtec, for patent infringement. VP claims that Imtec sold a number of dental implant devices, including "threaded" implants, "angled abutment" implants, and "push-in" implants, which infringed various patents held by VP.

Imtec moves to dismiss for lack of personal jurisdiction and improper venue. As evidence that jurisdiction is absent, Imtec states that: (1) it does not have a "regular and established" place of business in New Jersey; (2) it does not have an office or any employees in the state; (3) it has no authorized dealers, manufacturers or distributors in the state; (4) it has no sales agents, salesperson, wholesaler, broker or other type of sales representative in the state; (5) between 1994 and August 1999, it never attended a trade show or other conference in the state; and (6) it has never maintained a New Jersey telephone listing. Def. Brf. at 3. It asserts that the only link it has to the state are "minimal" sales of the threaded and angled abutment implants to New Jersey dentists. Imtec argues that these unsolicited, isolated sales, typically for less than $ 400, are insufficient to grant either general or specific personal jurisdiction.

VP responds that Imtec's repeated sales to New Jersey dentists, combined with Imtec's commercial Internet site which can be accessed from the state, constitute "continuous, substantial and systematic" contacts with the forum that give rise to general personal jurisdiction. Plaintiff adds that Imtec's actual sales of allegedly infringing [*4] products in the forum state are also sufficient to grant this Court specific jurisdiction over Counts I, II, & IV. As for the "push-in" implants, which were never sold in-state, VP argues that Imtec has sent at least one catalog advertising this product to New Jersey. Plaintiff asserts that this offer to sell an allegedly infringing product in the forum state gives the Court specific jurisdiction over this type of implant (Count III).

Legal Discussion

Personal Jurisdiction

If a defendant challenges an action for lack of personal jurisdiction, the burden is on the plaintiff to prove, by a preponderance of the evidence, facts sufficient to establish personal jurisdiction. *Carteret Savings Bank, FA v. Shushan*, 954 F.2d 141, 146 (3d Cir. 1992). Moreover, the plaintiff must sustain its burden of proof "through sworn affidavits or other competent evidence," and not on bare pleadings alone. *Time Share Vacation Club v. Atlantic Resorts, Ltd.*, 735 F.2d 61, 67 n.9 (3d Cir. 1984). The plaintiff must show that this Court can maintain jurisdiction over the defendant consistent with due process. *DeJames v. Magnificence Carriers, Inc.*, 654 F.2d 280, 284(3d Cir.), cert. denied, 454 U.S. 1085, 70 L. Ed. 2d 620, 102 S. Ct. 642 (1981). In deciding a motion to dismiss for lack of personal jurisdiction, the Court must construe disputed facts in favor of the plaintiff and accept them as true. *Shushan*, 954 F.2d at 142.

A federal court assessing whether jurisdiction may be exercised over a defendant must look to the long-arm statute of the state in which it sits. Fed. R. Civ. P. 4; *Mellon Bank (East) PSFS, National Ass'n v. Farino*, 960 F.2d 1217, 1223 (3d Cir. 1992). Rule 4:4-4 of the New Jersey Court Rules grants jurisdiction to the courts of this state "to the uttermost limits permitted by the United States Constitution," *Avdel Corp. v. Mecure*, 58 N.J. 264, 268, 277 A.2d 207 (1971), "limited only by the due process constraints of the Fourteenth Amendment." *DeJames*, 654 F.2d at 284.

In New Jersey, to subject a nonresident party to personal jurisdiction, due process requires that party "have certain minimum contacts with it such that the maintenance of the suit does not offend 'traditional notions of fair play and substantial justice.'" *International Shoe Co. v. Washington*, 326 U.S. 310, 90 L.Ed. 95, 66 S. Ct. 154 (1945). In this regard, the plaintiff must demonstrate "with reasonable particularity" that the Court has either specific jurisdiction, where the cause of action arises from or relates to the defendant's activities in the forum state, or general jurisdiction, where the defendant has continuous and systematic conduct in the forum state. *Dollar Savings Bank v. First Security Bank of Utah*, 746 F.2d 208, 211 (3d Cir. 1984); *Giangola v. Walt Disney World Co.*, 753 F. Supp. 148, 154 (D.N.J. 1990).

Once a court has found that a defendant's contacts with the forum state are sufficiently significant to confer jurisdiction to the forum, "in appropriate cases" the court may evaluate other facts. *Burger King*, 471 U.S. 462, 476-77, 85 L. Ed. 2d 528, 105 S. Ct. 2174 (1985). These factors include "the burden on the defendant, the forum State's interest in adjudicating the dispute, the plaintiff's interest in obtaining convenient and effective relief, the interstate judicial system's interest in obtaining the most efficient resolution of controversies, and the shared interest of the several States in furthering fundamental substantive social policies." *Id.*

General Jurisdiction

As said, to assert general jurisdiction, a plaintiff must demonstrate that the defendant's contacts with the forum are so "continuous and substantial" that the defendant should "expect to be haled into court on any cause of action." See *Weber v. Jolly Hotels*, 977 F. Supp. 327 (D.N.J. 1997) (citing *Helicopteros Nacionales de Colombia S.A. v. Hall*, 466 U.S. 408, 80 L. Ed. 2d 404, 104 S. Ct. 1868 (1984)). Here, the issue is whether the sale of approximately $9,500 in dental implants to New Jersey dentists and an Internet site accessible from New Jersey are enough connection to support general jurisdiction.

1. Sales

Imtec argues that the sales were "isolated," "unsolicited" and "irregular," that the orders were filled in and shipped from Oklahoma "without the assistance of a network of distribution and in-state promotional efforts"; that the customers paid by credit card and had no ongoing accounts with the company; and that the orders were always shipped "F.O.B." Def. Brf. at 9. Consequently, it asserts that these sales cannot support the exercise of general jurisdiction over the company. VP counters that "over a period of years, [Imtec] has solicited and accepted direct orders from New Jersey and shipped the accused product directly to New Jersey." VP avers that Imtec made approximately "23 sales of accused products directly to customers in New Jersey" and shipped at least one catalog to the state. Pl. Brf. at 4 n.2.

As noted, the exercise of general jurisdiction "is consistent with due process only when the plaintiff has satisfied the 'rigorous' burden of establishing that the defendant's contacts are continuous and substantial." *Osteotech, Inc. v. Gensci Regeneration Sciences, Inc.*, 6 F. Supp. 2d 349, 353 (D.N.J. 1998). Defendant's small sales and its demonstrated lack of any sales structure—offices or agents—within the forum state do not satisfy this "rigorous" burden and indicate that the exercise of general jurisdiction is improper. The Court finds that plaintiff has failed to demonstrate the continuity of contact necessary to exercise general personal jurisdiction over Imtec on the basis of $9,500 in sales to New Jersey dentists over a five-year period.

2. Internet

"There are three areas into which Internet use can be categorized" for the purpose of determining whether the exercise of personal jurisdiction is permitted. *Mieczkowski v. Masco Corp.*, 997 F. Supp. 782, 786 (E.D. Tex. 1998) (citing *Zippo Mfg. Co. v. Zippo Dot Com, Inc.* 952 F. Supp. 1119 (W.D. Pa. 1997)). At one end of the spectrum are cases where individuals can directly interact with a company over their Internet site, download, transmit, or exchange information with the company, and enter into contracts with the company via computer. In such cases, the exercise of personal jurisdiction is appropriate. *See CompuServe, Inc. v. Patterson*, 89 F.3d 1257 (6th Cir. 1996); *Decker v. Circus Circus Hotel*, 49 F. Supp. 2d 743, 748 (D.N.J. 1999); *Weber v. Jolly Hotels*, 977 F. Supp. 327 (D.N.J. 1997). At the other end of the continuum are cases in which the defendant "has done nothing more than advertise on the Internet." *Mieczkowski*, 997 F. Supp. at 786; *Bensusan Restaurant Corp. v. King*, 937 F. Supp. 295 (S.D.N.Y. 1996), aff'd, 126 F.3d 25 (2d Cir. 1997). Such sites are called "passive" sites and personal jurisdiction is generally not found. *Mieczkowski*, 997 F. Supp. at 786. In the middle are cases where parties can interact with the defendant company but may not be able to contract with it over the Internet site. *Id*. In these cases, whether jurisdiction can be found is determined by "examining the level of interactivity and commercial nature of the exchange of information that occurs on the website." *Zippo*, 952 F. Supp. At 1124 (citing *Maritz Inc. v. Cybergold, Inc.*, 947 F. Supp. 1328 (E.D. Mo. 1996)); *see also Decker*, 49 F. Supp. 2d at 748.

Imtec's Internet site, http://www.imtec.com/imtec, contains: (1) company and product descriptions; (2) distributor information; (3) ordering information; and (4) a catalog request form that can be filled out and electronically transmitted to the company. A customer, then, may browse the products and order a catalog but cannot purchase implants from the company over the Internet. The site, therefore, falls into the middle category. After reviewing the company's level of involvement with its customers via the computer, the Court determines that this site will not support the exercise of general personal jurisdiction over the defendant. Potential customers can send e-mail to customer support personnel but cannot place orders via the computer. They must instead either contact an authorized sales representative or call the company at a local (Oklahoma) or "800" number. The only "active" connection that a potential customer has with the company via computer is a form to order a catalog. This level of interaction, simply put, is not "continuous" or "systematic" enough to find general personal jurisdiction on the basis of the Internet site. *See generally Smith v. Hobby Lobby Stores, Inc.*, 968 F. Supp. 1356 (W.D. Ark 1997) (computer advertisement where defendant did not "contract to sell any goods or services" insufficient to confer jurisdiction).

Specific Jurisdiction

Specific jurisdiction over defendant Imtec is appropriate if VP's cause of action arises directly from defendant's actions in the forum state. *See Osteotech*, 6 F. Supp. 2d at 354; *Giangola v. Walt Disney World*, 753 F. Supp. 148, 154 (D.N.J. 1990). The Court "must examine the relationship among the defendant, the forum and the cause of action to determine whether the defendant had 'fair warning' that it could be brought to suit here." *Osteotech*, 6 F. Supp. 2d at 354 (citing *Shaffer v. Heitner*, 433 U.S. 186, 53 L. Ed. 2d 683, 97 S. Ct. 2569 (1977)). Further, "forum-related conduct must form the basis of the alleged injuries and resulting litigation." *Id.* (citing *Helicopteros Nacionales de Colombia S.A. v. Hall*, 466 U.S. 408, 80 L. Ed. 2d 404, 104 S. Ct. 1868 (1984)). The Federal Circuit has adopted this test for determining jurisdiction in patent cases. *See Akro Co. v. Luker*, 45 F.3d 1541, 1545-46 (Fed. Cir. 1995).

Imtec argues that its limited sales in New Jersey "have not been so deliberate and purposeful so as to provide a basis for the exercise of personal jurisdiction." Def. Brf. at 7 (citing *Asahi Metal Indus. Co. v. Superior Court of Ca.*, 480 U.S. 102, 94 L. Ed. 2d 92, 107 S. Ct. 1026 (1987)). Imtec relies on the absence of a sales structure and advertising within the state and its method of shipping F.O.B. in support of its contention that the sales were "random or fortuitous acts." *Id.* (citing *Burger King Corp. v. Rudzewicz*, 471 U.S. 462, 85 L. Ed. 2d 528, 105 S. Ct. 2174 (1985)). VP answers that Imtec "acted purposefully and directed its activities into New Jersey by consummating the sales and shipping products directly to New Jersey dentists." Pl. Brf. at 4. VP estimates that at least 23 sales of allegedly infringing products to New Jersey dentists occurred. VP adds that Imtec has solicited additional sales within the forum; the company sent at least one catalog to the state and maintains a catalog order form on its Internet site. *Id.*

In patent cases, "the law is clear that, where a defendant infringer is shown to have sold the allegedly infringing product in the forum state, the forum may exercise [specific] personal jurisdiction over the the defendant." See *Osteotech*, 6 F. Supp. 2d at 354 (citing *Beverly Hills Fan Co. v. Royal Sovereign Corp.*, 21 F.3d 1558 (Fed. Cir. 1994)). Regardless of the quantity of products sold or the shipping method used, the sale of patented products to buyers in the forum state creates specific personal jurisdiction over an out-of-state seller. See generally *North Am. Philips Corp. v. American Vending Sales, Inc.*, 35 F.3d 1576, 1579-80 (Fed. Cir. 1994) (finding that goods shipped to sellers F.O.B. were sold in the purchaser's state); *Beverly Hills Fan Co.*, 21 F.3d at 1570 (finding jurisdiction over patent case where sales made to customers in the forum state). Here, Imtec sold two of the three allegedly infringing products to New Jersey purchasers. The Court finds that it can exercise specific personal jurisdiction over Imtec for these sales (Counts I, II & IV of VP's complaint).

Imtec argues and VP concedes, however, that one type of implant, the "push-in" implant was never sold to New Jersey dentists. In support of specific personal jurisdiction over the patent dispute for this product, VP alleges that the company "offered to sell" the "push-in" product within the state in violation of 35 U.S.C. sec. 271(a).

The Court may exercise specific jurisdiction over Imtec for the "push-in" count of the complaint, Count III, if it offered to sell the allegedly infringing product in the forum state. *See 3 D Sys., Inc. v, Aarotech Labs., Inc.,* 160 F.3d 1373, 1378-79 (Fed. Cir. 1998). Offers to sell may be formal or they may consist of "generating interest in a potential infringing product to the commercial detriment of the rightful patentee." *Id.* at 1379 (finding that price quotes were offers to sell despite disclaimers). The 3D court found that because defendant's price quote letters contained "a description of the allegedly infringing merchandise and the price at which it can be purchased," the letters were offers to sell. *Id.* Mere advertisements directed to a national audience, however, are not "offers to sell" within a particular forum. *See ESAB Group, Inc. v. Centricut, LLC*, 34 F. Supp. 2d 323, 333 (D.S.C. 1999); *see, e.g., Intel Corp. v. Silicon Storage Tech., Inc.*, 20 F. Supp. 2d 690 (D. Del. 1998). Rather, specific product descriptions and pricing information must be "purposefully circulated" to residents of the forum state. See ESAB, 34 F. Supp. 2d at 333; *Lifting Tech., Inc. v. Dixon Indus., Inc.*, 1996 U.S. Dist. LEXIS 21852, No. 96-68, 1996 WL 653391, at *5 (D. Mont. Aug. 27, 1996) (national magazine advertisements sent to forum state combined with price quote letters sent to resident constituted an "offer to sell" in forum state); *see also Decker*, 49 F. Supp. 2d at 750.

Here, Imtec may have sent one catalog to a New Jersey dentist. *MacDonald* Aff. at P 4. Plaintiff, however, does not describe the specific catalog sent to New Jersey nor state whether this catalog contains a description of and pricing information for the "push-in" implant. The company's Internet site which does contain specific product descriptions of "push-in" implants with their catalog order numbers does not contain pricing information. Thus, the Internet site is not an "offer to sell." See 3 D, 160 F.3d at 1379 ("offer to sell" must contain "a description of the allegedly infringing merchandise and the price at which it can be purchased").

Plaintiff has the burden to prove, by a preponderance of the evidence, facts sufficient to establish personal jurisdiction. *Carteret Savings Bank, FA v. Shushan*, 954 F.2d 141, 146 (3d Cir. 1992); *see also Stranahan Gear Co. v. NL Indus., Inc.*, 800 F.2d 53, 58 (3d Cir.1986)(cursory allegation in affidavit does not satisfy burden of proof). Plaintiff has failed to meet this burden for Count III of VP's complaint. Because the Court cannot conclude that Imtec ever offered to sell the allegedly infringing "push-in" implant within this state, it may not exercise specific personal jurisdiction over an infringement suit for this product. See *Osteotech*, 6 F. Supp. 2d at 354 ("forum-related conduct must form the basis of the alleged injuries and resulting litigation"). Plaintiff's motion to dismiss for lack of personal jurisdiction over a conflict involving the "push-in" implants is granted.

Venue

Venue is governed by 28 U.S.C. sec. 1400(b):

Any civil action for patent infringement may be brought in the judicial district where the defendant resides or where the defendant has committed acts of infringement and has a regular and established place of business.

In 1988, Congress broadened the corporate residence standard under the general venue statute, 28 U.S.C. sec. 1391(c), to state that a corporate defendant resides in any judicial district where it is subject to personal jurisdiction. This residence standard applies to the patent venue statute. *See V.E. Holding Corp. v. Johnson Gas Appliance Co.*, 917 F.2d 1574, 1578 (Fed. Cir. 1990). Accordingly, venue is proper here for those Counts over which this Court can exercise personal jurisdiction (Counts I, II, & IV).

Request to Sever [omitted]

Conclusion

Imtec's motion to dismiss for lack of personal jurisdiction is denied for Counts I, II, & IV and is granted for Count III. Consequently, venue is proper in this judicial district for the Counts over which the Court has jurisdiction. Imtec's request to sever is placed before the magistrate judge.

Case Questions

1. Explain the difference between jurisdiction and venue.

2. According to the court, what are the three areas by which Internet use can be categorized?

Exercises

1. Using the Internet locate the Minnesota warning regarding cyber crimes.

2. Research your own state law regarding the application of its long-arm jurisdiction to cyberspace.

3. Briefly discuss some problems that might arise in formulating an international treaty to regulate cyberspace.

4. Indicate how you would determine whether an e-business is transacting business in your state.

5. What is your opinion of American courts applying U.S. Constitutional standards to foreign nationals?

6. Research your own jurisdiction to determine the methods that may be employed to serve process on an out-of-state Internet company.

7. Differentiate between personal, in rem and quasi-in-rem jurisdiction.

8. How does subject matter jurisdiction differ from jurisdiction over the parties?

9. What are the basic differences between civil and criminal law?

10. Relate the concept of due process with jurisdiction and service of process.

Related Websites

Ftc.gov
Fcc.gov
kentlaw.edu/cyberlaw/

Appendix A

Convention on Cybercrime

Chapter Three

CONSTITUTIONAL LAW ISSUES

Chapter Overview

The **United States Constitution** is the supreme law of the land, meaning that all statutes, regulations and other rules must meet the standards imposed by the Constitution in order to be valid and enforceable. Simply because a legislative body has enacted a law does not mean that that law can be enforced if its provisions fail to pass constitutional scrutiny. Pursuant to one of the most prominent judicial decisions in the United States, *Marbury v. Madison*, it is the function of the judiciary to determine whether the actions of the legislative and executive branches of government meet constitutional safeguards.

A comprehensive discussion of constitutional law is beyond the scope of this text; however, as indicated in the previous chapter, the rapid advance of technology has forced legal scholars to apply traditional legal concepts to new problems created by cyberspace. As jurists attempt to draft legislation that specifically addresses these new technological concerns they must keep one eye trained to the Constitution so that new laws adhere to the mandates of individual rights and liberties. Bearing in mind this problem of adaptation of old law to new science, several areas of constitutional concern have surfaced with regard to cyberspace.

One of the rights of an individual that is held to be a fundamental constitutional right is the right to individual privacy. This right ensures that a person will be free from intrusion into his or her seclusion, meaning that a person has a fundamental right to be left alone. With respect to cyberlaw this right may be violated when an individual's personal information can be accessed by strangers by means of the Internet, or his or her seclusion invaded by junk e-mail.

Arguably the major constitutional challenge to the unfettered use of the Internet involves the First Amendment right of freedom of speech. **Freedom of speech** can be defined as the right of a person to say or write whatever he or she thinks without fear of governmental retaliation. However, the right to free speech is not unlimited, and exceptions have been carved out to protect persons from certain unprotected speech such as obscene or defamatory statements and materials that may lessen the reputation of a person. In this context, the Internet has been a medium for the transmission of both protected and unprotected free speech.

As these constitutional questions are addressed in this chapter, it is important to bear in mind some of the jurisdictional issues discussed in the previous chapter. The U.S. Constitution is only applicable to United States citizens and those persons who seek the protection and advantages of the United States' laws. The Constitution does not apply to those persons who are neither physically present in the United States nor who have a direct impact in the United States, and therein lies the problem. Because the Internet is global in scope, a note placed on a bulletin board based in Saudi Arabia may have a direct and immediate effect in Dubuque. How the courts, countries and persons involved handle this problem of potential international conflict dramatize the turmoil that can develop when different legal systems collide.

The Right to Privacy

Basically, the right to privacy is the right of a person to be left alone. The Constitution itself is silent on this point, but the issue of a constitutional basis of a right to privacy has long been held to exist, not directly in the Constitution but rather under the penumbra, or shadow, of the constitutional provisions.

The first mention of a "right to privacy" appeared in 1890 in a law review article authored by Louis D. Brandeis, a former Justice of the United States Supreme Court. The concept of a right to privacy has historically been based on a broad interpretation of two specific Amendments to the Constitution: the Fourth and the Ninth.

The Fourth Amendment states that people have the right to be secure in their persons, property and homes, and have a right to be free from unreasonable searches and seizures. This Amendment forms the basis of the requirement that the police obtain a search warrant to enter a person's house.

The Ninth Amendment simply states that the enumeration of certain rights does not deny other rights that are retained by the people. It should be noted at the outset that neither of these Amendments specifically uses the word "privacy"; they do not create such a right and, most importantly, these Amendments only apply to governmental actions and do not specifically protect persons from the private actions of other individuals. Therefore, the question must be addressed as to how this right to privacy applies to cyberlaw.

The answer is twofold. First, directly related to the interpretation of the Fourth and Ninth Amendments is the governmental use of the Internet in a fashion that could violate constitutional guarantees. Significantly, this means that whereas the government is permitted to use computers to collect personal data about individuals who are either citizens or resident in the United States, the government may only gather such information if it can demonstrate a compelling need and that such information is necessary for a legitimate governmental purpose.

Example: In order to provide a person with Social Security benefits the government must determine that the individual is entitled to such benefits by having worked a requisite number of quarters and having contributed to the Social Security Fund during that period. The government may use computer technology to gather such information to assist in the payment of such benefits.

However, the government may still be precluded from transferring such data for a nonessential use without the individual's consent. In order to prevent such unwarranted dissemination, the federal government has enacted several statutes over the past decades that are applicable or directly related to computer information gathering. These federal statutes are:

1. **The Fair Credit Reporting Act of 1970,** which mandates that credit reports on individuals be fair and accurate and provides sanctions against transmitting such credit information without the person's consent. Further, the statute permits the individual to obtain information about his or her credit report from the credit agencies that maintain them, and this includes online inquiries.

Example: *The ABC Credit Agency has been asked to prepare a credit report on an individual. The agency used the person's name and Social Security number to access information about her by means of the Internet. Some of the information is publicly available, but other data was retrieved by accessing information stored by another agency. Such use of the Internet could be considered a violation of the person's rights under the Fair Credit Reporting Act.*

2. **The Cable Communication Protection Act of 1984** prohibits a cable operator from disseminating information about a subscriber without the subscriber's consent. Many computer applications permit the user to have cable programs transmitted directly to the computer, and therefore this statute could directly affect privacy rights in cyberspace. This act applies to both private citizens and the government.

3. **The Computer Fraud and Abuse Act of 1986** was enacted specifically to address problems associated with computer use. This statute makes it a crime to access computer data stored in government computers. In the interest of privacy the statute also makes it a crime for an individual to access personal data about another person that is stored in a government file, such as Social Security information noted above.

4. **The Electronic Communication Privacy Act of 1986**, which protects the sanctity of electronic communications including not only e-mail but all other forms of information that is electronically transmitted. This act applies to individuals as well as the government, but includes four exemptions to the act for which interception is permitted:

   a) ***Internet Service Providers***, the companies that create and market Internet access services for its customers, may interrupt such communications as is necessary in order to maintain the quality of such service. However, the provider may not randomly interrupt such communications, nor sell or disseminate any information so gathered. This exception is designed exclusively to permit the provider to maintain its product.

Example: *A customer has complained to her Internet service provider that her e-mail messages arrive in a garbled format. The provider may intercept the customer's e-mail to discover what the transmission problem may be without violating the provisions of the act.*

   b) ***Consent***, which applies whenever the user has granted permission to have his or her transmissions intercepted.

Example: *When he was first employed, a stockbroker was informed by his employer that it would periodically monitor his computer to determine the quality and quantity of his work, and he agreed to this when he accepted employment. The employer, by monitoring his e-mail, has discovered that he is using the company's computer to send and receive pornographic e-mails. The company fires him. The employee cannot claim that his rights were violated because he had agreed to such interceptions as one of the terms of his employment.*

   c) ***Business Exception***, which permits businesses to interrupt employees computer transmissions that occur at work on the company equipment, as in the example above.

   d) ***Law Enforcement***, meaning that the government and law enforcement agencies may intercept and monitor electronic communications in the same manner that they may tap telephone calls, provided that they first obtain an appropriate warrant.

Example: *The police have obtained information by which they believe that a named individual has been using his computer to arrange illegal drug sales. The police are able to obtain a warrant to intercept this person's e-mail to monitor his money transfer transactions.*

5. **The Video Privacy Protection Act of 1986** extends the Cable Communications Protection Act to videocassettes and CDs that are used by computers.

Example: *A customer decides to purchase some CDs from her favorite online retailer. Later, without the customer's permission, the online retailer sells the customer's name and e-mail address to another company that wants to acquire a potential customer list of people interested in purchasing CDs. This unauthorized sale of the customer's information would be a violation of the Video Privacy Protection Act.*

6. **The Privacy Act of 1994** applies to data that identifies a person by name, number, or other means of personal identification. This act applies to the Internet whenever such identifying information is stored in a computer file. In such situations, before the information can be disseminated, the information-storing agency must obtain the written consent of the individual and provide the individual with all information stored about him or her at the individual's request, as well as permitting the individual to correct any errors appearing in such data.

Example: *An HMO maintains all of its medical records on participants coded by the patient's name and Social Security Number. The HMO is precluded, under the provisions of the Privacy Act, from disseminating such information without the patient's consent, and the patient has the right to see all such information about him or her that the HMO stores.*

Specifically relating to these statues is the problem of e-businesses maintaining records on persons who access their sites. A **cookie** is a device that stores the e-mail information of any person who accesses a given website. This information stored on the cookie may then be used by the e-business or sold to other businesses to create a customer/user file. Because the cookie contains personal identifying information (the e-mail name) such dissemination without the consent of the user may violate the above-discussed statutes.

In addition to the constitutional and specific statutory protections against invasions of privacy, the right to privacy has also been recognized as right under traditional concepts of tort law. A **tort** is a civil wrong, redress for which does not fall under any other legal doctrine. In the context of tort law protection against an invasion of privacy, the law recognizes that a person may suffer an invasion of privacy in any of four ways:

1. Intrusion upon the person's solitude or into the person's private affairs. A person is entitled to be free from unwanted interference into his or her personal life. The elements of this tort are:
   a) an act of prying or interference
   b) the act would be objectionable to a reasonable person
   c) the interference involves activity or information that is generally considered to be private.

Example: *A woman wants to send her aunt an e-mail message. When she goes online she discovers that she has over 30 unsolicited e-mail advertisements. This problem of junk e-mail is referred to as **spamming**. The senders acquired the woman's e-mail address by purchasing that information from other e-businesses whose sites the woman has accessed. At this point in time, except for certain limited states that have passed anti-spamming statutes, this invasion of the woman's solitude may be capable of being redressed under traditional tort law principles.*

2. Public disclosure of an embarrassing or private fact. The elements of this tort are:
   a) private information about a person
   b) that a reasonable person would object to having disclosed.

Example: *A website prints a notice about a college athlete's sexual preference. If such information is confidential and was divulged without the athlete's consent, the athlete's right to privacy may have been violated.*

3. Placing a person in a **false light**. This tort involves:
   a) disseminating facts that put a person in a false light
   b) those facts are objectionable
   c) malice (if the person is a public figure).

Example: *A woman is arrested for firing a gun in a restaurant. The newspaper prints the name of her boyfriend who was in the restaurant with her in a way that intimates that he was involved in her act, which is not true. The boyfriend may have a cause of action against the paper for placing him in a false light.*

4. The appropriation of a person's name or likeness for personal advantage. This tort involves the unreasonable use of another's image for commercial advantage.

Example: *A t-shirt manufacturer prints a shirt with the image of a famous actress on the front, which it sells on the Internet. If the actress did not authorize such use, her privacy was invaded.*

Note however, that this fourth type of tort is inapplicable if a person uses a personal likeness for his or her own advantage. This is known as the **right of publicity**, meaning that if the actress from the previous example printed up a shirt with her own likeness on it to sell on her publicity tours, her likeness has not been "appropriated."

There are several other tort law principles that apply to the right to privacy:
   a) The right to privacy does not exist if the person has given his or her consent to the action in question.
   b) The right does not attach if the information is considered a news event.
   c) To assert the right, the violation must appear in a **permanent publication**, which is defined as something fixed or permanently available. With respect to cyberlaw, because almost all data from the Internet can be downloaded, Internet use would probably meet this requirement.
   d) Some jurisdictions hold that privacy can only be invaded if the publication of the information results in financial gain to the wrongdoer, so each jurisdiction's law must be individually analyzed.
   e) If a person is considered to be a **public figure**, he or she may have lost such privacy rights (see below).

The cyberlaw problems associated with the right to privacy are being addressed by the legislatures, the courts, and the international community as specific questions arise.

Obscenity

The First Amendment to the Constitution prohibits Congress from abridging the freedom of speech or of the press. These prohibitions are deemed applicable to the individual states through the Fourteenth Amendment. However, these freedoms are not absolute, and certain types of expression are not protected by the Constitution. One such exception that has particular import for cyberlaw is speech that is considered to be obscene.

Obscenity is defined as a description or depiction of sexual conduct that, taken as a whole by the average person, applying contemporary community standards, appeals to a prurient interest in sex in a patently offensive manner, and which does not have serious literary, artistic, political or scientific value using a national standard. To determine whether a given item is obscene, each of three elements must be individually examined.

1. *Appealing to the prurient interest.* To meet this element, the material considered as a whole must appeal to a prurient interest in sex. Such interest relates to material that appeals to a shameful interest in sex, but does not apply to mere lust. That interest must be determined by reference to the "average" person. This element may create a problem with respect to cyberspace where the material disseminated over the Internet is sent to such diverse areas as Los Angeles, California, and Teheran, Iran. How can a court determine the "average" for a global community?

Further, this requirement may be modified if the material is designed for an identified discrete group, such as masochists, rather than the community at large. In such circumstances the court will decide whether the material appeals to the prurient interest of that identified group. Also, the material must be viewed in its entirety—it cannot be considered to be appealing to prurient interests if only one small portion may appeal to prurient interests but, when taken as a whole, the entire work does not.

Example: Certain passages in a 900-page novel appeal to the prurient interest. These passages, combined, total 20 pages of the entire work. Under these circumstances the novel would not be considered obscene.

2. *Patently offensive.* To determine the offensiveness of the material, the work must offend the affected community, not the nation as a whole. Once again, with the global impact of the Internet, how is the appropriate "community" to be identified?

Example: A website transmits pictures of nude women which are downloaded in both Miami and Mecca. Which community determines whether the pictures are patently offensive?

3. *Lacking serious social value.* In common parlance this element is generally referred to as "redeeming social value." However, merely having some redeeming value is insufficient to conclude that the material is not obscene. The court must assess a work's serious literary, artistic, political or scientific value using a national standard. With worldwide distribution over the Internet, what is the "nation"?

Questions regarding the serious content of a work are considered to be questions of fact to be determined by a jury. However, determining whether a given work is obscene is only one side of the coin; for cyberlaw application, the greatest problem arises with respect to regulating what has become known as **cyberporn**. To date, the United States has enacted four statutes in an attempt to regulate obscenity in cyberspace.

In 1996 Congress enacted the **Communications Decency Act** to protect minors from pornography, making it a crime to knowingly transmit obscene material in foreign or interstate commerce by means of an interactive computer service. The act applies both to adults and **minors**, persons under the age of eighteen. That same year the **Child Pornography Prevention Act** was passed which makes it a crime to knowingly produce child pornography by means of computer technology. This statute applies regardless of whether the persons depicted are in fact children or adults who give the physical appearance of children.

Example: *An adult film producer offers films for sale on his website. Some of the films depict adults who resemble teenagers being seduced by older men and women. This use of the Internet would violate the Child Pornography Prevention Act.*

Two more statutes were enacted in 1998 specifically designed to protect children from accessing pornography on the Internet. The **Child Online Protection Act of 1998 (COPA)** requires persons who provide "harmful" material by means of the Internet to create methods of determining the age of the consumer before allowing access to the material, and the **Protection of Children from Sexual Predators Act** makes it a crime for anyone to attempt to use the Internet for the purpose of child pornography or sexual abuse. (See Appendix B.)

Example: *An "adult" website offers pornographic magazines for sale over the Internet. The site owner accepts all credit card sales over the Internet without attempting to determine the age of the card user. This activity would violate the provisions of COPA if a minor buys a magazine in this fashion.*

The problem of cyberporn has become closely associated with **cybercrime**, crimes committed on or by using the Internet, and these problems will be specifically addressed in Chapter Six of this text. For the purposes of this chapter on constitutional law issues in cyberspace, it is important to remember that whereas the Internet, when used as a means of transmitting speech, is protected by constitutional guarantees, not all speech is afforded such protection. The U.S. Constitution does not protect speech that is considered to be obscene. However, problems arise with respect to regulating such unprotected speech because of the jurisdictional problems discussed in Chapter Two as well as the fact that there is no international body or consensus with respect to regulating obscenity on the Internet and cyberporn is global in impact. (See Convention on Cybercrime, Appendix A)

Defamation

Just as with speech that is considered obscene, speech that is deemed defamatory is also not protected by the U.S. Constitution.

Defamation is a statement about a person that has been communicated to another which results in the lessening of the reputation of the person about whom the statement is made. Defamation may be either oral or written. Oral defamation is called **slander**, whereas written defamation is called **libel**. Defamatory statements transmitted by means of the Internet are considered to fall within the category of libel.

In order to prove defamation, the following elements must be evidenced:

1. The statement is defamatory, which means that it impugns an individual's reputation and/or exposes the individual to public hatred, contempt, or ridicule. If the statements are defamatory on their face, they are deemed to be **defamatory per se**; if the defamatory aspect of the statement is only defamatory by relating it to other facts it is **defamatory per quod** and it must be shown that the person to whom the statement was made was aware of those outside facts.

Example: *Telling a third person that a named woman is a prostitute is considered defamation per se; telling a third person that a named woman works at a certain company might be defamation per quod if that company were a brothel and the third person knew that fact.*

2.   The statement must be "of or concerning" the person who claims the injury. In other words, the statement must identify the person who is allegedly being defamed.

Example: Saying "that man" is a liar does not concern a particular person if not coupled with other statements identifying who "that man" is.

3.   There is publication, which means that the statement is communicated to a third person, someone other than the speaker or the person about whom the statement refers.

Example: E-mailing John and calling him a thief is not publication. However, if the sender e-mails a courtesy copy of that statement to a friend of John's, that would be publication to a third person.

4.   There is damage to the reputation of the person. If the person is already held in low regard by the third person, the statement may not have lessened his or her opinion of the allegedly defamed person.

If the statement is considered to be defamation per se, damages, or injury, are automatically presumed, whereas defamation per quod requires proof of actual injury to the defamed person.

It must be noted that statements that might be considered objectionable about an ordinary person may not provide relief if the person who is the subject of the statement is considered to be a **public figure**, someone who is generally known. In order to maintain a suit of defamation involving a public official, the defamed person must prove, in addition to the above-indicated elements, that the statement was both false and made with malice towards the defamed person.

Example: An Internet service provider publishes a news item about a right-wing politician that states that the politician was found drunk in a bordello. Even though the politician's reputation may be lessened, because the politician is a public figure if the statement is true and not reported maliciously, the service provider will not be held liable.

The law recognizes four defenses to a charge of defamation:

1.   Consent. If the person who is the subject of the statement has agreed to its publication, he or she may not later sue for defamation.
2.   Truth. Truth of the facts stated is always a defense.
3.   Absolute privilege. This applies if the speaker has a **privilege**, a legal right, to make the statement. The following are considered to fall within this defense:
     a) statements made as part of a judicial proceeding
     b) statements made as part of a legislative proceeding
     c) statements made as part of an executive proceeding
     d) statements made by a broadcaster under circumstances in which the broadcaster is "compelled" to make the statement under the concept of the fair use of the airways

Example: The Internet provider who disseminated the statement about the politician in the preceding example may be compelled to permit the politician to reply during which the politician makes a defamatory statement about the reporter. The provider cannot be charged with defamation.

    e) statements made between spouses because such statements are not considered to be made to "the public"

  4. Qualified privilege. These privileges include the following:
    a) reports of public proceeding in which the defamatory statement is made
    b) statements that are made in the public interest
    c) statements made in defense of the owner's right
    d) statements made to a person who has an interest in the information, such as an employer seeking information about a prospective employee
    e) statements in which the speaker and the hearer have a common interest in having the information.

Pursuant to the provisions of the Communications Decency Act, an interactive service provider is not considered to be the speaker or publisher of the statement where it is made by another content provider. This means that the provider is only liable for statements of its own that it publishes.

Various problems arise with respect to seeking relief if one is the victim of defamation on the Internet, the primary one being that of jurisdiction. It must first be determined where the statement was made and where it was received in order to meet the publication requirement. Further, even if that could be ascertained, the question remains as to the appropriate court to hear the matter and/or enforce any ultimate judgment. As with most areas of cyberlaw, the courts and the legislatures must attempt to grapple with the problems of applying traditional law to nontraditional technology.

Chapter Review

The United States Constitution provides for certain enumerated and implied rights for individuals who come within its protections. Among these rights that have a direct impact on cyberlaw include the right to privacy, the right to be free from obscene material and the right to be free from being defamed.

The right to privacy mandates that a person is to be free from any intrusion into his or her seclusion or private affairs. Whenever such an interest is affected by means of computer technology, it enters into the sphere of cyberlaw. This right may be violated when personal data stored on a database is accessed without authority or personal information about a person is disseminated over the Internet without consent.

Although the Constitution guarantees persons the right to express themselves freely without fear of governmental retribution, not all speech is so protected. Statements that are obscene, those that appeal to a prurient interest in sex and which have no redeeming social value, are not protected and persons who disseminate obscene material over the Internet violate both the Constitution and specific laws that penalize such activity.

Finally, a person is precluded from making a defamatory statement about another. If such a statement is made over the Internet, the transmitter may be subject to a civil suit by the person so defamed for lessening his or her reputation in the community.

Key Terms

Cable Communications Protection Act of 1984—Federal law that prohibits the dissemination about a subscriber by a provider without the subscriber's consent

Child Online Protection Act (COPA) of 1998—Federal law designed to protect children from accessing pornography on the Internet

Child Pornography Prevention Act—Federal law making it a crime to produce child pornography by means of computer technology

Communications Decency Act of 1996—Federal law making it a crime to transmit pornography in foreign or interstate commerce by means of computer technology

Computer Fraud and Abuse Act of 1986—Federal law making it a crime to access government data banks

Cookie—Computer device that keeps track of all persons who access a given website

Cybercrime—Crime committed by means of a computer or computer technology

Cyberporn—Pornography transmitted over the Internet

Defamation—Libel or slander

Defamation per quod—A statement that is only defamatory if referenced to material not appearing in the statement

Defamation per se—Statements that are defamatory on their face

Electronic Communication Privacy Act of 1986—Federal law designed to extend privacy protections to electronic communications

Fair Credit Reporting Act of 1970—Federal law designed to prohibit unauthorized transfer of a person's credit history

False Light—Disseminating information that puts a person in a false light

Freedom of Speech—Constitutional guarantee

Libel—Written defamation

Obscenity—Material that appeals to prurient interests

Privacy Act of 1994—Federal law that protects transferring information that identifies people by name, number, or other unique identifier

Privilege—Legal right

Protection of Children from Sexual Predators Act of 1996—Federal law to protect children from sexual abuse involving computer use

Public Figure—Person who is known and recognized by the community

Right of Publicity—A person can profit from his or her own likeness

Right to Privacy—Right to be left alone that is assumed to be a constitutional guarantee

Slander—Oral defamation

Spamming—Junk e-mail

Tort—Civil wrong

United States Constitution—Supreme law of the land

Video Privacy Protection Act of 1986—Federal law that extends the Cable Communications Privacy Act to videos and CDs

Edited Cases

The *Comcast* case is presented to discuss whether there is a constitutional prohibition restricting local authorities' ability to require a cable company to provide equal Internet access to all of its subscribers. The second case, *In re Application of the United States of America*, discusses the alleged conflict between the Cable Communication Policy Act and the Electronic Communications Privacy Act.

Comcast Cablevision of Broward County, Inc., and Advocate Communications, Inc.,
D/B/A Advanced Cable Communications, v. Broward County, Florida,
Tci Tkr of South Florida, Inc., and Mediaone of Greater Florida,Inc.,
v. Broward County Florida
124 F. Supp. 2d 685 (S.D. Fla. 2000)

THIS CAUSE is before the Court upon cross-motions for summary judgment. The Court has reviewed the extensive factual submissions and excellent memoranda of law filed by the parties, and heard oral argument.

Introduction

The issue presented in this case is whether the First Amendment to the United States Constitution restricts the authority of local government to require a cable television system which offers its subscribers high-speed Internet service to allow competitors equal access to its system. Broward County, a political subdivision of the State of Florida, has adopted an ordinance that requires any cable system franchisee to provide any requesting Internet service provider access to its broadband Internet transport services on rates, terms, and conditions at least as favorable as those on which it provides such access to itself.

The County contends that the ordinance is necessary to level the playing field among competitors and guarantee its citizens access to a diversity of Internet service providers, further justifying the ordinance as part of the price for use of the public rights-of-way. The cable companies targeted by the ordinance contend that they are entitled to the speech and press protections of the First Amendment and that it is not within the County's power to decide the programming available on their systems. For the reasons that follow, I conclude that the ordinance unconstitutionally abridges freedom of speech and the press.

Background

A. The Ordinance

On July 13, 1999, at the prompting of GTE, a telephone company offering competing services, the Broward County Commission adopted Ordinance No. 1999-41. The ordinance, which is applicable to all County granted cable franchisees, states:

Nondiscriminatory Access Required. Subject to technical feasibility, Franchisee shall provide any requesting Internet Service Provider access to its Broadband Internet Access Transport Services (unbundled from the provision of content) on rates, terms, and conditions that are at least as favorable as those on which it provides such access to itself, to its affiliate, or to any other person. Such access shall be provided at any technically feasible point selected by the requesting Internet Service Provider.

Ordinance No. 199-41, Sec. 1.02, Access to Broadband Internet Access Transport Services, Exhibit A to Plaintiffs Comcast and Advanced Cable's Appendix to Statement of Material Facts in Support of Summary Judgment.

The ordinance was adopted by a 4-3 majority of the County Commission. The Commission's staff recommended against adopting the ordinance.

B. The Debate

1. Broadband

"Broadband" refers to technology that allows users to access the Internet at speeds significantly higher than the modems typically used today. Currently, many Americans who use the Internet do so at speeds less than 56 kbps. Broadband technology allows users access at speeds that range from fifty to several hundred times faster. This increased speed will provide for a range of enhanced services and, in all likelihood, will change the way consumers communicate, shop, educate, and entertain. It is estimated that approximately two million Americans presently have access to broadband technology. By 2008, that number is predicted to reach 78 million. *See A Staff Report to William E. Kennard, Chairman, Federal Communications Commission on Industry Monitoring Sessions Convened by Cable Services Bureau*, October 1999, Broadband Today, at 9. The increasing demand for broadband services has been driven by the explosive growth of the Internet, which has risen from 10 million users in 1995, to 150 million worldwide users in 1999. *See id.*at 16.

2. Cable Broadband

The cable industry is transforming from closed cable systems that feature one-way delivery of analog television signals to two-way interactive broadband systems, involving a hybrid of coaxial and fiber optic technologies. Historically, cable networks were constructed to provide only video programming services that required only one-way transmission of signals. Until recently, a typical one-way cable system provided approximately 50 channels of analog video. The network was a full coaxial system with a centralized headend, trunk lines leading to the neighborhoods, and distribution lines carrying the signal to the consumer.

Today, coaxial systems are being replaced by hybrid systems referred to as hybrid fiber-coaxial or "HFC." The replacement of coaxial cable with fiber optic cable enables cable operators to deliver applications at very high data rates.

These new networks allow a cable operator to offer more than 100 analog video channels, hundreds of digital video channels, as well as provide capacity for Internet access, telephony and other services. With respect to Internet access, upgraded cable systems can carry data up to several hundred times faster than transmission using dial-up modems over ordinary telephone lines, and a hundred times faster than ISDN (integrated services digital network) telephone lines. Because a cable network is a shared medium, these speeds vary depending on the number of actual subscribers using the Internet connection at the same time. *See id.*

3. Telephone Company Broadband

Digital Subscriber Line (DSL) is the telecommunications carriers' version of broadband access. With DSL, the average analog connection of 56.6 kbps can be increased to 1.5 Mbps or higher.

DSL technology upgrades the performance of the standard copper line connecting most homes and businesses to carry high capacity data transmission. The technology expands the amount of frequency used over the copper line, whereby the line's higher frequencies are used to transmit the data and the lower frequencies are free to transmit voice or fax transmissions. Thus, DSL is able to function on a line simultaneously with standard voice and fax services and avoids the installation of a separate line. Since the technology works over the existing telephone system, DSL is significantly less expensive to deploy on a broad scale than new fiber or cable construction.

There are two general categories of DSL service, symmetrical and asymmetrical. Symmetrical versions offer the same data rates upstream and downstream and are well suited for business applications. Asymmetrical versions offer different data rates upstream and downstream and are best suited for residential users who receive a lot of data but do not originate or send much. One version, asymmetric digital subscriber line (ADSL), allows a user to simultaneously browse the Internet or watch a movie while talking on the telephone. It is said that ADSL provides a competitive advantage over cable modem Internet access in the following areas:

- Simultaneous fast Internet and voice/fax capabilities over a single telephone line.
- Data security over a dedicated point-to-point line which is not available over a shared medium such as cable.
- Dedicated bandwidth that guarantees performance regardless of the number of users on the network unlike cable modems where actual performance deteriorates as the number of users increases.

4. Wireless: Fixed and Satellite

Fixed wireless providers are using their existing microwave networks to transmit high-speed Internet services. Fixed wireless providers avoid the high costs and delays associated with laying fibers or upgrading cable networks and can therefore enter the market quickly at relatively low costs. The technology also presents obstacles, however, most notably the line of sight requirements between the transmitter and receiving antenna.

There are several satellite providers that are constructing systems and plan to start offering two-way broadband satellite services by 2001. With their unlimited coverage, satellite systems will offer broadband access to virtually any part of the United States. *See id.* at 21-22.

5.   National Broadband Policy

In 1996, Congress directed the Federal Communications Commission (FCC), in section 706 of the Telecommunications Act, to monitor the development of broadband capability and, if necessary, to take steps to accelerate the deployment of broadband capability. *See generally Advanced Services Report*, 14 FCC Rcd 2398 (1999). Section 706(c) is entitled "advanced telecommunications capability," which Congress defined "without regard to any transmission media or technology, as high speed, switched, broadband telecommunications capability that enables users to originate and receive high-quality voice, data, graphics, and video telecommunications using any technology." Pub.L. No. 104-104, Title VII, sec. 706(c), 110 Stat. 153 (1996) (reproduced in the notes under 47 U.S.C. sec. 157).

In February 1999, the FCC released its initial report concerning advanced communications capability as directed by the Congress. *See Advanced Services Report, supra*. In its 1999 report, the FCC found that there is reasonable and timely deployment of broadband capability and that there was no need at that time for regulatory intervention in the broadband market. *See id.* at sec. 101. The Commission announced that it would continue to closely monitor the deployment of broadband and planned to issue additional reports on broadband deployment during each calendar year. *See id.* at sec. 19.

The FCC also considered the issue of Internet access in considering the merger of AT&T, at the time the nation's largest long-distance telephone provider, and Telecommunications, Inc., one of the largest cable television operators. In its order approving the transfer of licenses from TCI to AT&T, the FCC rejected any open access condition, citing the emergence of competing methods of high-speed Internet access. It found "that the equal access issues raised by the parties to this proceeding do not provide a basis for conditioning, denying, or designating for hearing any of the requested transfers of licenses and authorizations." *See Applications for Consent to the Transfer Control of Licenses and Section 214 Authorizations from TCI to AT&T*, 14 FCC Rcd 3160, 1999 WL 76930 (F.C.C.) (1999) ("Transfer Order"). The FCC concluded that "while the merger is unlikely to yield anti-competitive effects, we believe it may yield public interest benefits to consumers in the form of a quicker roll-out of high-speed Internet access services." *Id.* at sec. 94.

In October 1999, the Cable Services Bureau of the FCC released a report on the state of the broadband industry. With respect to broadband cable access, the Report concluded:

The Bureau is not persuaded that consumers are at risk of cable establishing a bottleneck monopoly in broadband services in the absence of immediate regulatory action. There have been no developments since the release of the Section 706 Report earlier this year to alter the Commission's conclusion that no monopoly exists. Moreover the monopoly argument wrongly assumes that cable is the only viable broadband pipe available in the near term to provide Internet access to the home. As deployment of DSL, satellite and wireless advances in large part spurred by rapid cable modem deployment, consumers will have alternative platforms to use for high-speed data access, telephony and video services. We have already seen evidence that these alternative technologies are attracting new subscribers at an exponential rate, and that prices for these new services are falling.

C. Activities of the Plaintiffs

MediaOne Florida is a wholly owned subsidiary of MediaOne Group, Inc., a holding company that owns numerous subsidiaries (collectively "MediaOne") providing cable services to subscribers in various regions of the United States. In 1999, MediaOne Group announced a plan to merge with AT&T, and the FCC has granted approval to the merger. See Memorandum Opinion and Order, In the Matter of Application of Consent to the Transfer of Control of Licenses and Section 214 Authorizations From MediaOne Group, Inc., Transferor, to AT&T Corp., Transferee, CS Docket No. 99-251 (June 6, 2000) P 1 ("MediaOne Merger Order").

In its cable franchise areas, MediaOne offers (or has made plans to offer) a high-speed interactive cable modem service called "RoadRunner" as a programming option available to its cable subscribers for an extra charge (as are other programming options such as HBO or certain movie channels). The RoadRunner programming service provided by MediaOne contains content, applications (*e.g.*, games and chat boards), and Internet connectivity. RoadRunner provides MediaOne with a network of computers and facilities to deliver these services to cable systems.

TCI TKR is a wholly owned subsidiary of Tele-Communications, Inc. ("TCI"). TCI is a national cable company that provides cable services to millions of subscribers across the country through its local subsidiaries. In 1998, TCI announced a plan to merge with AT&T Corp. The merger was consummated in March 1999. See Memorandum Opinion and Order, In the Matter of Application for Consent to the Transfer of Control of Licenses and Section 214 Authorizations from Tele-Communications, Inc., Transferor, to AT&T Corp., Transferee, CS Docket No. 98-178 (Feb. 17, 1999) PP 5-8 ("TCI Merger Order").

TCI and others formed a company now named Excitesec.Home ("sec.Home") to develop content for cable modem services and to develop a network of computers and facilities to deliver the content and Internet connectivity to TCI's cable systems. Separately, TCI has entered into arrangements with the *Chicago Tribune* and others to supply local news and content for TCI's cable modem service. In its cable franchise areas throughout the country, TCI offers (or has made plans to offer) sec.Home to its cable subscribers as a single integrated programming option available for an extra charge.

TCI's cable modem offering is made pursuant to an exclusive contract with sec.Home, and MediaOne's offering is made pursuant to an exclusive contract with RoadRunner. These contracts remain in effect until 2002. sec.Home and MediaOne's RoadRunner service allow subscribers high-speed access to the Internet and all publicly available content on it. This includes the web pages of America Online, Mindspring, and all other ISPs. Thus, TCI and MediaOne subscribers, by paying the monthly rate for sec.Home or RoadRunner service, can access any information or ontent that is publicly available anywhere on the Internet, regardless of the source of that information or content.

TCI and MediaOne acquire or produce news, information, and advertising content and publish it on the respective "first pages" of the sec.Home and RoadRunner services they offer subscribers. The "first page" is the default screen that TCI and MediaOne subscribers see when they access TCI's sec.Home or MediaOne's RoadRunner service.

All subscribers to the sec.Home or RoadRunner programming receive and are exposed to the "first page" and its content when they initially access the service. This is also the case each time thereafter, unless the subscriber changes the "first page."

Sec.Home and RoadRunner subscribers can change the "first page" they see when they access the Internet from MediaOne's "first page," for example, to America Online's or any other ISP's. However, most sec.Home and RoadRunner subscribers choose to retain the "first pages" produced by TCI and MediaOne as their default start-up screen.

TCI and MediaOne both sell the right to advertise on their "first pages" and use the revenues to subsidize the transmission cost of their cable modem services.

Because of the passage of the ordinance, TCI and MediaOne have halted all plans to offer their respective cable modem programming options to customers in unincorporated Broward County. MediaOne Florida has announced that it will not offer cable modem services in unincorporated Broward County as long as the ordinance remains in effect. TCI TKR has also postponed plans to offer such services in Broward pending the outcome of this litigation, placing its plans to upgrade its systems in unincorporated Broward County at the bottom of its prioritization list. MediaOne is currently offering and providing two-way RoadRunner service to subscribers in incorporated sections of Broward County, where the ordinance does not apply.

Analysis

A. It is now well established that regulation of cable operators implicates both the Free Speech and Free Press clauses of the First Amendment. *See, e.g., Turner Broadcasting System, Inc. v. F.C.C. (Turner I,.* 512 U.S. 622, 114 S. Ct. 2445, 129 L. Ed. 2d 497 (1994); *Leathers v. Medlock*, 499 U.S. 439, 111 S. Ct. 1438, 113 L. Ed. 2d 494 (1991); *City of Los Angeles v. Preferred Communications, Inc,* 476 U.S. 488, 106 S. Ct. 2034, 90 L. Ed. 2d 480 (1986). Through "original programming or by exercising editorial discretion over which stations or programs to include in its repertoire," cable programmers and operators "seek to communicate messages on a wide variety of topics and in a wide variety of formats." *Turner I*, 512 U.S. at 636, 114 S. Ct. at 2456 (quoting *Preferred Communications*, 476 U.S. at 494, 106 S. Ct. at 2037).

In this case, the plaintiff cable operators seek to offer broadband Internet service. Along with movies, weather, sports, news and entertainment programming, such as the Weather Channel, HBO, VH1 and CNN, the Plaintiffs have selected an Internet service—Advanced Communications has selected ISP Channel; MediaOne has selected RoadRunner; and TCI, along with others, has founded sec.Home. Each selection offers distinctive programming and format. According to the Plaintiffs, their choices were made from an array of opportunities and reflected a choice based upon content. Their choice required them to forego other programming because of the physical limitations of their system. They plan to market their Internet provider as an integral part of their overall programming. Under their business plan, advertising is sold to create income for their Internet service in addition to payments from their subscribers.

The Plaintiffs now have exclusive contracts with their Internet providers. Pursuant to the contracts, the Internet providers participated in the installation of equipment to establish the system. The Plaintiffs advise that as these exclusive contracts expire, they are considering the addition of other Internet providers as part of their offering. They say this is driven by audience demand for some services. They consider some Internet providers unacceptable because of offensive or hateful programming. The Plaintiffs say they are not, and do not want to become, a transport service, and that their offerings are a matter of choice.

Broward County acknowledges that a cable operator may be entitled to protection for its own content, but contends that the transmission mechanism employed by the cable operator enjoys no First Amendment protection and may be separated out for regulation. "Plaintiffs are 'singled out' because of their possession of a unique facility—the transmission conduit—not because of anything they say, do not say, or wish to say." Broward County's Reply and Response at 2. According to the County, the cable operators possess "a valuable conduit" that "should be shared among content providers to create the conditions for vigorous competition, innovation, and consumer choice." *Id.* at 2. The County claims to regulate "only trade practices and not speech." *Id.* at 4.

The County argues that its ability to regulate is not constrained by the Plaintiffs' business plan. The County contends that it has the authority to separate the provision of Internet service from the transportation mechanism owned by the cable companies and offers this hypothetical to explain its approach:

Suppose to reduce noise and pollution, the County granted one delivery company a public franchise to deliver newspapers each morning. That company then "ties" the delivery franchise to its own newspaper—it adopts a rule that the consumer must purchase its newspaper in order to receive delivery of any other newspaper.

According to the County, its action "untying" these services would be "economic regulation" not subject to heightened First Amendment scrutiny. The "flaw" in the argument of the cable operators, claims the County, is that "it mistakes the truck for the newspapers—the delivery service (or transmission) for the content." *Id.*

B. The Supreme Court, however, has repeatedly held that "liberty of circulating is as essential to [freedom of the press] as liberty of publishing; indeed, without the circulation, the publication would be of little value." *Ex Parte Jackson*, 96 U.S. 727, 733, 24 L. Ed. 877 (1877); *see also City of Lakewood v. Plain Dealer Pub. Co.*, 486 U.S. 750, 768, 108 S. Ct. 2138, 2150, 100 L. Ed. 2d 771 (1988) ("The actual 'activity' at issue here [placement of newsracks] is the circulation of newspapers, which is constitutionally protected."); *Lovell v. City of Griffin, Ga.*, 303 U.S. 444, 452, 58 S. Ct. 666, 669, 82 L. Ed. 949 (1938) ("The ordinances [prohibiting distribution of circulars] cannot be saved because it relates to distribution and not to publication."). Liberty of circulating is not confined to newspapers and periodicals, pamphlets and leaflets, but also to delivery of information by means of fiber optics, microprocessors and cable. "The press in its historic connotation comprehends every sort of publication which affords a vehicle of information and opinion." *Id.*

In arguing that the conduit or transmission capability of speech can be separated from its content, the County ignores the relationship between the two. Although all would agree that the First Amendment protects freedom of thought and expression, it is equally true that thought is nonverbal and necessarily requires speech to be communicated. Moreover, technology extends the senses, permitting faster communication beyond reach of the human voice. The printed word brought uniformity and repeatability and permitted widespread circulation through books and then newspapers. The increasing speed of information gathering and publication also has created new forms of arranging and circulating information affecting not only the physical appearance of the press but also the prose of those contributing to it. For example, movies, by speeding up the mechanical, moved us from sequence to configuration and structure while the immediacy of radio and television has eliminated distance and time. In short, content and technology are intertwined in ways which make analytical separability difficult and perhaps unwise.

The present case involves broadband technology. Broadband cable Internet service brings instant two-way communication that can accommodate tremendous amounts of information in video, audio, and printed form. Undoubtedly, it will affect our economy and culture, as have the other technologies for human expression. As Marshall McLuhan said over thirty years ago, to a substantial extent, "the medium is the message." Marshall McLuan, *Understanding Media: The Extension of Man*, McGraw-Hill (1964). If so, the question then becomes, can government regulate the technology of expression without also changing its meaning?

C. The Broward County ordinance operates to impose a significant constraint and economic burden directly on a cable operator's means and methodology of expression. The ordinance singles out cable operators from all other speakers and discriminates further against those cable operators who choose to provide Internet content. The ordinance has no application to wireless, satellite, or telephone transmission or other providers of Internet service. In these respects, the ordinance operates in much the same manner as the use tax held to violate the First Amendment in *Minneapolis Star and Tribune Co. v. Minnesota Com'r of Revenue*, 460 U.S. 575, 103 S. Ct. 1365.

A primary purpose of the First Amendment is "to preserve an untrammeled press as a vital source of public information." *Grosjean*, 297 U.S. at 250, 56 S. Ct. at 449. The free press clause protects not only the words which appear on a newspaper's pages, but its printing and circulation as well. As Justice Stewart has written:

The Free Press guarantee is in essence a structural provision of the Constitution. Most of the other provisions in the Bill of Rights protect specific liberties or specific rights of individuals: freedom of speech, freedom of worship, the right to counsel, the privilege against compulsory self-incrimination, to name a few. In contrast, the Free Press Clause extends protection to an institution. Potter Stewart, "Or of the Press," 26 Hastings L.J. 631, 633 (1975) (emphasis added). Under the First Amendment, government should not interfere with the process by which preferences for information evolve. Not only the message, but also the messenger receives constitutional protection.

The Broward County ordinance invidiously impacts a cable operator's ability to participate in the information market. The cable operator, unlike a telephone service, does not sell transmission but instead offers a collection of content. Like a newspaper, a cable operator sells advertising to defray the costs of its service. Advertising allows an operator to keep subscriber rates lower than would otherwise be the case, an attraction in obtaining the critical mass of subscribers necessary to pay for the sizable investment in physical plant. See Affidavit of Thomas Cullen P 11, Exhibit I, Plaintiffs Comcast and Advanced Cable's Appendix to Statement of Material Facts in Support of Summary Judgment (Volume II).

The business plan adopted by the cable operators is not the only one possible and may not succeed. Some Internet service providers, for example, Altavista, offer free access to the Internet relying only on advertising for revenues. This model is more similar to that used by broadcast television or radio. See Declaration of Janusz A. Ordover PP 140-43, Exhibit B, Declarations in Support of Plaintiff TCI TKR of South Florida, Inc. and MediaOne of Greater Florida, Inc.'s Cross-Motion for Summary Judgment. Others may rely solely on subscriber fees. The imposition of an equal access provision by operation of the Broward County ordinance both deprives the cable operator of editorial discretion over its programming and harms its ability to market and finance its service, thereby curtailing the flow of information to the public. It distorts and disrupts the integrity of the information market by interfering with the ability of market participants to use different cost structures and economic approaches based upon the inherent advantages and disadvantages of their respective technology.

D. The impact of the access requirement on a cable operator and the application of First Amendment analysis to the ordinance can be demonstrated by slightly changing the hypothetical posed by the County in its memorandum supporting summary judgment. Suppose the Broward County Commission, concerned about the ability of consumers to gain access to classified advertising and other sources of information, adopted an ordinance requiring *The Ft. Lauderdale News* and *Sun Sentinel* to deliver *The Miami Herald*, *The New York Times*, and the printed material of anyone who made a request on the same terms as it delivered its own newspaper. Could such an ordinance withstand scrutiny under the First Amendment?

Since Broward County's access regulation is only triggered by a cable operator's decision to offer an Internet information channel, it is very similar to the Florida law which led to the Supreme Court's decision in *Miami Herald Pub. Co. v. Tornillo*, 418 U.S. 241, 94 S. Ct. 2831, 41 L. Ed. 2d 730 (1974). That case involved a Florida law which provided for a right of reply to every attack upon a candidate for office which appeared within the newspaper. The reply was required to be in as conspicuous a place and in the same kind of type as the charges that prompted the reply, provided it could not take up more space than the charge which prompted the reply. The argument of the proponents of that measure are echoed by the County's arguments here—that government has an obligation to ensure that a wide variety of views reach the public. It was argued that concentration of ownership and the expense of entry into publishing had resulted in a loss of any ability by the public to respond or contribute in any meaningful way to debate on issues. One-newspaper towns had become the rule, said access proponents, with effective competition operating in only four percent of large cities.

The Supreme Court unanimously rejected these arguments, finding that an enforceable right of access brings about a direct confrontation with the express provisions of the First Amendment. *See id.* at 254, 94 S. Ct. at 2838. As the *Tornillo* Court explained:

A newspaper is more than a passive receptacle or conduit for news, comment, and advertising. The choice of material to go into a newspaper, and the decisions made as to the limitations on the size and content of the paper, and treatment of public issues and public officials—whether fair or unfair—constitute the exercise of editorial control and judgment. It has yet to be demonstrated how government regulation of this crucial process can be exercised consistent with First Amendment guarantees of a free press as they have evolved this time.

Id. at 258, 94 S. Ct. at 2840. It is ironic that a technology, which is permitting citizens greater ease of access to channels of communication than has existed at any time throughout history, is being subjected to the same arguments rejected by the Supreme Court in *Tornillo*. Broward County's ordinance intrudes upon the ability of the cable operator to choose the content of the cable system and imposes a cost in time and materials in order to make available the space that may be demanded. The result has been that cable operators have not provided Internet service in unincorporated Broward County. Compelled access like that ordered by the Broward County ordinance both penalizes expression and forces the cable operators to alter their content to conform to an agenda they do not set. *See generally Pacific Gas and Elec. Co. v. Public Utilities Com'n of California*, 475 U.S. 1, 106 S. Ct. 903, 89 L. Ed. 2d 1 (1986).

E. The history of the First Amendment also informs its command. For, as Justice Holmes stated, "[a] page of history is worth a volume of logic." *New York Trust Co. v. Eisner*, 256 U.S. 345, 41 S. Ct. 506, 65 L. Ed. 963 (1921).

Upon introduction of the printing press, Henry VIII proclaimed that the prices of books must be reasonable, that foreign books not be sold in England, and that printers must have royal permission to set up shop. The charter of the Stationer's Company prohibited all printing except by members of the company or those having a special license from the crown. The first newspapers were also met by licensing prosecutions of unlicensed news-sheet printers and the power of the crown to grant privileges of monopoly. *See F. Siebert, Freedom of the Press in England 1476-1776 (1965); see also, 2 J. Story, Commentaries on the Constitution of the United States*, sec. 1882 (5th ed.1891).

The licensing of books and newspapers expired in England in 1694. However, in 1712, Parliament imposed a tax upon newspapers and advertisements. In 1765, stamps sent to the colonies for newspaper duties were a precipitating factor for the American Revolution. *See Grosjean*, 297 U.S. at 246-48, 80 L. Ed. at 666-68.

When the Constitution was proposed without an explicit guarantee of freedom of the press, the anti-federalists objected. Richard Henry Lee, one of Virginia's leading anti-federalists, had been a signer of the Declaration of Independence and president of the Continental Congress. Within a month after adjournment of the constitutional Convention, he published what quickly became the most popular and influential anti-ratificationist tract, *Letters from the Federal Farmer*. Subsequently, he published *An Additional Number of Letters*, which included a discussion of freedom of the press:

All parties apparently agree, that the freedom of the press is a fundamental right, and ought not to be restrained by any taxes, duties, or in any manner whatever. Why should not the people, in adopting a federal constitution, declare this, even if there are only doubts about it . . . Printing, like all other business, must cease when taxed beyond its profits; and it appears to me, that a power to tax the press at discretion, is a power to destroy or restrain the freedom of it. There may be other powers given, in the exercise of which this freedom may be affected; and certainly it is of too much importance to be left thus liable to be taxed, and constantly to constructions and inferences. A free press is the channel of communication as to mercantile and public affairs; by means of it the people in large countries ascertain each others' sentiments; are enabled to unite, and become formidable to those rulers who adopt improper measures.

Richard Henry Lee, "Letter XVI, January 20, 1788," in *An Additional Number of Letters from the Federal Farmer to the Republican* 151-53 (Chicago: Quadrangle Books, 1962) (1788); see also Leonard W. Levy, *Freedom of the Press from Zenger to Jefferson* 142-44 (Carolina Academic Press, 1996). Concerns voiced by the anti-Federalists led to the adoption of the Bill of Rights, including the First Amendment, in 1791.

History tells us that governments, democracies as well as monarchies, have been quick to exercise control over new technology for expression, from the printing press to broadcast television, to cable. Regulation has been directed not only at the content of the message, but at the method of its delivery. The founders of the nation who wrote the Constitution and insisted it include the First Amendment had immediate experience as a guide. Further, the First Amendment, as they wrote it, leaves no room for equivocation. "Congress shall make no law . . . abridging the freedom of speech or of the press . . . ."

In encountering new media technologies of our own era, it would be wise to remember the history of the First Amendment as well as the old adage that "those who cannot remember the past are condemned to repeat it." George Santayana, *The Life of Reason* [1905-1906], Reason in Common Sense.

F. In *Turner I*, the Supreme Court held that cable operators are generally entitled to the same First Amendment protection as the print media. The standard adopted by the Court in *Red Lion Broadcasting Co. v. F.C.C.*, 395 U.S. 367, 89 S. Ct. 1794, 23 L. Ed. 2d 371 (1969), which was grounded on the scarcity of broadcasting frequencies, was held inapplicable to cable. *See Turner I*, 512 U.S. at 637, 114 S. Ct. at 2456. "The rationale for applying a less rigorous standard of First Amendment scrutiny to broadcast regulation . . . does not apply in the context of cable regulation." *Id.* at 639, 114 S. Ct. at 2457. "Application of the more relaxed standard of scrutiny adopted in *Red Lion* and the other broadcast cases is inapt when determining the First Amendment validity of cable regulation." *Id.*

Nevertheless, in *Turner I*, the Court upheld the must-carry provisions adopted by the FCC which require carriage of local broadcast stations on cable systems. The Court determined that the applicable standard to evaluate the must-carry provisions was the intermediate level of scrutiny applicable to content-neutral restrictions that impose an incidental burden on speech. However, the reasons given by the Court for applying intermediate rather than strict scrutiny do not apply in this case.

First, unlike the must-carry rules which applied to virtually all cable operators in the country, the Broward County ordinance applies only to the select few that seek to operate broadband Internet service. This ordinance is targeted only at the Plaintiffs, and it is likely to result in the elimination of broadband cable Internet service in unincorporated Broward County. The ordinance was adopted at the behest of a telephone company seeking to eliminate or hamper a competitor.

Moreover, differential treatment is not justified by some special characteristic of the medium being regulated. In *Turner I*, the Supreme Court found that when an individual subscribes to cable, the physical connection between the television set and the cable network gives the cable operator bottleneck or gatekeeper control over most (if not all) of the television programming that is channeled into the subscriber's home. 512 U.S. at 656, 114 S. Ct. at 2466. According to the Court, cable operators possessed "bottleneck monopoly" power that threatened the "viability of broadcast television." Id. at 661, 114 S. Ct. at 2468. This was the reason the Court found *Tornillo* not to control the must-carry provisions.

Cable operators control no bottleneck monopoly over access to the Internet. Today, most customers reach the Internet by telephone. Those who obtain access through cable can use the Internet to reach any Internet information provider. After inquiry, the FCC has concluded that it does not foresee monopoly, or even duopoly in broadband Internet services. See Advanced Services Report. The "bottleneck" theory offers no justification for less than heightened scrutiny of the Broward County ordinance.

Finally, the Court found that the must-carry regulations did not force the cable operators to alter their own message or create a risk that a cable viewer might assume that ideas or messages of the broadcaster were endorsed by the cable operator. The Court pointed out that cable had a long history of serving as a conduit for broadcast signals and that broadcasters were required by FCC regulation to identify themselves at least once every hour. The Court stated that no aspect of must-carry would cause a cable operator to avoid controversy and by so doing diminish the free flow of information and ideas. *See Turner I*, 512 U.S. 622 at 655-56, 114 S. Ct. 2445 at 2465-66, 129 L. Ed. 2d 497.

In contrast, there is no history of cable operators serving as a conduit for Internet service providers. During oral argument, counsel for Broward County estimated that there may be around 5,000 Internet service providers at present, and unlike broadcasters, there is no limit on the number that might demand access. Nor is there any reason to expect that Internet information services granted access to the cable system would not be offensive to the operator and its subscribers. The cable operator under the ordinance would be required to adopt technology which would allow its system to identify each subscriber's choice of Internet service provider so that equal access could be provided and accommodate the demands of the service providers, all in contravention of existing contracts. The Broward County ordinance, unlike the must-carry regulations of the FCC, threaten to diminish the free flow of information and ideas.

For these reasons, I believe this case falls within the rule of *Tornillo, Minneapolis Star* and *Tribune Co.*, and *Pacific Gas and Elec. Co.* and therefore strict scrutiny is required. However, if I am mistaken, the ordinance fails content-neutral scrutiny as well.

G. Under *U. S. v. O'Brien*, 391 U.S. 367, 88 S. Ct. 1673, 20 L. Ed. 2d 672 (1968), a content-neutral regulation will be sustained if:

It furthers an important or substantial governmental interest; if the governmental interest is unrelated to the suppression of free expression; and if the incidental restriction on alleged First Amendment freedoms is no greater than is essential to the furtherance of that interest.

When the government defends a regulation on speech it must demonstrate that the harm it seeks to prevent is real, not merely conjectural, and that the regulation will alleviate the harm in a direct and material way. *See Edenfield v. Fane*, 507 U.S. 761, 770-71, 113 S. Ct. 1792, 1800-01, 123 L. Ed. 2d 543 (1993). A court may not simply assume that an ordinance will advance the asserted state interests sufficiently to justify its abridgment of expressive activity. *See City of Los Angeles v. Preferred Communications*, 476 U.S. 488 at 496, 106 S. Ct. 2034 at 2038, 90 L. Ed. 2d 480. While a legislative body is entitled to substantial deference, in First Amendment cases the deference afforded to legislative findings does not foreclose independent judgment of the facts bearing on an issue of constitutional law. *See Landmark Communications, Inc. v. Virginia*, 435 U.S. 829, 843, 98 S. Ct. 1535, 1543-44, 56 L. Ed. 2d 1 (1978).

Broward County argues that its ordinance is necessary to ensure competition by providing ISP's access to the "essential facility" operated by the cable operations. *See, e.g., Defendant* Broward *County's Memorandum of Law in Support of the County's Motion for Summary Judgment* at 4, 6. According to the County, its ordinance was designed to ensure "competition" and "diversity" in cable broadband Internet services, and the cable operators "are thwarting such competition and diversity by using their exclusive control over the cable 'pipeline' . . . ." *Defendant Broward County's Reply to Plaintiffs' Memoranda of Law* at 23.

However, the harm the ordinance is purported to address appears to be nonexistent. Cable possesses no monopoly power with respect to Internet access. Most Americans now obtain Internet access through use of the telephone. Local telephone companies provide dial up Internet access to over 46.5 million customers, whereas all cable companies combined currently provide Internet services to only about two million customers. *See G. Arlen, 11% First-Quarter Growth Lifts U.S. Online Audience to 50.27 Million*

Customers, 5% Use High Speech Access, Telecom Reports Int'l (April 2000) (available at www.tr.com). The FCC has predicted that traditional telephone lines "will remain the principal means of accessing the Internet" in the near term. *Broadband Today* at 23. AOL, the most dominant ISP with over 24 million subscribers, and other predominantly dial-up ISPs have more than 90% of residential Internet users as customers. *See id.* at 32.

With respect to advanced telecommunications capability or broadband, the FCC estimated that there were approximately one million subscribers as of December 31, 1999. Of these, approximately 875,000 subscribed to cable based services, 115,000 subscribed to asymmetric DSL, with the remaining attributed to other media. Since late 1998, cable increased subscribers approximately three-fold and local telephone companies increased their DSL subscription approximately four-fold. *See FCC News Release*: *FCC Issues Report on the Availability of High-Speed and Advanced Telecommunications Services*, 2000 FCC LEXIS 4041 (Aug. 3, 2000).

The FCC, the agency charged by Congress with the responsibility of monitoring the deployment of broadband technology, has concluded that the preconditions for monopoly in the consumer market for broadband appear absent. According to the FCC, there are, or likely will soon be, a large number of potential entrants into the residential market using different technologies such as DSL, cable modems, and utility fiber to the home, satellite, and radio. The FCC does not foresee the consumer market for broadband becoming a sustained monopoly or duopoly. *See Advanced Services Report* at sec. 48, 52.

In contrast to the FCC, Broward County has conducted no inquiry. The County has proffered no substantial evidence demonstrating that actual harm exists that could justify infringement of First Amendment interests. "The mere assertion of a dysfunction or failure in a speech market, without more is not sufficient to shield a speech regulation from the First Amendment . . . ." *Turner I*, 512 U.S. at 640, 114 S. Ct. at 2458. It has not been demonstrated that the Broward County ordinance furthers a substantial governmental interest. Therefore, even applying content-neutral intermediate scrutiny, the ordinance violates the First Amendment.

Conclusion

For the foregoing reasons, it is

> ORDERED and ADJUDGED that the cross-motions for summary judgment filed by Plaintiffs Comcast Cablevision of Broward County, Inc., Advanced Cable Communications, TCI TKR of South Florida, Inc. and MediaOne of Greater Florida, Inc. (DE 103 and DE 108) are GRANTED. The Motion for Summary Judgment filed by Defendant Broward County, Florida (DE 90) is DENIED. Since Ordinance No. 199-41 violates the First Amendment, it is unconstitutional and cannot be enforced.

> Final Judgment shall be entered in favor of the Plaintiffs.

Case Questions

1. How does the county argue that the cable operators are singled out for special treatment?

2. According to the court, under what circumstance will regulation of free speech be sustained?

In Re Application of The United States of America
158 F. Supp. 2d 644 (D. Md. 2001)

Pending before the Court is Cablevision Systems Corporation's (Cablevision's) Motion to Quash or Otherwise Modify the Court's Order Dated May 10, 2001 (Paper No. 2). I have considered Cablevision's Motion and the Government's response. I previously issued a Memorandum and a separate Order under seal addressing these matters, and by separate Order today I vacate same, and the issues raised in Cablevision's May 10 Motion are now resolved herein and by the accompanying Order. The parties, although given the opportunity, have not requested that the Court's rulings be sealed. No hearing is necessary. See D. MD. R. 105.6.

Cablevision is a cable television company that also owns and operates Optimum Online and Optimum at Home, cable modem services that operate over cable lines and provide subscribers with high speed Internet and related services. On May 10, 2001, the Court ordered Cablevision to disclose to the Government certain information about its customers or subscribers and to refrain from telling any other person about the existence of the Order, the Government's application for the Order, or the investigation itself. It issued this Order pursuant to the authority granted in the Electronic Communications Privacy Act, 18 U.S.C. sec.sec. 2703, 2705. Cablevision has moved to quash or modify that Order on the theory that the Cable Communications Policy Act of 1984, as amended, 47 U.S.C. sec. 551, would make it civilly liable for disclosing subscriber information without personally notifying the subscribers of the disclosure.

Cablevision asserts that the Cable Communications Policy Act conflicts with the Electronic Communications Privacy Act. The former provides that a cable subscriber must be notified when the cable operator discloses "personally identifiable information" to a governmental entity and subjects the operator to civil liability for failing to provide such notice, see 47 U.S.C. sec. 551. It provides in pertinent part:

(c) Disclosure of personally identifiable information

(1) Except as provided in paragraph (2), a cable operator shall not disclose personally identifiable information concerning any subscriber without the prior written or electronic consent of the subscriber concerned and shall take such actions as are necessary to prevent unauthorized access to such information by a person other than the subscriber or cable operator. (2) A cable operator may disclose such information if the disclosure is—

. . . (B) subject to subsection (h) of this section, made pursuant to a court order authorizing such disclosure, if the subscriber is notified of such order by the person to whom the order is directed . . . .

. . . (h) Disclosure of information to governmental entity pursuant to court order

A governmental entity may obtain personally identifiable information concerning a cable subscriber pursuant to a court order only if, in the court proceeding relevant to such court order—

. . . (2) the subject of the information is afforded the opportunity to appear and contest such entity's claim.

47 U.S.C. sec. 551 (1991 & 2000 Supp.). The Electronic Communications Privacy Act, by contrast, specifically authorizes a court to order that a provider of electronic communications service or remote computing service not disclose the existence of a court order issued pursuant to 18 U.S.C. sec. 2703 that requires it to produce personal information about the subscriber or customer. See 18 U.S.C. sec. 2705(b). It provides in pertinent part:

> A governmental entity acting under section 2703 . . . may apply to a court for an order commanding a provider of electronic communications service or remote computing service to whom a . . . court order is directed, for such period as the court deems appropriate, not to notify any other person of the existence of the . . . court order. The court shall enter such an order if it determines that there is reason to believe that notification of the existence of the . . . court order will result in—
>
> 1) endangering the life or physical safety of an individual;
> 2) flight from prosecution;
> 3) destruction of or tampering with evidence;
> 4) intimidation of potential witnesses; or
> 5) otherwise seriously jeopardizing an investigation or unduly delaying a trial.

There is little authority addressing this apparent conflict, and almost none purporting to resolve it. Cf. *United States v. Kennedy*, 81 F. Supp. 2d 1103, 1111 (D. Kan. 2000) (observing that question of whether Acts conflicted was one of first impression but not deciding question). In the case of In re Application of the United States of America for an Order Pursuant to 18 U.S.C. 2703(d), 36 F. Supp. 2d 430 (D. Mass. 1999), the district court discussed the apparent conflict between the Acts but did not resolve it. *See id.* at 433. The court reasoned that the issue of the cable company's liability was not ripe for resolution because the cable company did not oppose the Government's application for the order. *See id.* The present case is different, however, because Cablevision has contested the Order by filing its motion to quash or otherwise modify the Order. Moreover, although the issue of Cablevision's civil liability may not be ripe, the question of whether this Court's Order complies with federal law, specifically the Cable Communications Policy Act, is very much before the Court.

Faced with an apparent statutory conflict, courts have a duty to construe the statutes as consistent so far as the language permits. *See Morton v. Mancari*, 417 U.S. 535, 551, 41 L. Ed. 2d 290, 94 S. Ct. 2474 (1974) explaining that

> "the courts are not at liberty to pick and choose among congressional enactments, and when two statutes are capable of co-existence, it is the duty of the courts, absent a clearly expressed congressional intention to the contrary, to regard each as effective"). As the Supreme Court and the Fourth Circuit have recognized, repeals by implication are disfavored. *See Radzanower v. Touche Ross & Co.*, 426 U.S. 148, 154, 48 L. Ed. 2d 540, 96 S. Ct. 1989 (1976) (citation omitted); *McLean v. Central States, Southeast & Southwest Areas Pension Fund*, 762 F.2d 1204, 1209 (4th Cir. 1985). In the absence of an affirmative expression of an intent to repeal an earlier enacted statute, courts will find that Congress has implicitly repealed an earlier statute by enacting a later one only when there is an "'irreconcilable conflict' [between the statutes] in the sense that there is a positive repugnancy between them or that they cannot mutually coexist." *Radzanower*, 426 U.S. at 155.

The Government attempts to reconcile the Acts by asserting that the Cable Communications Policy Act does not apply to nontelevision services involving two-way communications, reasoning that the Act defines "cable service" as "the one-way transmission to subscribers of . . . video programming or . . . other programming service, and . . . subscriber interaction, if any, which is required for selection or use of such video programming or other programming service." 47 U.S.C. sec. 522(7). The privacy provisions of the Act, however, apply to "cable operators," see 47 U.S.C. sec. 551, which is defined to include entities that "control or [are] responsible for the management and operation of . . . a cable system." 47 U.S.C. sec. 522(7). A cable company that provides cable modem service over a cable system is therefore a "cable operator" and subject to the privacy provisions of the Act. The Court has endeavored to construe the Act in such a way as to avoid the statutory conflict, but has been unable to do so without doing violence to the intent of Congress as expressed in the language of the statute.

There is an "irreconcilable conflict" between the notice provisions of the earlier enacted Cable Communications Policy Act and the later enacted Electronic Communications Privacy Act. The Cable Communications Policy Act, which established privacy protections for subscribers to services provided by cable television companies, provides that a cable operator may disclose "personally identifiable information concerning any subscriber without the prior written or electronic consent of the subscriber concerned" pursuant to a court order authorizing such disclosure only "if the subscriber is notified of such order by the person to whom the order is directed." 47 U.S.C. sec. 551(c)(1), (2)(B). It further provides that "[a] governmental entity may obtain personally identifiable information concerning a cable subscriber pursuant to a court order only if, in the court proceeding relevant to such court order . . . the subject of the information is afforded the opportunity to appear and contest such entity's claim." 47 U.S.C. sec. 551(h)(2). When, however, the subscriber also receives cable modem services from the cable company, such as Internet or electronic mail services, the Electronic Communications Privacy Act also applies. That Act provides that a court that orders a provider of electronic communications service or remote computing service to disclose personal information about a subscriber to a governmental entity "shall" enter an order "commanding" the provider not to disclose the existence of the court order if the governmental entity requests such an order and the Court finds certain circumstances to exist. *See* 18 U.S.C. sec. 2705(b). In short, the Cable Communications Policy Act requires that the cable company notify a subscriber of a court order that requires it to disclose personal information about the subscriber, whereas the Electronic Communications Privacy Act requires a court, under circumstances set forth in 18 U.S.C. sec. 2705(b), to bar a cable company that provides an electronic communications service or remote computing service from notifying a subscriber to that service of such an order.

When a court orders production of personal information regarding a subscriber to an electronic communications service or remote computing service from a cable company that is also the provider of the electronic communications service or remote computing service and the circumstances that require a court to issue a confidentiality order under 18 U.S.C. sec. 2705(b) exist, these Acts impose conflicting obligations upon the cable company. In such circumstances, there is an irreconcilable conflict between the statutes. Because Congress enacted the pertinent provisions of the Electronic Communications Privacy Act after it enacted the pertinent provisions of the Cable Communications Policy Act, compare Electronic Communications Privacy Act of 1986, Pub. L. No. 99-508, sec. 201, 100 Stat. 1848 (1986) (adding 18 U.S.C. sec.sec. 2703 & 2705 on October 21, 1986), with Cable Communications Policy Act of 1984, Pub. L. No. 98-549, sec. 2, 98 Stat. 2794 (1984) (adding 47 U.S.C. sec. 551 on October 30, 1984), I hold that the Electronic Communications Privacy Act implicitly repealed those provisions of the Cable Communications Policy Act that require that a subscriber to an electronic communications service or remote computing service provided by a cable company be given notice of a court order directing the cable company to disclose personal information about the subscriber to a governmental entity.

For the foregoing reasons, Cablevision's motion will be denied. A separate Order will issue.

Case Questions

1. What is the primary conflict between the two statutes that the court is asked to address?

2. What is your opinion of the ultimate resolution reached by the court in this case? Discuss.

Exercises

1. In your opinion why was a right to privacy not specifically included in the Constitution?
2. How would a person prove that a defamatory statement was actually communicated to a third person by means of the Internet? Could this invade the recipient's privacy?
3. What do you believe is the rationale behind the privileges to defamation? Discuss.
4. Discuss some factors you would use to determine the appropriate community standards for a cyberporn problem.
5. Indicate some problems that might be encountered in regulating child pornography in cyberspace.
6. What do you think should be the legal response to spamming? How would this meet a constitutional challenge?
7. Differentiate between libel and slander.
8. Locate *Marbury v. Madison* on the Internet and read the decision.
9. Discuss some of the restrictions that are placed on a person's freedom of speech.
10. Read *Intel Corp. v. Hamidi*, 114 Cal. Rptr. 2d 244 (2001) for a discussion of freedom of speech and what is called "cybertrespass."

Related Websites

Legalethics.com
Gse.ucla.edu/iclp/hp.html

Appendices

Appendix A, Convention on Cybercrime
Appendix B, Children's Online Protection Act of 1998 (COPA)

Chapter Four

ONLINE BUSINESS OPERATIONS

Chapter Overview

One of the greatest perceived advantages of modern computer technology is the ability to conduct business online. This business aspect of cyberspace has impacted the way manufacturers sell and consumers buy. As more and more households acquire computer capabilities, the greater the growth of the phenomenon of electronic business.

From the entrepreneur who wishes to expand a business to a worldwide market, to the service professional who prefers to work in a "virtual office" where each employee in a given office may be physically located all over the country, to the householder who wants to pay bills without leaving home, the world of e-business has provided the modern answer to the problems of transacting business.

E-commerce, as the term is generally used, refers to any business enterprise that is conducted online. Basically any business can operate online once it has acquired a **domain name**, a unique identifying group of words that refers to a specific company (see Chapter Five). The domain name is used to access the business' website, and once that site is "hit," or accessed by a consumer, the business is up and running. However, simply setting up the appropriate website does not automatically create an effective **e-business** (a business that is conducted online). Certain problems have arisen with respect to the operation of a business online, and this chapter will address three specific areas of e-commerce that have been identified as engendering legal challenges.

The first problem associated with conducting business online is the problem of contract formation. A **contract** is an agreement between two or more persons which, if it meets all legal standards, creates enforceable rights and obligations between the parties. In the traditional business setting contracts are formed when the parties orally agree or sign a written contract. In an electronic setting the parties' only contact may be by means of e-mail, and the problem arises with respect to the validity of the intent of the parties and their signatures. Further, because of new methods of operation associated with cyberspace, certain specific types of contracts have been generated to address defined cyberspace problems such as creating joint ventures or partnerships online, protecting the integrity of the business operations and outsourcing agreements.

The second problem facing an e-business is how the business will be financed, both with respect to raising capital to fund the enterprise as well as securing agreements to receive payments from customers and clients. Traditional legal concepts have had to be redefined and expanded to meet new technological changes in this area of business operations.

Finally, concerns have arisen with respect to the taxability of the business, which may have no traditional tax base. A business is not only responsible for the taxes on the income it generates but also may be liable for collecting sales taxes on the products it sells. Also, there is a question with respect to which authority has tax jurisdiction over the business.

This chapter will examine these three areas of conducting an online business: forming valid contracts electronically, financing the e-business, and meeting the business' tax liability.

Contracting with an Online Business

Basic Contract Principles

To be valid and enforceable, all contracts must meet six requisite elements, which are:

1. offer
2. acceptance
3. consideration
4. legality of the subject matter
5. contractual capacity of the parties
6. contractual intent of the parties.

Although a detailed examination of basic contract principles is beyond the scope of this text, a brief discussion of these elements may prove helpful in elucidating the problems associated with applying traditional legal theories to modern technology.

1. **Offer**. An **offer** is a proposal by one party to another manifesting a present intent to enter into a valid contract. All contracts must start with a valid offer.

Example: A woman goes online and discovers that she has an e-mail from her former school. When she opens it up she finds a message from the dean asking her to teach a class as an adjunct. This request from the dean, if it is specific with respect to certain essential details, would constitute an offer to enter into a valid contract.

To be valid, the offer must be certain and definite with respect to all of its essential terms, including:
   a. price
   b. subject matter of the contract
   c. the parties to the agreement
   d. the time in which the obligations must be performed.

For most offers, each of these terms must be specified; the court cannot create a contractual term for the parties. However, the court will, if the parties are silent on a point, assume a "reasonable" price and time of performance. Note however, for persons who are deemed to be **merchants**, those who regularly deal in the type of goods that form the subject matter of the contract, the **Uniform Commercial Code (UCC)**, a statute adopted in every state, changes this requirement. Under the UCC, merchants may neglect to specify a price and leave that term open for later negotiation without defeating the formation of a valid contract.

2. **Acceptance**. **Acceptance** is the manifestation of assent to the terms of the offer. Once an acceptance is given, the contract is formed. Under common law principles, the acceptance must exactly match the terms of the offer. This is known as the **mirror image rule**. Any variance in the terms terminates the offer and creates a **counter-offer**, which may or may not be accepted by the person who proffered the original offer. Note, however, that an exception exists under the UCC for merchant traders, whereby variance in the acceptance can create the contract if the original offeror does not object to the change within ten days.

Example: A building contractor contacts a piping supplier that he has used for the past eight years. He orders 3000 yards of a particular pipe at 50 cents per yard, the price he has paid in the past. The supplier e-mails back, agreeing to sell the contractor the 3000 yards of the pipe at 55 cents per yard. If the contractor does not object, a contract has been formed for 3000 yards of pipe at 55 cents per yard because both parties are merchant traders.

Pursuant to traditional contract doctrines, an acceptance is effective when properly dispatched by an authorized means of communication. A **rejection** of the offer, whereby the offer is declined, is effective when actually received. This doctrine is called the **mailbox rule**. However, modern authorities apply the rule according to the reasonable expectations of the parties. This rule has some particular cyberspace applications which will be discussed below.

3. **Consideration. Consideration** is the bargain element of the contract, the contract's subject matter. Legally defined, consideration is a benefit conferred of a detriment incurred at the request of the other party. To be valid, each party to a contract must give and receive something of legal value: **mutuality of consideration**. If there is no mutuality, there is no contract.

Example: A student purchases a textbook from Amazon.com. The student gives consideration in the form of payment and receives consideration in the form of the text. Amazon.com gives consideration in the form of the book and receives payment in return. This is a valid contract with mutuality of consideration.

4. **Legality of the Subject Matter**. A contract may not be formed for an unlawful purpose, a concept that is self-explanatory. An example of an unlawful contract would be two dot.com companies joining together to violate the antitrust laws.

5. **Capacity of the Parties**. To be valid, the parties to the contract must have **contractual capacity**, meaning that they understand the nature of the agreement and are deemed legally old enough to enter into valid contracts. Generally, all adults, persons over the age of eighteen, are deemed to be of an age to contract. Persons between the ages of fourteen and eighteen are called **minors** and may be able to avoid the contractual obligations at their option. Persons younger than fourteen are considered, legally, incapable of forming a valid contract.

The person's ability to comprehend the nature of the contract is a factual question which must be decided on a case-by-case basis.

Problems associated with minors entering into agreements online have evolved with respect to purchasing obscene material. Statutes now require vendors of questionable publications to determine prior to the online sale the age of the purchaser. However, it is difficult for the vendor to ascertain the validity of the proof provided online when all the transactions are performed with no face-to-face contact. (See Chapter Three.)

6. **Contractual Intent**. To be valid and enforceable, the parties must be able to demonstrate that they each knew and intended the terms of the agreement and that they voluntarily and knowingly entered into that contract. If a person was defrauded into entering the agreement, or one side misrepresented the subject matter, this element of intent will be lacking. Intent is always a difficult element to prove, even in traditional settings, and specific problems associated with electronic fraud will be dealt with in the final chapter of this text discussing cybercrime.

Once all of these elements coalesce, a valid contract is formed, and each side has legally enforceable rights and obligations.

Online Contract Formation

One problem of negotiating and completing a contract online that has been identified and addressed is that of giving validity to **electronic signatures**, signatures that are transmitted over the Internet. Because most business contracts are written, with the parties affixing their signatures to note acceptance, validating electronic signatures has become an urgent matter to be resolved in transacting online business.

To date, only Massachusetts has not passed some form of law to provide legal recognition of electronic signatures. In 1996 the World Conference of Commissioners on Uniform Laws began formulating a proposed uniform act dealing with electronic signatures, and the result is the **Uniform Electronic Transactions Act (UETA)**. This proposed uniform act states that when any law requires a signature in writing, an electronic signature will be deemed to meet this requirement and, in a concept parroting the Uniform Commercial Code, attempts to permit parties to create their own practices and procedures to further online business transactions.

However, UETA is fairly limited in scope:

1. UETA only applies to "electronic records and electronic signatures relating to a transaction." "Transaction" is defined as "an action or set of actions arising between two or more persons relating to the conduct of business, commercial or governmental affairs." The statute is designed to be given a broad interpretation so that it validates retail transactions and consumer transactions as well as contracts between merchants.

2. UETA is designed to be permissive, meaning that the parties are always free to establish their own procedures, which would have precedence over UETA provisions on that given point.

3. UETA exempts the following transactions from its provisions:
    a) Testamentary documents
    b) Articles 3, 4, 4A, 5, 6, 7, 8, 9 and most of 1 of the UCC
    c) The Uniform Computer Information Transactions Act
    d) Any other law specified by the statute enacting UETA.

Basically, UETA provides legal validity to transactions that are concluded by means of an electronic signature, stating that such electronic signature is to be given the legal effect of any other valid form of writing seal, and states that legal effect may not be denied simply because the transaction was effectuated electronically.

Based on the foregoing, UETA impacts basic contract formation in three significant ways:

1. It provides that a valid contract can be formed by the exchange of e-mail, either alone or in concert with other methods of communication such as faxes or traditional writings.

2. Contracts may be formed by software that is programmed to create agreements, such as the licensing agreements appearing at the start of most software when it is being loaded.

3. A contract may be formed by a person completing a form appearing on a website.

These provisions do not alter traditional contract theories, but simply apply them to the new technology.

UETA has also grappled with the electronic aspects of the mailbox rule discussed above. Pursuant to UETA, an electronic message is deemed sent when it is properly addressed to the recipient to the information processing system identified by the recipient, is capable of being processed by such system, and enters a processing system outside the control of the sender. The message is deemed received when it enters the processing system of the recipient if that system is capable of reading the message.

Example: *A person sends an e-mail acceptance to a recipient using WordPerfect9. The recipient's computer is only programmed to read Word and cannot decipher the message. In this instance there is no receipt. However, if the recipient's processing system could read WordPerfect9, even if that is not the program generally used by the recipient, the message will be deemed received under UETA.*

The electronic signature is considered to be the person's signature if he or she is responsible for sending it.

UETA has provided certain rules to cover situations in which the parties may have made an error in their transmissions. First, if the parties have agreed on security protections and one side has failed to use these procedures, any error that could have been detected by using that procedure will be held against the nonconforming party. Second, if the transaction concerned both an individual and an electronic program (such as a person agreeing to a pre-packaged purchase of a good or service online), any error by the individual in filling out the electronic form will not be held against him or her if the program did not provide a means of correcting input errors prior to transmission. And third, these provisions are subject to any other contract law in effect concerning contract error.

Finally, if a signature is required to be notarized, the electronic signature of a notary will be considered to meet this requirement pursuant to UETA.

UETA is not a federal statute, only a proposed uniform law, and each jurisdiction is free to adopt or reject UETA in whole or in part. However, as with the UCC which is a similar statute, it is assumed that eventually all the states will enact UETA in one form or another. At the time of this writing, 37 states and the District of Columbia have adopted UETA and it is being reviewed by nine other states and the Virgin Islands.

On the federal level, in 2000 the **Electronic Signature in Global and National Commerce Act (E-sign)** was passed into law. The statute applies to "any signature, contract or record," but is voluntary except with respect to federal and state government agencies. In order to come within the purview of E-sign, the transaction must occur in interstate commerce in order to meet basic Constitutional standards with respect to applying federal laws. However, because of the global aspect of cyberspace, it is most probable that this initial requirement will be easily met. Under E-sign any transaction that affects interstate commerce may not be denied effect simply because it is in an electronic format.

E-sign does not apply to the following:

a. testamentary documents
b. family law matters
c. the UCC except for section 1-107 and 1-207, and Articles 2 and 2A
d. court documents
e. documents accompanying the transportation of hazardous materials
f. certain other documents concerning rights and benefits to utilities, housing and health.

Unlike UETA, E-sign contains some consumer protection provisions, notably an opt-out provision whereby a consumer must provide affirmative consent to receive records electronically.

These two statutes are concerned with giving validity to agreements entered into by means of computer technology. However, certain types of contracts have particular applicability to the Internet.

Contracts to Protect a Website

In order to protect the integrity of a website, most e-businesses have created contracts to specify the terms and conditions of use of the website that must be agreed to by the user prior to the user being able to access more than just the site's homepage. Typically, the user is alerted to the agreement by a hyperlink on the homepage. Some of these agreements are merely informational and are constructively deemed to be agreed to by the person using the site. Other forms of these agreements require interaction with the user that creates a contract as discussed above. However, the specifics of each such agreement will depend upon the needs and wishes of the website owner. Some of the most commonly encountered provisions in these agreements are:

a. Use of copyrighted and trademarked materials. To protect the intellectual property rights of the website owner, the limitations on the use of such materials must be specified. This provision should also alert the user to potential suits for copyright and trademark infringement if the permitted use is violated. A complete discussion of intellectual property rights and cyberlaw appears in the following chapter.

b. Warranties. A **warranty** is a guarantee as to the nature and quality of a product or service given by the provider. Unless the website owner is selling a good that is governed by the warranty provisions of the Uniform Commercial Code, the website owner should include a warranty section designed for Internet use. The **Uniform Computer Information Transactions Act (UCITA)** provides sample warranty clauses. The website for this act is law.upenn.edu/library/ulc/ulc.htm.

c. Hyperlinking agreement. These provisions govern the right to link, or access, from one site to another. Many terms and use agreements provide specific limitations and disclaimers with respect to hyperlinking use.

Outsourcing Contracts

Because of the fluidity of computer technology and software, many e-businesses have chosen to outsource to third persons some of the services more traditional companies provide themselves. These outsources can prove to be extremely cost effective and, because of the speed of the Internet, do not interrupt or delay the provision of such services to customers.

Some of the provisions that may commonly appear in an outsourcing agreement are:

a. Duties and obligations of the vendor. As with all contracts, the rights and responsibilities of the parties should be detailed so that all parties are aware of their contractual obligations. This provision may have special importance if the only contact between the e-business and the outsource vendor is by means of the Internet.

b. Licensing agreement. If the contract includes the licensing of property that is subject to intellectual property right protections, the terms of the permitted use of that property should be delineated.

c. Warranties and representations. Because the vendor is acting on behalf of the e-business and the products and services it is offering are not within the e-business' control, both sides should determine what will be the nature and quality of the products and services so that neither side will be held responsible for the other side's failure to meet a legal obligation with respect to the ultimate product or service.

d. Service. The e-business must receive adequate assurances that the vendor can meet all of the service needs of the business including payment of fees and royalties and resolution of conflicts.

e. Response time. Because the vendor is basically the representative of the e-business, it becomes important to determine a maximum amount of time that the vendor has to respond to problems on behalf of the e-business.

f. Privacy. As discussed in prior chapters, privacy and protection of information have become major issues with respect to Internet use. Any agreement between a vendor and an e-business should include clauses that protect each side's privacy needs and protection of its records.

g. Insurance. Recently insurance carriers have started issuing **anti-hacking insurance** to compensate for any loss resulting from the unauthorized access of a website. An e-business may require a vendor to maintain such a policy for its protection.

In addition to these provisions, all typical contract provisions would be operative.

Franchise Agreements

A **franchise** is a contractual relationship in which one party licenses another to use its name, marketing and resources to operate a business under the umbrella of the first party's reputation and expertise. The party who licenses the interest is the **franchisor**, and the party who operates the business under the license is the **franchisee.** A common example of a franchise agreement is McDonald's, which licenses its name to independent operators who manage their own restaurants under the McDonald logo in consideration of paying McDonald's a fee. McDonald's provides the marketing, supplies, logos and so forth.

Franchises are regulated under the auspices of the **Federal Trade Commission (FTC),** which promulgates rules and regulations to protect consumers and franchisees from potential fraud. Pursuant to FTC rules, a franchisor must furnish potential franchisees with written disclosures that include basic financial information similar to that mandated for Registration Statements by the Securities and Exchange Commission (see below). The FTC provides a basic format that can be followed to meet this requirement known as the **Uniform Franchise Offering Circular (UFOC).** Under the FTC rules there is no filing requirement, only disclosure. The purpose of this disclosure is to protect potential franchisees before they invest by providing them with essential financial information so that they may assess potential benefits and detriments of the franchise agreement.

The FTC Franchise Rules impose six specific requirements with respect to offering a franchise:

1. The franchisor must make basic financial disclosure regarding its general financial position.

2. The franchisor must substantiate all alleged earnings.

3. The franchisor must disclose the number and/or percentage of its franchisees who have made any advertised claims with respect to any anticipated benefits of the agreement.

4. A standard form franchise agreement must be provided.

5. The franchisor is required to refund deposits and interest payments made by investors subject to any conditions stated in its disclosure statement.

6. No oral or written claim may be made that cannot be substantiated.

Pursuant to a traditional franchise agreement, the franchisor offers the right to use its trademark, service mark and trade name on goods and services; it receives control over the franchisee's methods of operation, and requires the franchisee to make specific payments to the franchisor. In many instances the franchise agreement also specifies geographic locations, meaning that within that designated area the franchisor may not franchise another person who would compete with the first franchisee.

Franchises impact cyberlaw in two significant areas: disclosure and licensing. Pursuant to proposed FTC rules, a franchisor may make disclosure by means of the Internet. Internet is defined very broadly by the rule to include all communications transmitted by means of computers, telephones, faxes and other electronic devices. The rule also requires franchisors to include their e-mail addresses and Internet homepages, if any, and the cover page of the disclosure statement. The rule permits disclosure on the Internet in one of two ways:

1. The potential franchisee may agree to receive all disclosure information electronically.
2. The potential franchisee may have a written paper summary document to supplement the electronic disclosure.

To meet the requirements of electronic disclosure, the electronic document must be capable of being printed and the electronic document must be self-contained, meaning that the potential franchisee must be able to read each page of the disclosure statement without any other method other than by scrolling the screen. The franchisor must retain a copy of all such electronic disclosures for a three-year period.

The second area of cyberlaw significance concerns the geographic limitation provisions of standard franchise agreements. The Internet is totally global, meaning that any consumer, regardless of his or her actual geographic location, may access a website. If a franchisee has a store with a geographic limitation area of ten blocks, but a consumer living three blocks away from the site of the store can access the franchisor's homepage to make a purchase, this homepage may infringe on the franchisee's contract right. This practice is referred to as **encroachment**. However, franchisors may argue that using an alternative method of business is not an infringement on such rights. To date there is no definitive answer to this problem, but because of the Internet's unlimited geographic impact, it is expected that this practice will be the focus of much future legal action.

Financing the E-business

Once a business has decided that it is going to create and maintain an online presence, its fundamental problem, as with all businesses, is securing the entity's financial integrity. To operate a successful business, the business must be both adequately capitalized and capable of assuring a steady cash flow to maintain operations. These two aspects of e-business will be addressed in this section of the text.

Funding an E-business

An online entity, as with all business ventures, is financed in a manner consistent with its legal status. A sole proprietorship receives capital from its owner's contribution or loans the owner personally guarantees. Partnerships are financed similarly to sole proprietorships except with two or more contributor/owners. However, limited partnerships, corporations and limited liability companies may receive financing by an alternative method—selling an interest in the business operation to investors. These investments in a business are called **securities**, which represent an investor's contractual-proprietary interest in the venture. For the most part, the majority of the securities in existence are **shares**, certificates that represent a proportional ownership interest in a business.

Whenever a business enterprise decides to raise capital by **issuing** (selling) securities to the public, that issuance is governed by various federal and state statutes, generically referred to as **Blue-Sky laws**. The two primary federal statutes that govern the sale of securities to the general public are the **Securities Act of 1933** and the **Securities Exchange Act of 1934**.

The 1933 Act mandates that, for companies coming within the purview of the statute, prior to offering securities for sale to the public, the company must file a **Registration Statement** with the government that provides all the information necessary to give a clear financial picture of the company. The Registration Statement must include a **prospectus**, a document detailing all the information about the offering including potential risk factors for the investors, as well as a complete description of the company, its property, its managers, and its current owners. The Registration Statement must also include information regarding the company's income earnings, by-laws, major contracts and historical and prospective financial status.

Certain companies are exempt from the registration requirement of the Securities Act. These companies are described as a **small business securities offering**, which are:

   a.   companies that are exclusively engaged in intrastate commerce
   b.   companies that do not seek to be publicly held (**private placements**)
   c.   **small corporate offering registrations (SCOR)**, those corporations that only want to raise $1 million in a 12-month period with no secondary offering
   d.   California Limited Offering Exemption for companies organized under California law that do more than half their business in California.

Also, there are simplified filing procedures for corporations that plan to raise less than $25 million.

The 1934 Act created the **Securities and Exchange Commission (SEC)** to oversee the operation of the 1933 Act. The SEC regulates all companies that register a security offering with the SEC, that have at least $10 million in assets and at least 500 shareholders, or whose shares are sold on a national exchange.

With respect to the Internet and security regulation, over a decade ago the SEC created a program called **EDGAR** (electronic database gathering, analysis & retrieval) for the electronic filing of all registration information. The prior requirement of paper filing has been completely eradicated by the introduction of EDGAR. EDGAR can be accessed at www.sec.gov/edgar.htm.

Further, in order to raise capital by means of a public offering, companies are now permitted to offer the securities for sale on the Internet, called an **Internet securities offering (ISO)** or **direct public offering (DPO)**. The ability of a company to make a public offering of its shares on the Internet came about in 1995 pursuant to an SEC release (33-7233) [www.sec.gov/rule/concem/33-7233.txt]. To make such an Internet offering, the SEC requires that the offering provide the potential investor with all of the same information he or she would receive by a more traditional offering method, such as a prospectus, financial status and so forth. To meet the SEC requirements the issue must

- provide timely and adequate notice of the details of the offering, which means sending a notice by e-mail or post office or if a person has expressed interest by means of a website—the website alone does not act as "notice"

- the investor must be able to have easy access to the information on the site, and

- there must be some evidence of delivery of the notice (see above for contract delivery).

A potential investor can consent to delivery of the material by electronic means but the business must be able to evidence the actual receipt of the information by the investor.

Being able to make public offerings by means of the Internet greatly increases a business' potential for raising capital because the Internet can reach far more people than the traditional methods of direct mailings and newspaper ads. Internet offerings also provide a medium for selling securities on a global basis for a relatively moderate (compared to traditional methods) marketing cost. However, such offerings also raise jurisdictional problems with respect to the applicability of U.S. securities laws to foreign offerings made online and to meeting the requirements of the securities laws of all nations whose residents access the information. As has been discussed before, as with most legal issues relating to cyberspace, the problem of jurisdiction always raises its specter for both applicability and enforcement of a specific nation's laws.

Receiving Payment for an E-business

An e-business is primarily concerned, once it is up and operating, with generating income from the online sale of its products or services. Excluding cash, which obviously could not occur online, merchants receive payment by means of commercial paper or credit cards.

Commercial paper, also referred to as **negotiable instruments**, is an instrument designed to promote commerce by acting as a cash substitute. Commercial paper is divided into two categories: **notes**, which are two-party instruments whereby one person agrees to pay a specified sum to another on or by a given date, and **drafts**, which are three-party instruments in which one person authorizes a second to pay a sum certain to a third person on the first person's behalf. A typical example of a draft is a check. Commercial paper is governed by the provisions of Article 3 of the Uniform Commercial Code.

To transfer commercial paper, the parties must sign the instrument and, as discussed above, problems may arise if the instrument is electronically created. Under the provisions of UETA it is possible to create and transfer commercial paper electronically because UETA mandates that electronic signatures are to be given the same legal effect as traditional signatures. However, Article 3 of the UCC does not apply e-signs except for promissory notes that secure an interest in real property (mortgages). This means that, for jurisdictions that have adopted the appropriate version of UETA, an e-business may be able to receive payment by an electronically transmitted negotiable instrument.

The second method of securing payment for sales is by means of credit cards. An e-business may enter into agreements to accept credit cards by means of a **merchant service agreement** with a financial institution that issues the credit card. At the present time, this method of payment has proven to be the most practical for e-businesses. However, there are several factors involved with these agreements to which the e-business must be alerted:

- Most of these agreements permit each side to withdraw funds without notifying the other in advance.

- Credit card transactions involve a certain degree of the risk of loss if the cards are fraudulently used or the cardholder defaults. Merchant service contracts should specify which party bears the loss, or how the loss is to be apportioned.

- There are no laws specifically designed, at the present time, to cover online credit card use. Therefore, all of the current federal regulations regarding credit cards apply to the Internet and must be addressed.

- Credit card payments usually involve a time delay between the period of the charge and the actual payment by the cardholder's bank to the merchant; debit cards, on the other hand, automatically deduct funds from the purchaser's account which make the funds immediately available to the merchant. The merchant service agreement should detail the type of card that will be made available.

- Banks usually charge a **settlement fee** to the merchant that represents the difference between the amount charged and the revenue earned by the bank. Banks usually charge a greater fee if the cardholder was not "present" at the credit transaction, which includes online sales as well as telephonic and direct mail orders. These fees must be taken into account when the e-business is negotiating the contract.

For the most part, online credit card sales are no different from credit card sales through other venues, but for e-business they represent the majority of their sales revenues and therefore merchant service contracts must be carefully analyzed.

Taxation and E-business

One problem facing the governmental taxing authorities, in light of the rapidly expanding technological business world, is how to apply traditional tax laws to these new business formats. Many traditional tax laws do not operate well in terms of e-commerce. To address this issue, on the federal level, Congress enacted the **Internet Tax Freedom Act** in 1998. This statute prohibits Internet access taxes and any new taxes from being imposed on Internet access. This legislation does not affect state tax laws; states are perfectly free to impose sales taxes on in-state sales regardless of whether the sale results from an in-person, direct mail, or Internet transaction. The Internet Tax Freedom Act also establishes an Advisory Committee on Electronic Commerce to develop proposals to enable the government to tax Internet business in a reasonable manner.

Generally, there are four alternative proposals being posited to address the problem of taxing e-businesses. These proposals are:

1. a **use tax**, which is a form of a sales tax that is paid not by the vendor as is traditional, but by the customer who would be required to remit to the taxing authority a percentage of the purchase price of the goods acquired by means of an Internet sale. Some jurisdictions have already required taxpayers to report the cost of purchases they have made on the Internet.

2. **third-party collection** whereby an independent clearing house would be created through which all Internet sales would be reported prior to the sale. This clearinghouse would then compute the tax, inform the vendor who would then add the tax to the purchase price, collect such tax, and then remit it to the appropriate authority. However, because of the varying tax rates among all the states and foreign countries, it may be practically impossible to calculate the appropriate tax to be collected.

3. a **national sales tax**, which would be a uniform sales tax to be imposed throughout the country preempting all local sales taxes. This proposal has, for obvious reasons, not been favored by state and local authorities, who would have to seek allocation of the taxes collected from the federal government.

4. a **proxy tax**, which would eliminate the sales tax as such by imposing a tax on Internet use. This proposal has also met with resistance from the cyberspace community because it feels it would have a chilling effect on the growth of e-commerce.

Further, in addition to the problem of determining which form of tax may be appropriate for Internet sales, a secondary issue involves locating the Internet vendor. Because of the global reach of cyberspace, traditional tax theories that demand some form of presence with the taxing jurisdiction may be totally obliterated by the Internet. Not only may it be practically impossible to locate the precise physical location of the e-vendor, it may be impossible to exercise jurisdiction over a vendor located outside the United States (Chapter Two).

As a consequence, as the government attempts to raise revenues by means of ever-increasing Internet sales, it must develop new and technologically appropriate methods of determining and imposing the tax burden.

Chapter Review

One of the major benefits of the new technology is its ability to provide business with a new medium for generating sales. E-business has become the favorite venue for the expansion of commercial enterprises.

Operating a business online has generated three specific cyberlaw business problems:

1. how can contracts be validly formed online;
2. how can the e-business finance its operations; and
3. how can the government tax the revenues generated from e-sales?

Over the past few years several statutes have been enacted to give validity to signatures transmitted online so as to enable businesses to form enforceable contracts in cyberspace. Without this legal recognition of electronic signatures it would be virtually impossible to form enforceable contracts online.

Financing an e-business is now possible by means of electronic transmissions, both in terms of filing Registration Statements with the SEC in order to sell securities to the public, as well as offering securities for sale directly to the public by means of the Internet. Further, e-businesses can receive revenue from sales consummated over the Internet by using merchant service agreements in the same fashion as catalog and telephone sales are completed.

The most problematic area of e-commerce lies in the government's ability to tax e-sale revenues. To date, no specific proposal has been adopted with respect to the collection of sales taxes for e-sales, but several options are being considered which would impact both the expense and regulation of e-commerce.

Key Terms

Acceptance—Manifestation of assent to an offer to contract

Anti-hacking Insurance—Insurance to remedy losses occasioned by unauthorized access into the insured databases

Blue-Sky Laws—Securities laws

Commercial Paper—Cash substitute regulated by Article 3 of the UCC

Consideration—The bargain element of a contract

Contractual Capacity—The legal ability to enter into a valid contract

Counteroffer—Variance in the terms of an acceptance that creates a new offer from the original offeree to the original offeror

Direct Public Offering—Attempting to sell securities directly to potential investors without using a broker

Domain Name—Unique identifier for a website

Draft—Three-party negotiable instrument

E-business—Business operated by means of computer technology

E-commerce—Business conducted over the Internet

EDGAR—EC program to file Registration Statements

Electronic Signature—Signature created and transmitted on the Internet

Electronic Signature in Global & National Commerce Act (E-Sign)—Federal law giving legal validity to signatures created in cyberspace

Encroachment—Commercially invading exclusive territory under a franchise agreement

Federal Trade Commission—Federal agency that oversees fair trade practices

Franchise—License use of protected property rights

Franchisee—Person who acquires a franchise license

Franchiser—Person who grants a franchise license

Internet Securities Offering—Direct offering of securities to potential investors by means of the Internet

Internet Tax Freedom Act—Federal law prohibiting imposition of taxes on Internet access

Issue—Security that is available for purchase by the public

Mailbox Rule—To create a valid contract, the acceptance must be sent by an authorized means of communication

Merchant—One who regularly trades in the type of goods subject of a sales contract

Merchant Service Agreement—Contract that establishes the use of credit cards for Internet sales

Minor—Person between the ages of 14 and 18

Mirror Image Rule—Under the common law the requirement that an acceptance cannot vary the terms of the offer

Mutuality of Consideration—To have a valid contract both sides must give and receive something of legal value

Negotiable Instrument—Commercial paper

Note—Two-party commercial paper

Offer—Proposal to enter into a valid contract

Private Placement—Security offering to a small group of investors

Prospectus—Document detailing information about a company that wishes to offer its securities for sale to the public

Proxy Tax—Tax that would eliminate a sales tax for Internet sales

Registration Statement—Document that must be filed with the SEC prior to a public offering of securities

Rejection—Declining a contractual offer

Securities Act of 1933—Federal blue-sky law

Securities and Exchange Commission—Government agency that regulates the sale of corporate securities

Securities Exchange Act of 1934—Federal statute that created the SEC

Settlement Fee—Charge by financial institution imposed for making credit card payments to the vendor

Share—Stock

Small Business Securities Offering—SEC exception to registration requirement

Small Corporation Offering Registration (SCOR)—Simplified registration for qualifying small businesses

Third-Party Collection—Using a clearinghouse to determine sales tax for Internet sales

Uniform Commercial Code—Statute that regulates various areas of commerce including the sale of goods between merchants and commercial paper

Uniform Computer Information Transactions Act (UCITA)—Statute that provides sample warranty clauses for e-sales

Uniform Electronic Transactions Act (UETA)—Statute concerning Internet contract formation

Uniform Franchise Offering Circular—Method of offering franchises for sale

Use Tax—Form of a sales tax remitted by the customer

Warranty—Contractual guarantee

Edited Cases

The following case decisions highlight some of the e-business problems currently being encountered. The first case, *CigarCafe, L.C. v. America Online, Inc.*, discusses some potential defenses to Internet contracts. The second decision, *Untied States of America v. Ivnanov*, concerns hacking into a business operation.

CigarCafe, L.C. v. America Online, Inc.
50 Va. Cir. 146 (1999)

This matter came on upon the Defendant's motion for Summary Judgment on all counts of the Amended Motion for Judgment, and on damages for lost profits, humiliation and embarrassment, compensatory damages, and punitive damages. Plaintiff requests Summary Judgment on Counts III and IV.

In its Amended Motion for Judgment, Plaintiff CigarCafe, L.C. (CigarCafe) seeks damages against Defendant America Online, Inc. (AOL) for fraudulent inducement to enter into Interactive Services Agreement (ISA) (Count I), fraudulent inducement to enter into Shopping Channel Agreement (SCA) (Count II), willful destruction of Plaintiff's business (Count III), civil relief for Computer Trespass, violation of sec. 18.2-152.4, Code of Virginia, 1950 (Count IV), breach of ISA (Count VI), and breach of SCA (Count VII).

Facts

Plaintiff and Defendant entered into a contract entitled Interactive Services Agreement, under which Plaintiff would have a "content" site, a location on the network for information about the product, advertising, and conversing with celebrities, and an electronic store on Defendant's network. The contract was entered into in April 1997, for a period of one year after extensive negotiations between the parties. The ISA provided that Defendant would cooperate in press releases, marketing, and advertising the sites, and would sell 25% of the advertising space for the sites. The ISA required both parties to cooperate and reasonably assist the other party in supplying material for marketing and promotional activities. Plaintiff was to pay Defendant 15% of revenue from sales and 25% of revenue from advertising.

Plaintiff alleges that Defendant, beginning soon after the agreement was entered into, engaged in various tortious actions. First, Plaintiff alleges that Defendant effectively sabotaged the Plaintiffs launching of the new site by refusing to approve press releases, which forced Plaintiff to cancel the scheduled launch party to which celebrities and news media had been invited. The next major problem arose when Plaintiff attended a conference held by Defendant. At the conference, Defendant announced that it would be effectively removing tobacco and alcohol from its network. Shortly thereafter, Defendant told Plaintiff that it had to "leave" the network. Defendant told Plaintiff that Plaintiff would be allowed to have an Internet site connected to the AOL network by a direct link, which allows access by clicking on an icon in AOL, but that it would not be on the network itself any longer. This also meant that Plaintiff lost the content aspect of its site. Defendant later called Plaintiff and told it that even that was not viable, and then shut down Plaintiff's site completely. Plaintiff was denied the option to reopen it off-network by AOL. These actions occurred in December of 1997 and January of 1998. Defendant argues that its actions were permissible under the contract and otherwise.

A. Counts I and II: Fraudulent Inducement

Facts, as well as inferences drawn from disputed and undisputed facts, are in dispute, including whether the misrepresentations were of present facts or future conduct. Defendant's Motion for Summary Judgment on both of these counts is overruled.

B. Count III: Willful Destruction of a Business

This Court previously determined that there was such a recognized tort in Virginia. Admittedly, the law on this subject is ambiguous. Under the facts of this case, however, a cause of action for willful destruction fails. The tort of wrongful destruction of a business must exist independently of a breach of contract. Here, the allegations do not amount to a separate tort.

Defendant argues that there is not a cause of action for destruction of a business, and the three cases cited by *Plaintiff, Anchor Co. v. Adams*, 139 Va. 388, 124 S.E. 438 (1924); *Peshine v. Shepperson*, 58 Va. 472, 17 Gratt. (58 Va.) 472 (1867); and *Kamlar Corp. v. Haley*, 224 Va. 699, 299 S.E.2d 514 (1983), do not create such a cause of action; rather these cases discuss destruction of a business purely in the context of the court's analysis of proof of damages.

Based on *Anchor Co. v. Adams*, 139 Va. 388, 124 S.E. 438 (1924), and *Peshine v. Shepperson*, 58 Va. 472, 17 Gratt. (58 Va.) 472 (1867), there appears to be a recognized cause of action in Virginia for willful destruction of business. In Peshine, the plaintiff sued defendant for trespass to property. In an attempt to pay off creditors, defendant, in collusion with plaintiff's clerk, entered the plaintiff's store after plaintiff had left for the evening, removed inventory from the store, sold the inventory to the creditors, and later told plaintiff what had been done. The court distinguished trespass to property committed without circumstances of aggravation, meaning no fraud, malice, oppression or other special aggravation, from trespass "well calculated to injure the credit and business standing of a merchant . . . ." In the latter situation, the court explained that "damages resulting from the injury to the credit and business standing of the plaintiff, and from the injury to his business" were recoverable. The court suggested that the jury, as long as it did not act with partiality or prejudice, would be free to give compensatory damages or damages "with a view to punishment." In this case, it appears that the cause of action was for trespass, and the destruction of business theory had to do with determining that the trespass was aggravated rather than without aggravation. However, in *Anchor Co.*, the Virginia Supreme Court summarized *Peshine* as "an action for destruction of a business by the illegal levy of an attachment." 139 Va. 388, 392, 124 S.E. 438 (1924). In that case, the destruction came about by the illegal levy.

In *Anchor Co.*, defendant assented to the assignment to defendant of a lease of a building used as a restaurant. During the lease, defendant began to make improvements to the property. Defendant erected scaffolding around the property and began removing the roof, adding several stories to the building and taking out partitions on the street floor. These conditions drove away customers and "made it impossible for the plaintiffs to continue their business . . . and were in plain disregard of the rights of its tenants." *Id.* at 390. The issue before the Court involved damages. The court explained that "the willful and unauthorized destruction of one's business is ground for the imposition of punitive damages on the wrongdoer." *Id.* at 392 (citing *Peshine v. Shepperson*, 58 Va. 472 (1867)). The court held that the circumstances justified imposition of punitive damages since defendant, without justification and in disregard of its contract, made it impossible for plaintiffs to continue their business. 139 Va. at 393.

Both *Peshine* and *Anchor Co.* appear to recognize destruction of business as recoverable, but as part of another wrongful act, tortious trespass and breach of contract, respectively. The willful destruction claims were important to damages because they demonstrated the existence of malice, willfulness, or other aggravation, thus allowing for certain damages.

In *Kamlar Corp. v. Haley*, 224 Va. 699, 299 S.E.2d 514 (1983), the Supreme Court of Virginia found that the trial court erroneously allowed the jury to consider punitive damages for breach of a purely contractual duty by defendant, Kamlar Co. In *Kamlar*, plaintiff sold his business assets to defendant and received a five-year employment contract to act as a manager of the company.

While serving as manager, plaintiff discovered a hydraulic pump he bought long before the sale of the business. He checked and found that it was not included on the list of assets in the contract for sale. Thus, he returned the pump for credit and kept the money for himself, supposedly believing that it belonged to him. Defendant discovered this, tried to make plaintiff confess to stealing, and refused plaintiff's offer to reimburse defendant if the company's officers determined that plaintiff was not the owner. Apparently, defendant's officers had reservations about plaintiff's management ability since the sale of the business, and defendant used this action by plaintiff as a pretext for firing him. As a general rule, damages for breach of contract are limited to pecuniary loss, and punitive damages are not recoverable. This rule does not apply "where the breach amounts to an independent, willful tort, in which event exemplary damages may be recovered under proper allegations of malice, wantonness, or oppression." *Id.* at 705 (quoting *Wright v. Everett*, 197 Va. 608, 90 S.E.2d 855 (1956)). "A breach of contract, accompanied by ulterior motives, in the absence of an independent tort" does not support a claim for punitive damages. 224 Va. at 706 (citations omitted). The court observed that "[s]ome jurisdictions permit punitive damages where the intent of the breaching party is 'malicious,' consisting of 'an evil or rancorous motive influenced by hate; the purpose being to deliberately and willfully injure the plaintiff . . .' but most jurisdictions have required that the plaintiff allege and prove facts amounting to an independent tort, before permitting the recovery of punitive damages." *Id.* (citations omitted). The court adopted the latter rule, which it explained was established in *Wright*. Thus, according to *Kamlar*, a plaintiff must allege a count of an independent, willful tort separately from a count alleging breach of contract. 224 Va. at 707.

The Court distinguished *Anchor Co. v. Adams*, where it allowed punitive damages for the willful destruction of a business, because the plaintiff alleged not only breach of contract, but independently tortious conduct as well. This conduct was the unlawful entry of the leased premises, the erection of scaffolding, removal of the roof and moving the partitions, "thus destroying the lunchroom business conducted by the tenant." *Kamlar* does not make clear whether the actions, which resulted in the destruction, were the tortious acts, or whether the destruction of the business itself was the tortious act. Since the Court described the destruction as defendant's apparently intended result of the other actions, it appears that the physical unlawful activities were the tort, whereas the destruction of the business was the resulting damage, and therefore relevant to a damages question only.

The dissent in *Kamlar* argued that the majority altered the rule, established in *Wright*, that punitive damages may be recovered in breach of contract actions "where the breach amounts to an independent, willful tort, in which event exemplary damages may be recovered under proper allegations of malice, wantonness, or oppression—as, for example, in actions for breach of marriage contracts." *Id.* (dissenting in part) (quoting *Wright v. Everett*, 197 Va. 608, 615, 90 S.E.2d 855, 860 (1956)). The dissent characterized the *Wright* line of cases as establishing that the breach need not be an actual tort, as the majority insisted, but rather "the breach must amount to or be analogous to a tort." The dissent noted that in *Anchor* plaintiff sued defendants for a breach of contract. In disregard of this contract, defendant began making improvements to the building which made access to the plaintiff's restaurant dangerous. 197 Va. at 608-09. The *Anchor* Court held that punitive damages could be imposed because, "[t]he defendant, in disregard of its contract, made it impossible for its tenants to continue their business . . . . Those responsible therefore were apparently either ignorant of the plaintiff's rights or else contemptuous of them." 197 Va. at 609 (quoting *Anchor Co. v. Adams*, 139 Va. at 392-93) (emphasis added)). The dissent suggested that, although h the plaintiff's claim was based on Defendant's tortious conduct, this conduct arose out of the breach of the contract in violation of plaintiff's rights, as opposed to a tort independent of that contract.

The Supreme Court of Virginia, in *Foreign Mission Board v. Wade*, 242 Va. 234, 409 S.E.2d 144 (1991), announced that *Kamlar* and *Wright* established the principle "that punitive damages are recoverable only if an independent tort is pleaded and proved. They do not, however, stand for the proposition that the breach of a contractual duty constitutes an independent tort." *Id.* at 241. The court acknowledged that a party's action can show both a breach of contract and a tortious breach of duty, "[b]ut the duty tortiously or negligently breached must be a common law duty, not one existing between the parties solely by virtue of the contract." *Id.*

In *R.M.A. v. McDevitt Street Bovis, Inc.*, 43 Va. Cir. 468 (1997), Judge Markow held that the plaintiff had failed to allege any breach of duties separate and independent from the contractual obligations. Plaintiff argued that it was sufficient to have alleged that defendant had a common law duty not to defraud plaintiff. Judge Markow responded, "[o]f course, there is a common law duty that one should not defraud another. Here, however, that duty [arose] from the contractual relationship. The particular instances of misrepresentation are duties and obligations specifically required by the contract. There is nothing which established that the duty breached is separate and independent from the contract . . . . If there were no contract, then there would have been no duties owed by defendant to plaintiff." The Judge held that plaintiff was limited to claiming damages for breach of contract. *Id.* at 471.

The dismissal of allegations of constructive and actual fraud in RMA was affirmed by the Virginia Supreme Court in *R.M.A. v. McDevitt Street Bovis, Inc.*, 256 Va. 553, 507 S.E.2d 344 (1998). The court explained that where the act or omission which, without a contractual obligation involved, would not give rise to a cause of action, then the action is founded upon contract. In contrast, where "the relation of the plaintiff and the defendants be such that a duty arises from that relationship, irrespective of the contract, to take due care, and the defendants are negligent, then the action is one of tort." *Id.* at 558. The Court acknowledged that it has allowed a party to show both a breach of contract and a tortious breach of duty, but that the duty breached must be a common law duty that does not exist solely because of the existence of a contract. *Id.* (citing *Foreign Mission Bd. v. Wade*, 242 Va. 234, 241, 409 S.E.2d 144, 148 (1991)). Plaintiff's claim for constructive fraud was dismissed, since its allegations amounted merely to allegations of negligent performance of the contract and "[a] tort action cannot be based solely on a negligent breach of contract." *R.M.A.*, 256 Va. at 559. The Court also affirmed the Circuit Court's dismissal of plaintiffs allegation of actual fraud since "each particular misrepresentation by McDevitt related to a duty or obligation that was specifically required by the . . . Contract." The Court distinguished a situation where an allegation involved fraudulent inducement. The court explained that fraud in the inducement, where a party makes a promise but at that time intends not to perform, constitutes actual fraud. *Id.* This discussion suggests that in the present case, Plaintiff could show an independent tort necessary for punitive damages by asserting fraud in the inducement. Plaintiff did assert fraud in the inducement and could recover punitive damages on those counts. However, this does not resolve whether Plaintiff can recover for willful destruction.

In the present case, Count III of CigarCafe's Amended Motion for Judgment alleges Willful Destruction of Plaintiff's business. The case law is ambiguous as to whether an independent cause of action exists for willful destruction, or rather such willful destruction provides only the requisite malice/aggravation necessary for an award of punitive damages in a breach of contract action. Based on *Kamlar*, this count falls regardless of which interpretation is adopted. Assuming willful destruction constitutes a common law tort in Virginia, *Kamlar* provides that this tort must exist independently of any breach of contract. The court acknowledged that a party's action can show both a breach of contract and a tortious breach of duty, "but the duty tortiously or negligently breached must be a common law duty, not one existing between the parties solely by virtue of the contract." *Id.* Count III alleges that the destruction occurred from one or more of the following acts: defendant's refusal to approve or issue a press release announcing Plaintiff's launch, refusal to sell advertising, the removal of Plaintiff's pop-up screen capability without notice and without a contractual basis to do so, refusal to promote any celebrities offered by Plaintiff, removal of the link of keyword "cigar" to a screen linked to Plaintiff's online area without notice, AOL's public statement of opposition to tobacco, and committing computer trespass and locking Plaintiff out of its two electronic stores. All of these actions, other than the trespass, merely constitute potential breaches of duties arising out of the contract, not separate torts. The allegation of computer trespass, while constituting a breach of the contract, is also an independent wrong. However, as is held further in this opinion letter, this statute does not apply to the facts of this case and Plaintiff has not properly alleged a common law trespass. Plaintiff's Motion for Summary Judgment on Liability on Count III is overruled.

Defendant's Motion for Summary Judgment on Liability on Count III is sustained. Count III is dismissed.

C. Count IV: Computer Trespass

Plaintiff requests civil relief under sec. 18.2-152.12, Code of Virginia, 1950, as amended for defendant's violation of sec. 18.2-152.4. Plaintiff alleges that Defendant committed computer trespass by evicting Plaintiff from the site and removing Plaintiff's "pop-up" images from the network, all in violation of Va. Code sec. 18.2-152.4. This statute provides that a person shall be guilty of the crime of computer trespass if he "uses a computer or computer network without authority and with the intent to: 1. Temporarily or permanently remove, halt [*153] or otherwise disable any computer data, computer programs, or computer software from a computer or computer network . . . [or] 3. Alter or erase any computer data, computer programs, or computer software." sec. 18.2-152.4(A).

Specifically, Plaintiff alleges that Defendant's actions in removing the pop-up screen functionality in the CigarCafe Online Area permanently removed computer data, programs, and/or software from a computer and/or computer network without authority, and altered and/or erased computer data, programs or software.

Plaintiff states that its programmer disabled the links because Defendant had a "gun to CigarCafe's head." In reality, Defendant's agent told Plaintiff that if Plaintiff would not remove the information, Defendant would. Plaintiff explains that Hoaglund, an employee of Plaintiff, was required by Defendant to remove certain links from the Clerk's store. With the threat that Defendant would disable the links themselves if Plaintiff did not do so, Hoaglund connected her computer to Defendant's computer and with a password transmitted data to the computer in AOL's facility. Plaintiff argues that the Computer Crimes Act definition of a computer network applies. sec. 18.2-152.2 defines computer network as "a set of related, remotely connected devices and any communications facilities including more than one computer with the capability to transmit data among them through the communications facilities." Defendant responds that this is an incredible interpretation.

Defendant disputes Plaintiff's conclusion that the statute's definition is consistent with the scenario in this case where Plaintiff's programmer used Plaintiff's computer to connect to Defendant's computers to make the required changes. Defendant argues that in order to violate the statute, it must use a computer or computer network to delete data from another party's computer. First, Defendant states that it neither used nor had access to Plaintiff's computers. One of Plaintiff's employees dialed in to a computer at an AOL facility and used a password to be connected with the computer that housed the Clerk's electronic store data that was erased. Defendant states that the alleged trespass occurred on Defendant AOL's computers at AOL's facility. Thus, there can be no violation of the Act because Defendant did not trespass upon, invade, interfere with or infringe on property belonging to Plaintiff. Defendant emphasizes that one of Plaintiff's employees electronically entered Defendant's computers and deleted data.

In real property law, an owner or landlord can be sued for trespass on the leased premises. *Johnson v. Marcel*, 251 Va. 58, 465 S.E.2d 815 (1996). In the present case, the ISA agreement provided that Plaintiff owned the Licensed Content and Defendant received a license to use, market, license, distribute, display, perform, transmit and promote the Online Area and Licensed Content contained in the AOL Network. See ISA, 1.2. In the SCA, Defendant owned the shopping channel. Defendant provided Plaintiff "promotional placement" as a merchant on this shopping channel. When activated, Plaintiff's site could be accessed via the World Wide Web or area on Plaintiff's Server. (Note that parties dispute whether Plaintiff's site was limited to the area or to both the area and the World Wide Web.) See SCA, Introduction. Plaintiff could be considered an owner of computer data, programs or software under the ISA and a lessee under the SCA. However, the ISA also provides that Plaintiff "owns all right, title and interest in and to the advertising and promotional spaces within the AOL Network." See ISA, paragraph 3.1.

Under the computer trespass statute and the statutory definitions, anyone who used a computer or network beyond his authority may be subject to computer trespass. "Uses" a computer or computer network is defined as: "attempts to cause or causes the withholding or denial of use of a computer program, data or software to another user." In the present case, Defendant was not just a user denying access to another user. Defendant owned the network and took away the pop-up privilege and Plaintiff's electronic store. These benefits were conferred to Plaintiff as part of a business relationship established through a contract. Defendant merely took away from Plaintiff the ability to continue using these benefits. Plaintiff had no right to these benefits, except by contract, and thus Defendant may or may not have breached the contract, but did not commit a crime in changing Plaintiff's contractual rights.

Plaintiff alleges that Defendant was using "a computer or computer network without authority" and with the intent to remove and delete certain data. Plaintiff argues that Defendant was "without authority" under the statute because Defendant had no "permission of the owner to use a computer, or used it in a manner exceeding such right or permission."

Owner means "owner or lessee of computer data, computer programs, or computer software or an owner, lessee, or licensee of computer data, computer programs, or computer software." Plaintiff asserts that it is the "owner" of the content that was erased through Defendant's threats and demands to Plaintiff. Plaintiff arguably qualifies for this definition in that it was a lessee or licensee of space on AOL's network. The ISA states that CigarCafe grants AOL exclusive license to use, market, license, etc., the Online Area and Licensed Content contained through the AOL Network. Subject to this license, CigarCafe retains all right, title to and interest in the Licensed Content. ISA, paragraph 1.2.

In order for the statute to apply, Defendant must have used a computer or computer network without authority, meaning it had "no right or permission of the owner to use a computer, or . . . [used] a computer in a manner exceeding such right or permission." sec. 18.2-152.2. Although the SCA contract between Defendant and Plaintiff gave Defendant the right to be involved in the CigarCafe site, Defendant did not have complete authority to do whatever it wanted to do with the site. The ISA contract, paragraph 1.4, provides:

AOL shall have the right to remove, or direct ICP [CigarCafe] to remove any Content which, as reasonably determined by AOL (I) violates AOL's then-standard Terms of Service . . . the terms of this Agreement or any other standard, written AOL policy or (II) is not specifically described on Exhibit B. [Exhibit B is a detailed description of the Online Area.]

AOL shall be entitled to require reasonable changes to the content, features and/or functionality within any screen or form created using AOL's proprietary form technology (a "Rainman Area") to the extent such Rainman Area will, in AOL's good faith judgment, adversely affect operations of the AOL Service.

Thus, the contracts provide that AOL must be reasonable. Defendant insists that it was reasonable to permanently remove, alter or erase data, software, or programs relating to Plaintiff's site from its own server. The removal of the pop-up screen functionality in

Plaintiff's Online Area or closure of the electronic stores was certainly not reasonable or unreasonable as a matter of law, as this will be a factual issue at trial. However, this Statute was not intended to apply to this situation. The parties entered into a contract. If we assume the statute is applicable, and if Defendant breached this contract by making unreasonable changes in bad faith, then Defendant would be liable for the crime of computer trespass. This would place too severe a burden on contracting parties. If a company like AOL ever breached a contract, such a breach would usually involve computer access, and such companies necessarily would be criminally liable, whereas breaches of contract in areas of commerce other than online would not have such penalties. The purpose of making computer trespass criminally punishable is "to deter efforts to access a computer, regardless of success." Daniel R. Burk, *Virginia's Response to Computer Abuses: An Act in Five Crimes*, 19 U. Rich. L. Rev. 85, 98 (1984). The purpose of subparagraph (A)(3), was "apparently . . . to snare 'hackers,' computer enthusiasts who use their computers to break into governmental, educational, or commercial computer systems." Robin K. Kutz, *Computer Crime in Virginia: A Critical Examination of the Criminal Offenses in the Virginia Computer Crimes Act*, 27 Wm. & Mary L. Rev. 783, 816 (1986).

Even if the Court accepts Plaintiff's argument that Defendant essentially removed and altered/erased the data itself by ordering Plaintiff to do it under alleged duress, Defendant did have a right to make such orders, if they were reasonable. Thus, Defendant was not using a computer in a manner exceeding its right or permission. There is no question that the manner Defendant used, in "requir[ing] reasonable changes to the content . . ." was permissible under the contract. Rather, Defendant may not have had the right, under contract, to order the removal of certain subject matter, like a pop-up screen or an electronic store, even though the manner of removal was correct. At most, Defendant would be liable for breach of contract for acting unreasonably under the contract.

In fact, in the Amended Motion for Judgment, Plaintiff states that Defendant removed the pop-up screen capability without notice to Plaintiff; failed to inform Plaintiff prior to the removal of the policy that the pop-up screen could only promote content and not products (the implication Plaintiff is probably trying to make is that Defendant had to inform Plaintiff of this limitation in the contract, and not later); and yet Defendant demanded payment of the creation of this pop-up screen function. These actions appear to comprise the alleged breach. See Plaintiff's Amended Motion for Judgment, paragraph 28. Consequently, Plaintiff's presence on the network or use of the network was not improper; rather, the specific listed acts may have been improper under the contract.

The definition for "without authority" in the original bill before the legislature read:

> A person is "without authority" when he has no right or authority and no reasonable grounds to believe that he has such authority. A person may be using a computer or computer network without authority even when he has the right to use the computer or computer network in some other manner or has the right to use or gain access to the same computer data or computer programs for another purpose which is authorized.

Burk, 19 U. Rich. L. Rev. at 96 (emphasis added) (quoting Draft Proposal of Virginia Computer Crimes Act's definition of "without authority"). This original language contained a defense for a defendant who could demonstrate that it had reasonable grounds to believe it had this authority. The omission of this language could be interpreted in one of two ways. The legislature deleted this language because it did not wish to provide a defendant a reasonableness defense, or it believed the language was unnecessary to preserve defendant's right to make such an argument. Daniel Burk, in his article, *Virginia's Response to Computer Abuses: An Act in Five Crimes*, 19 U. Rich. L. Rev. 85, 98 (1984), argues that the House Committee which modified the bill believed this phrase created an affirmative burden of proof on defendant. *Id.* (citing Draft Proposal of Virginia Computer Crimes Act's definition of "without authority"). The author argues that although the availability of a reasonable grounds defense was deleted, "in all probability, however, the defense of reasonable grounds will go to the general question of intent to commit the crime."

The provision on Computer Trespass is different in that the defendant must intend merely to commit the act of removing or deleting. There is no requirement that the defendant intend a wrong by removing or deleting. In contrast, the Computer Fraud statute, sec. 18.2-152.3, for example, requires that the defendant intend to obtain property or service by false pretenses, or intend to embezzle, commit larceny, or convert property of another. However, the criminal statute prohibiting trespass other than by computer is analogous. See sec. 18.2-119. This statute does not expressly require intent, however, "the statute has been construed to require proof of a willful trespass." *Jones v. Commonwealth*, 18 Va. App. 229, 232, 443 S.E.2d 189 (1994) (citations omitted). If the defendant entered another's land "in good faith under claim of right" although defendant was mistaken, and defendant did not use force, defendant will not be convicted of trespass. *Id.* (citing *Reed v. Commonwealth*, 6 Va. App. 65, 71, 366 S.E.2d 274 (1988)). A bona fide claim of right is "a sincere, although perhaps mistaken, good faith belief that one has some legal right to be on the property. The claim need not be one of title or ownership, but it must rise to the level of authorization." *Reed*, 6 Va. App. at 71. Whether a Defendant has a claim of right generally would be a factual question. However, in the present case, Defendant did have a right under the ISA to remove or order Plaintiff to remove content under certain circumstances, if reasonable, and to require reasonable changes to the content. Thus, Defendant had a clear contractual right to use the method it employed to remove and delete the data. The contracts required reasonableness in determining what content could be deleted and, according to Plaintiff, did not allow for the removal of the specific content that was ultimately removed. Again, this is a question of a breach of contract rather than criminal trespass. The contract allowed Defendant access that might otherwise have been trespass. If the access involved actions that violated the contract, then Plaintiff can recover for breach of contract.

The Computer Trespass statute also provides that "nothing in this section shall be construed to interfere with or prohibit terms or conditions in a contract or license related to computers, computer data, computer networks . . . ." sec. 18.2-152.4(D). Defendant argues that this amendment makes clear that the legislature did not intend to interfere with contractual rights. Plaintiff insists that the trespass statute does not interfere with or prohibit the terms in the ISA or SCA. This paragraph was added to the statute in 1998, after Defendant's alleged actions, thus Plaintiff argues that even if this amendment protects Defendant from culpability for criminal trespass, it does not apply to this case because the amendment was passed after the alleged computer trespass. Plaintiff asserts that a statute may not interfere with an existing contract or right of action. Plaintiff argues that Subsection B of sec. 18.2-152.4 is a substantive provision and thus may only be applied prospectively.

A statute must be construed prospectively, "unless a contrary intent is manifest, but the legislature may, in its discretion, pass retrospective and curative laws provided they do not partake of the nature of what are technically called *ex post facto* laws, and do not impair the obligation of contracts, or disturb vested rights." *Collins v. Dept. of Alcoholic Bev. Control*, 21 Va. App. 671, 678, 467 S.E.2d 279 (1996). In addition, these laws must be of the type that "the legislature might have passed in the first instance to act prospectively." *Id.* Substantive rights, like vested rights, are protected from retroactive application. *Brushy Ridge Coal Co. v. Blevins*, 6 Va. App. 73, 79, 367 S.E.2d 204 (1988). Substantive rights create duties, rights and obligations, whereas remedial or procedural laws establish methods of obtaining redress or enforcement of substantive rights. *Board of Sup. v. FCS Building Assn.*, 254 Va. 464, 467, 492 S.E.2d 634 (1997).

While retroactive application of a substantive right violates due process, it does not, as Plaintiff asserts, create an *ex post facto* law in violation of the United States Constitution, Article I, sec. 10, or in violation of the Constitution of Virginia, Article I, sec. 9. The prohibition against *ex post facto* laws applies "to penal statutes which disadvantage the offender affected by them." *Collins v. Youngblood*, 497 U.S. 37, 41, 111 L. Ed. 2d 30, 110 S. Ct. 2715 (1990).The U.S. Supreme Court has pronounced the two critical elements necessary for a criminal or penal law to be an *ex post facto* law: "it must be retrospective, that is, it must apply to events occurring before its enactment, and it must disadvantage the offender affected by it." *Weaver v. Graham*, 450 U.S. 24, 29, 67 L. Ed. 2d 17, 101 S. Ct. 960 (1981). No new punitive measure may be applied to a crime that has already taken place. *Lindsey v. Washington*, 301 U.S. 397, 401, 81 L. Ed. 1182, 57 S. Ct. 797 (1937). Thus, the amendment to sec. 18.2-152.4 would not be *ex post facto* because it in no way disadvantages the criminal defendant.

In this statute, it is true that the legislature does not explicitly allow retroactive application. However, the language of the amendment demonstrates that no right has been impeded or created.

As explained above, it appears that the intention of the statute was never to cover contractual situations like the one in this case. The legislature amended the statute to clarify what constitutes the crime of computer trespass. Even without this provision, the implication is that the statute does not apply to the present situation.

Further evidence that sec. 18.2-152.4(B) merely articulates the law that was in existence prior to this amendment, even though not previously articulated in the statute, is provided by the language of the amendment. The amendment states that "[n]othing in this section shall be construed to interfere with or prohibit terms or conditions in a contract . . . ." Thus, no new right is being given and no right of action is being taken away. Rather, the legislature is clarifying the effect of the statute to avoid confusion.

A mere violation of a contract is not covered under sec. 18.2-152.4, Computer Trespass of the Computer Crimes Act. Plaintiff's Motion for Summary Judgment is denied. Defendant's Motion for Summary Judgment on Liability on Count IV is sustained. Count IV is dismissed.

A. Lost Profits

The Virginia Supreme Court has announced the rule regarding lost profits:

When an established business, with an established earning capacity, is interrupted and there is no other practical way to estimate the damages thereby caused, evidence of the prior and subsequent record of the business has been held admissible to permit an intelligent and probable estimate of damages.

R. K. Chevrolet, Inc. v. Hayden, 253 Va. 50, 480 S.E.2d 477 (1997). "In Virginia, loss of future profits proximately caused by wrongful conduct, which results in the interruption or destruction of an established business, may be recovered from a tortfeasor, provided the lost profits are capable of reasonable ascertainment and are not uncertain, speculative, or remote. *Hop-In Food Stores v. Serv-N-Save, Inc.*, 247 Va. 187, 440 S.E.2d 606 (1994);

see United Constr. Wkrs. v. Laburnum, 194 Va. 872, 887, 75 S.E.2d 694 (1953) (finding that lost profits must be established with "reasonable certainty" and may not be remote, speculative, contingent or uncertain). Lost prospective profits due to a breach of contract may be recovered if proven with a reasonable degree of certainty, "but it is equally well settled that prospective profits are not recoverable in any case if it is uncertain that there would have been any profits, or if the alleged profits are so contingent, conjectural, or speculative that the amount thereof cannot be proved with a reasonable degree of certainty." *Sinclair v. Hamilton & Dotson*, 164 Va. 203, 211, 178 S.E. 777 (1935) (citations omitted).

The court distinguished between situations where the business was established as opposed to new. Where a breach of contract causes interference with or prevention of a business that is "a new or unestablished nonindustrial business, or one merely in contemplation, the anticipated profits from such business cannot be recovered, for the reason that it cannot be rendered certain that there would have been any profits at all from the conduct of such business." *Id.* In *Shopping Plazas v. Olive*, 202 Va. 862, 869, 120 S.E.2d 372 (1961), the court held that evidence of anticipated profits of a new business should not have been considered by the jury. The Court affirmed this ruling in *Goldstein v. Kaestner*, 243 Va. 169, 413 S.E.2d 347 (1992), and explained that damages could not be awarded based on evidence of projected profits from the operation of a gasoline station which never opened.

In *Blue Ridge Bank v. Veribanc, Inc.*, 866 F.2d 681 (1989), the Fourth Circuit acknowledged that lost profits for a new business were not recoverable. The court explained, however, that since the injury, lost profits could be recovered. Virginia case law appears to encompass within the definition of "new" businesses not only businesses that have not yet begun operation. *Coastland Corp. v. Third Nat. Mtg. Co.*, 611 F.2d 969 (1979) (emphasis added) (distinguishing between an established business and one that was a "new business, venture, or enterprise, or one merely in contemplation"); *Sinclair v. Hamilton & Dotson*, 164 Va. 203, 178 S.E. 777 (1935) (emphasis added) (holding that the "prospective profits of a new nonindustrial business or one merely in contemplation are too uncertain and speculative to form a basis for recovery"). Many of the Virginia cases involved businesses that were not yet in operation. Yet, based on the language of the cases, the rule appears to encompass businesses that have recently started as well as ones that had not begun to operate. In *Whitehead v. Cape Henry Syndicate*, 111 Va. 193, 197, 68 S.E. 263 (1910), the plaintiff's business had been in operation for one month but the court considered this a new business because it had not been in business long enough and had no such trade to show with reasonable certainty what, if any, profits would have been made. The court stated that this new business's profits "depended not only upon future bargains and states of the market, but upon other contingencies . . ." The Court defined an established business as one that "had been successfully conducted for such a length of time and had such a trade established that the profits thereof are reasonably ascertainable." In contrast "where a new business or enterprise is floated and damages by way of profit are claims for its interruption or prevention," damages will be denied. *Id.* Thus, the mere existence of a business does not imply that it is established.

Defendant AOL cites *Coastland Corp. v. Third Nat. Mtg. Co.*, 611 F.2d 969 (1979), as support for the assertion that future profits may not be recovered even though the parties made profit "projections." In that case, the court rejected Coastland's argument that because appellant received documentation with potential profits, and was thus aware of such profits, damages should have included those potential profits. *Id.* The court explained that "when an established business, with an established earning capacity, is interrupted and there is no other practical way to estimate the damages thereby caused, evidence of the prior and subsequent record of the business has been held admissible to permit an intelligent and probable estimate of damages." In contrast, new ventures are too speculative and depend upon "future bargains, the status of the market, and too many other contingencies to furnish a safeguard in fixing the measure of damages." *Id.*

Assuming that Plaintiff was an established business, evidence of future damages would be too speculative to be considered. "When an established business is interrupted and sustains loss, evidence of its past profits, and estimates of future profits derived there from, are admissible to permit an estimate of damages. *Murray v. Hadid*, 238 Va. 722, 732, 385 S.E.2d 898 (1989) (emphasis added) (citing *Krikorian v. Dailey*, 171 Va. 16, 30, 197 S.E. 442, 448 (1938)). In addition prospective profits are not recoverable in any case if it is uncertain that there would have been any profits . . . . *Id.* In the present case, Plaintiff had no past profits to derive future profits since it had not been profitable during its brief existence.

Plaintiff bases its claim for future lost profits solely on the "stipulation" or business plan between AOL and CigarCafe. According to CigarCafe this business plan consisted of a detailed analysis of Plaintiff's business plan prior to the contract's formation, "with AOL's MBAs sending CigarCafe's MBA back to the drawing board repeatedly to massage the numbers, result[ing] in a profit projection that AOL blessed and to which AOL stipulated." See CigarCafe's Memorandum of Points and Authorities in Opposition to AOL's Motion for Summary Judgment on Damages, p. 3(b)(1). Plaintiff argues that this stipulation overcomes the speculative nature of future profits for a new business. Plaintiff insists that the prospective profits were not speculative because they were in contemplation of the parties and because certain AOL employees anticipated these profits. In *ADC Fairways Corp. v. Johnmark Const. Inc.*, 231 Va. 312, 343 S.E.2d 90 (1986), the court held that plaintiff should not have been awarded lost profits because they were "completely speculative." Plaintiff calculated lost profits based on a certain percentage of his bid multiplied by the number of units that were to be completed for the project. The percentage was not included in the contract. *CigarCafe* suggests that the Court held this way because the percentage amount was arbitrary. However, the Court focused on the inability to determine what the future profits would be. It explained that this profit projection was nothing more than the profit plaintiff "hoped to make at the time of the bid. There was no evidence to establish that this is the profit that would have been made had Johnmark completed the project." *Id.* at 318.

In the present case, even though the business was in operation when the alleged breach of contract occurred, it did not fit the definition of "established" since it had not been in business for a long enough time to gauge its profits and, in fact, had not experienced any profits. Furthermore, plaintiff conceded in its CigarCafe's Memorandum of Points and Authorities in Opposition to AOL's Motion for Summary Judgment on Damages and in oral argument that the new business rule ordinarily would preclude a start-up company such as CigarCafe from recovering lost profits. Finally, even if the business was an established one, the damages must be capable of reasonable ascertainment and may not be uncertain, speculative, or remote.

Even assuming CigarCafe was an established business, a plan of projected profits developed by AOL and CigarCafe would be too speculative to use as evidence, considering CigarCafe's brief existence, its lack of any profits, its failure to assert any method for determining these damages and to provide expert witnesses.

Finally, future profits as estimated in the projections by Defendant were not guaranteed in the contract. The parties did not somehow agree or stipulate that these profits were guaranteed. These projected profits were merely a hope or expectation of profits. Defendant's Motion for Summary Judgment on Damages as to lost profits is sustained.

Case Questions

1. What is meant, legally, as the "willful destruction of a business?"

2. Briefly outline the court's discussion of proving lost profits.

United States of America v. Ivanov
175 F. Supp. 2d 367 D. Conn. (2001)

Background

Online Information Bureau, Inc. ("OIB"), the alleged victim in this case, is a Connecticut corporation based in Vernon, Connecticut. It is an "e-commerce" business which assists retail and Internet merchants by, among other things, hosting their websites and processing their credit card data and other financial transactions. In this capacity, OIB acts as a financial transaction "clearinghouse," by aggregating and assisting in the debiting or crediting of funds against each account for thousands of retail and Internet purchasers and vendors. In doing so, OIB collects and maintains customer credit card information, merchant account numbers, and related financial data from credit card companies and other financial institutions.

The government alleges that Ivanov "hacked" into OIB's computer system and obtained the key passwords to control OIB's entire network. The government contends that in late January and early February 2000, OIB received from Ivanov a series of unsolicited e-mails indicating that the defendant had obtained the "root" passwords for certain computer systems operated by OIB. A "root" password grants its user access to and control over an entire computer system, including the ability to manipulate, extract, and delete any and all data. Such passwords are generally reserved for use by the system administrator only.

The government claims that Ivanov then threatened OIB with the destruction of its computer systems (including its merchant account database) and demanded approximately $10,000 for his assistance in making those systems secure. It claims, for example, that on February 3, 2000, after his initial solicitations had been rebuffed, Ivanov sent the following e-mail to an employee of OIB:

> [name redacted], now imagine please Somebody hack you network (and not notify you about this), he download Atomic software with more than 300 merchants, transfer money, and after this did 'rm-rf/' and after this you company be ruined. I don't want this, and because this I notify you about possible hack in you network, if you want you can hire me and im allways be check security in you network. What you think about this?

The government contends that Ivanov's extortionate communications originated from an e-mail account at Lightrealm.com, an Internet Service Provider based in Kirkland, Washington. It contends that while he was in Russia, Ivanov gained access to the Lightrealm computer network and that he used that system to communicate with OIB, also while he was in Russia. Thus, each e-mail sent by Ivanov was allegedly transmitted from a Lightrealm.com computer in Kirkland, Washington, through the Internet to an OIB computer in Vernon, Connecticut, where the e-mail was opened by an OIB employee.

The parties agree that the defendant was physically located in Russia (or one of the other former Soviet Bloc countries) when, it is alleged, he committed the offenses set forth in the superseding indictment.

The superseding indictment comprises eight counts. Count One charges that beginning in or about December 1999, or earlier, the defendant and others conspired to commit the substantive offenses charged in Counts Two through Eight of the indictment, in violation of 18 U.S.C. sec. 371. Count Two charges that the defendant, knowingly and with intent to defraud, accessed protected computers owned by OIB and by means of this conduct furthered a fraud and obtained something of value, in violation of 18 U.S.C. sec.sec. 2, 1030(a)(4) and 1030(c)(3)(A). Count Three charges that the defendant intentionally accessed protected computers owned by OIB and thereby obtained information, which conduct involved interstate and foreign communications and was engaged in for purposes of financial gain and in furtherance of a criminal act, in violation of 18 U.S.C. sec.sec. 2, 1030(a)(2)(C) and 1030(c)(2)(B). Counts Four and Five do not pertain to this defendant.

Count Six charges that the defendant transmitted in interstate and foreign commerce communications containing a threat to cause damage to protected computers owned by OIB, in violation of 18 U.S.C. sec.sec. 1030(a)(7) and 1030(c)(3)(A). Count Seven charges that the defendant obstructed, delayed and affected commerce, and attempted to obstruct, delay and affect commerce, by means of extortion by attempting to obtain property from OIB with OIB's consent, inducing such consent by means of threats to damage OIB and its business unless OIB paid the defendant money and hired the defendant as a security consultant, in violation of 18 U.S.C. sec. 1951(a). Count Eight charges that the defendant, knowingly and with intent to defraud, possessed unauthorized access devices, which conduct affected interstate and foreign commerce, in violation of 18 U.S.C. sec.sec. 1029(a)(3).

Discussion

The defendant and the government agree that when Ivanov allegedly engaged in the conduct charged in the superseding indictment, he was physically present in Russia and using a computer there at all relevant times. Ivanov contends that for this reason, charging him under the Hobbs Act, 18 U.S.C. sec. 1951, under the Computer Fraud and Abuse Act, 18 U.S.C. sec. 1030, and under the access device statute, 18 U.S.C. sec. 1029, would in each case require extraterritorial application of that law and such application is impermissible. The court concludes that it has jurisdiction, first, because the intended and actual detrimental effects of Ivanov's actions in Russia occurred within the United States, and second, because each of the statutes under which Ivanov was charged with a substantive offense was intended by Congress to apply extraterritorially.

A. The Intended and Actual Detrimental Effects of the Charged Offenses Occurred Within the United States

As noted by the court in *United States v. Muench*, 694 F.2d 28 (2d Cir. 1982), "the intent to cause effects within the United States . . . makes it reasonable to apply to persons outside United States territory a statute which is not expressly extraterritorial in scope." *Id.* at 33. "It has long been a commonplace of criminal liability that a person may be charged in the place where the evil results, though he is beyond the jurisdiction when he starts the train of events of which that evil is the fruit." *United States v. Steinberg*, 62 F.2d 77, 78 (2d Cir. 1932). "The Government may punish a defendant in the same manner as if [he] were present in the jurisdiction when the detrimental effects occurred." *Marc Rich & Co., A.G. v. United States*, 707 F.2d 663, 666 (2d Cir. 1983).

The Supreme Court has quoted with approval the following language from Moore's International Law Digest:

> The principle that a man, who outside of a country willfully puts in motion a force to take effect in it, is answerable at the place where the evil is done, is recognized in the criminal jurisprudence of all countries. And the methods which modern invention has furnished for the performance of criminal acts in that manner has made this principle one of constantly growing importance and of increasing frequency of application.

Ford v. United States, 273 U.S. 593, 623 (1927). Moreover, the court noted in Rich that:

> It is certain that the courts of many countries, even of countries which have given their criminal legislation a strictly territorial character, interpret criminal law in the sense that offenses, the authors of which at the moment of commission are in the territory of another State, are nevertheless to be regarded as having been committed in the national territory, if one of the constituent elements of the offence, and more especially its effects, have taken place there. The S. S. Lotus, 1927 P.C.I.J., ser. A, No. 10, at 23, reprinted in 2 *Hudson, World Court Reports*, 23, 38 (1935).

Here, all of the intended and actual detrimental effects of the substantive offenses Ivanov is charged with in the indictment occurred within the United States. In Counts Two and Three, the defendant is charged with accessing OIB's computers. Those computers were located in Vernon, Connecticut. The fact that the computers were accessed by means of a complex process initiated and controlled from a remote location does not alter the fact that the accessing of the computers, *i.e.*, part of the detrimental effect prohibited by the statute, occurred at the place where the computers were physically located, namely OIB's place of business in Vernon, Connecticut.

Count Two charges further that Ivanov obtained something of value when he accessed OIB's computers, that "something of value" being the data obtained from OIB's computers. In order for Ivanov to violate sec. 1030(a)(4), it was necessary that he do more than merely access OIB's computers and view the data. *See United States v. Czubinski*, 106 F.3d 1069, 1078 (6th Cir. 1997) ("Merely viewing information cannot be deemed the same as obtaining something of value for purposes of this statute." . . . This section should apply to those who steal information through unauthorized access . . . ."). The indictment charges that Ivanov did more than merely gain unauthorized access and view the data. Ivanov allegedly obtained root access to the OIB computers located in Vernon, Connecticut. Once Ivanov had root access to the computers, he was able to control the data, e.g., credit card numbers and merchant account numbers, stored in the OIB computers; Ivanov could copy, sell, transfer, alter, or destroy that data. That data is intangible property of OIB. *See Carpenter v. United States*, 484 U.S. 19, 25 (1987) (noting that the "intangible nature [of confidential business information] does not make it any less 'property' protected by the mail and wire fraud statutes"). "In determining where, in the case of intangibles, possession resides, the measure of control exercised is the deciding factor." *New York Credit Men's Ass'n v. Mfrs. Disc. Corp.*, 147 F.2d 885, 887 (2d Cir. 1945).

At the point Ivanov gained root access to OIB's computers, he had complete control over that data, and consequently, had possession of it. That data was in OIB's computers. Since Ivanov possessed that data while it was in OIB's computers in Vernon, Connecticut, the court concludes that he obtained it, for purposes of sec. 1030(a)(4), in Vernon, Connecticut. The fact that Ivanov is charged with obtaining OIB's valuable data by means of a complex process initiated and controlled from a remote location, and that he subsequently moved that data to a computer located in Russia, does not alter the fact that at the point when Ivanov first possessed that data, it was on OIB's computers in Vernon, Connecticut.

Count Three charges further that when he accessed OIB's computers, Ivanov obtained information from protected computers. The analysis as to the location at which Ivanov obtained the information referenced in this count is the same as the analysis as to the location at which he obtained the "something of value" referenced in Count Two. Thus, as to both Counts Two and Three, it is charged that the balance of the detrimental effect prohibited by the pertinent statute, *i.e.*, Ivanov's obtaining something of value or obtaining information, also occurred within the United States.

Count Six charges that Ivanov transmitted a threat to cause damage to protected computers. The detrimental effect prohibited by sec. 1030(a)(7), namely the receipt by an individual or entity of a threat to cause damage to a protected computer, occurred in Vernon, Connecticut, because that is where OIB was located, where it received the threat, and where the protected computers were located. The analysis is the same as to Count Seven, the charge under the Hobbs Act.

Count Eight charges that Ivanov knowingly and with intent to defraud possessed over ten thousand unauthorized access devices, i.e., credit card numbers and merchant account numbers. For the reasons discussed above, although it is charged that Ivanov later transferred this intangible property to Russia, he first possessed it while it was on OIB's computers in Vernon, Connecticut. Had he not possessed it here, he would not have been able to transfer it to his computer in Russia. Thus, the detrimental effect prohibited by the statute occurred within the United States.

Finally, Count One charges that Ivanov and others conspired to commit each of the substantive offenses charged in the indictment. The Second Circuit has stated that "the jurisdictional element should be viewed for purposes of the conspiracy count exactly as we view it for purposes of the substantive offense . . . ." *United States v. Blackmon*, 839 F.2d 900, 910 (2d Cir. 1988) (internal citations and quotation marks omitted). *See also United States v. Kim*, 246 F.3d 186, 191, n.2 (2d Cir. 2001) (noting that jurisdiction over a conspiracy charge depends upon jurisdiction over the underlying substantive charge). Federal jurisdiction over a conspiracy charge "is established by proof that the accused planned to commit a substantive offense which, if attainable, would have violated a federal statute, and that at least one overt act has been committed in furtherance of the conspiracy." *United States v. Giordano*, 693 F.2d 245, 249 (2d Cir. 1982). Here, Ivanov is charged with planning to commit substantive offenses in violation of federal statutes, and it is charged that at least one overt act was committed in furtherance of the conspiracy. As discussed above, the court has jurisdiction over the underlying substantive charges. Therefore, the court has jurisdiction over the conspiracy charge, at a minimum, to the extent it relates to Counts Two, Three, Six, Seven or Eight.

Accordingly, the court concludes that it has subject matter jurisdiction over each of the charges against Ivanov, whether or not the statutes under which the substantive offenses are charged are intended by Congress to apply extraterritorially, because the intended and actual detrimental effects of the substantive offenses Ivanov is charged with in the indictment occurred within the United States.

B.   Intended Extraterritorial Application

The defendant's motion should also be denied because, as to each of the statutes under which the defendant has been indicted for a substantive offense, there is clear evidence that the statute was intended by Congress to apply extraterritorially. This fact is evidenced by both the plain language and the legislative history of each of these statutes.

There is a presumption that Congress intends its acts to apply only within the United States, and not extraterritorially. However, this "presumption against extraterritoriality" may be overcome by showing "clear evidence of congressional intent to apply a statute beyond our borders . . . ." *U.S. v. Gatlin*, 216 F.3d 207, 211 (2d Cir. 2000). "Congress has the authority to enforce its laws beyond the territorial boundaries of the United States. Whether Congress has in fact exercised that authority in [a particular case] is a matter of statutory construction." *Equal Employment Opportunity Comm. v. Arabian American Oil Co.*, 499 U.S. 244, 248 (1991) (internal citations omitted) ("ArAmCo").

The defendant is charged with substantive offenses in violation of 18 U.S.C. sec. 1951, 18 U.S.C. sec. 1030 and 18 U.S.C. sec. 1029, and with conspiracy in violation of 18 U.S.C. sec. 371.

1. 18 U.S.C. sec. 1951: The Hobbs Act

The Hobbs Act provides, in pertinent part, as follows:

> Whoever in any way or degree obstructs, delays, or affects commerce or the movement of any article or commodity in commerce, by robbery or extortion or attempts or conspires so to do, or commits or threatens physical violence to any person or property in furtherance of a plan or purpose to do anything in violation of this section shall be fined under this title or imprisoned not more than twenty years, or both.

The Supreme Court has stated that the Hobbs Act "speaks in broad language, manifesting a purpose to use all the constitutional power Congress has to punish interference with interstate commerce by extortion, robbery or physical violence." *Stirone v. United States*, 361 U.S. 212, 215 (1960). The Court has not had occasion to decide whether the "broad language" of the Hobbs Act expresses a congressional intent to apply the statute extraterritorially. However, the Third Circuit, relying in part on Stirone, concluded that:

> Even if none of the [defendants'] overt acts had occurred in this country . . . Congress could give the district court jurisdiction under the commerce clause so long as [the defendants'] activities affected [the victim's] commercial ventures in interstate commerce within the United States. *See Stirone v. United States*, 361 U.S. 212, 215, 80 S. Ct. 270, 272, 4 L. Ed. 2d 252 (1960) (Hobbs Act utilizes all of Congress's commerce clause power and reaches even a minimal interference with commerce) . . . ."

Based on the foregoing, this court concludes that the Hobbs Act encompasses not only all extortionate interference with interstate commerce by means of conduct occurring within the United States, but also all such conduct which, although it occurs outside the United States, affects commerce within the borders of the United States. Therefore, it is immaterial whether Ivanov's alleged conduct can be said to have taken place entirely outside the United States, because that conduct clearly constituted "interference with interstate commerce by extortion," *Stirone*, 361 U.S. at 215, in violation of the Hobbs Act. Consequently, the court has jurisdiction over this charge against him.

2.   18 U.S.C. sec. 1030: The Computer Fraud and Abuse Act

The Computer Fraud and Abuse Act ("CFAA") was amended in 1996 by Pub. L. No.
104-294, 110 Stat. 3491, 3508. The 1996 amendments made several changes that are
relevant to the issue of extraterritoriality, including a change in the definition of
"protected computer" so that it included any computer "which is used in interstate or
foreign commerce or communication." 18 U.S.C. sec. 1030(e)(2)(B) (Emphasis added).
The 1996 amendments also added subsections (a)(2)(C) and (a)(7), which explicitly
address "interstate or foreign commerce," and subsection (e)(9), which added to the
definition of "government entity" the clause "any foreign country, and any state,
province, municipality or other political subdivision of a foreign country."

The plain language of the statute, as amended, is clear. Congress intended the CFAA to
apply to computers used "in interstate or foreign commerce or communication." The
defendant argues that this language is ambiguous. The court disagrees. The Supreme
Court has often stated that "a statute ought, upon the whole, to be so construed that, if it
can be prevented, no clause, sentence, or word shall be superfluous, void, or
insignificant." *Regions Hosp. v. Shalala*, 522 U.S. 448, 467 (1998) (internal citations and
quotation marks omitted). In order for the word "foreign" to have meaning, and not be
superfluous, it must mean something other than "interstate." In other words, "foreign" in
this context must mean international. Thus, Congress has clearly manifested its intent to
apply sec. 1030 to computers used either in interstate or in foreign commerce.

The legislative history of the CFAA supports this reading of the plain language of the
statute. The Senate Judiciary Committee issued a report explaining its reasons for
adopting the 1996 amendments. S. Rep. No. 357, 104th Congr., 2d Sess. (1996). In that
report, the Committee specifically noted its concern that the statute as it existed prior to
the 1996 amendments did not cover "computers used in foreign communications or
commerce, despite the fact that hackers are often foreign-based." *Id.* at 4. The Committee
cited two specific cases in which foreign-based hackers had infiltrated computer systems
in the United States, as examples of the kind of situation the amendments were intended
to address:

For example, the 1994 intrusion into the Rome Laboratory at Grifess Air Force Base in
New York, was perpetrated by a 16-year-old hacker in the United Kingdom. More
recently, in March 1996, the Justice Department tracked down a young Argentinean man
who had broken into Harvard University's computers from Buenos Aires and used those
computers as a staging ground to hack into many other computer sites, including the
Defense Department and NASA.

Id. at 4-5. Congress has the power to apply its statutes extraterritorially, and in the case of
18 U.S.C. sec. 1030, it has clearly manifested its intention to do so.

3.   18 U.S.C. sec. 1029: The Access Device Statute

Section 1029 of Title 18 of the United States Code provides for the imposition of
criminal sanctions on any person who uses, possesses or traffics in a counterfeit access
device "if the offense affects interstate or foreign commerce." 18 U.S.C. sec. 1029
(2000). As noted above, there is a centuries old canon of statutory construction to the
effect that a statute should be construed so that no word or phrase is rendered
superfluous. *See, e.g., Platt v. Union Pac. R.R. Co.*, 99 U.S. 48, 58 (1878) (noting that the
"rules of statutory construction declare that a legislature is presumed to have used no
superfluous words."). Therefore, based on the same reasoning applied above in the

discussion of sec. 1030, the court concludes that the plain language of sec. 1029 indicates a congressional intent to apply the statute extraterritorially.

The parties agreed at oral argument that the legislative history of 18 U.S.C. sec. 1029 mirrors that of sec. 1030. Therefore, the discussion above of the congressional intent behind sec. 1030 also applies to sec. 1029. Accordingly, the court finds that this section, too, was intended to apply extraterritorially.

4. 18 U.S.C. sec. 371: The Conspiracy Statute

The Second Circuit has recently noted that where the court has jurisdiction over the underlying substantive criminal counts against a defendant, the court also has jurisdiction over the conspiracy counts. *See Kim*, 246 F.3d at 191, n.2. A court may "infer the extra-territorial reach of conspiracy statutes on the basis of a finding that the underlying substantive statute reached extra-territorial offenses, even though the conspiracy charges came under separate code sections . . . ." *United States v. Evans*, 667 F. Supp. 974, 981 (S.D.N.Y. 1987) (internal quotation marks and citations omitted). *See also United States v. Yousef*, 927 F. Supp. 673, 682 (S.D.N.Y. 1996) ("Extraterritorial jurisdiction over a conspiracy charge depends on whether extraterritorial jurisdiction exists as to the underlying substantive crime."). Because the court finds that each of the underlying substantive statutes in this case was intended by Congress to apply extraterritorially, it also finds that it has jurisdiction over the conspiracy charge.

Conclusion

For the reasons set forth above, the defendant's Motion to Dismiss for Lack of Subject Matter Jurisdiction [Doc. # 34] is hereby DENIED.

Case Question

1. Pursuant to which statutes does the court obtain jurisdiction in this case?

Exercises

1. Obtain a copy of a franchise agreement and analyze its provisions.

2. Access EDGAR to see how SEC filings are now made.

3. What proposals would you make to design an appropriate method of taxing Internet sales?

4. Briefly explain the six requisite elements to create a valid contract.

5. Analyze how you would try to protect against credit card fraud on the Internet.

6. Discuss some of the defenses to contract formation discussed in the CigarCafe case presented above.

7. How might the ability to make payments over the Internet effect e-business? Discuss.

8. Briefly discuss how franchising works.

9. Discuss the requisite elements to create a valid contract.

10. Briefly outline some provisions of outsourcing contracts.

Related Websites

Berkmancenter.org
Perkinscoie.com/resources/ecomm/ecomm.htm

Chapter Five

INTELLECTUAL PROPERTY LAW ISSUES

Chapter Overview

As a general statement, **intellectual property** can be viewed as the tangible and intangible results of the creative brain process. For example, when an artist completes a painting, that physical object—the painting—is considered to be a tangible work of art. **Tangible property** refers to all items that can be touched and/or moved and which have intrinsic value. Conversely, when a scientist creates a new scientific process, even though the paper on which that process is written down may be an item of physical property, the property's value does not lie in the paper but in the idea represented on that paper, which is considered to be intangible property. **Intangible property** refers to items that have little intrinsic value but are representative of something of value. The paper on which the scientific process is written has limited value, but its worth lies in the application of the scientific equation.

The United States government grants property right protections to creators of intellectual property by allowing the creator the exclusive right to the fruits of his or her creative process for a statutorily specified period of time. This governmental grant of a property right falls into three broad categories: copyrights, trademarks and patents. The purpose behind the government's grant is to recognize creativity by rewarding the creator the exclusive right to dispose of such property as he or she wishes in the hope of encouraging even greater creative activity. However, in order to make the fruits of the intellectual process available to the general public to inspire others to create, these governmental grants of exclusive use are finite in duration.

The tremendous growth in popularity of the Internet over the past decade has engendered significant problems for the holders of intellectual property rights. Because so much material is either directly designed for computers and/or computer use or is disseminated by means of the Internet, an increasing concern over the appropriate method of regulating intellectual property in cyberspace has evolved. This chapter will examine the law regarding copyrights, trademarks and patents as they apply to cyberspace, as well as discuss some proposals that have been posited that are directly geared to resolving some of these intellectual property cyberlaw problems.

Copyrights

A **copyright** is a property right that is derived from other forms of property rights because it is not directly concerned with the ownership of a material object. A copyright is a governmental grant of exclusive use of a work of art or literature that is granted to the creator. This right may be owned and transferred by the holder. Copyrights may be obtained for the following types of "creations":

- literary works such as books, plays and articles
- musical creations such a songs
- recordings, records and CDs
- photographic works such as motion pictures, photographs, prints and so forth
- works of art and sculpture.

The authority of the federal government to grant a copyright emanates from the United States Constitution, and in 1790 the United States Congress enacted the first federal copyright legislation. This initial copyright law has been modified by both statute and judicial opinion to embrace the new technology which has expanded the concept of a "creative work." The most recent legislative enactment of the copyright law was the **Sonny Bono Copyright Term Extension Act**. Pursuant to this statute, most copyrights granted on or after January 1, 1978, exist for the life of the creator plus 70 years. This means that the creator is able to transfer his or her right by will or intestate succession to heirs who in turn may transfer the right until 70 years after the creator's death. At that point the copyrighted work belongs in the **public domain**, meaning that anyone is free to reproduce the work.

Example: A novelist has copyrighted all of his works. The first work was copyrighted in 1984. The writer dies in 2011, and in his will he leaves all of his copyrights to his daughter. The copyrights will remain in effect until 2081 (70 years after the novelist's death). If the daughter dies in 2070, she, in turn, may will the copyrights until they expire in 2081.

Having a copyright means that the holder has the *exclusive* right to the use of the work. This exclusive right includes the right to

- reproduce the work
- create later works based on the original work
- perform the work
- destroy the work
- distribute the work.

Example: An author writes a short story that she copyrights. She decides to disseminate the story on a website that she has created. Once the work is on the site, the problem arises with respect to her ability to prevent others from copying the work and exploiting it without her consent, which would be a violation of her copyright.

However, even though the holder of the copyright has the exclusive rights enumerated above, reproduction may still be permitted without the holder's consent if the use is deemed to be a fair use. **Fair use** refers to the use of a copyrighted work for the purpose of news reporting, research, criticism or comment. To determine whether such use is a fair use, the courts generally look at the following factors:

- the purpose and character of the use
- the type of work that has been copyrighted
- the economic effect of such use on the copyright holder
- the proportion of the total work that is being used.

Example: A legal scholar has just published a lengthy legal text on the history of the United States Supreme Court. A law student writes an article for her school law review in which she comments on the text, quoting many passages in detail. Such use of the copyrighted text will probably be considered a fair use because it is meant for scholarship and commenting on the copyrighted work.

In order to establish the copyright, the work must first be reduced to a copyrightable form, which is statutorily referred to as a **fixed creative work**. Originally, many works could not be copyrighted because they could not be reduced to a fixed format; an example would be a choreographed dance. However, as technology advanced, the law adapted so that now any work that can be reduced to a fixed format in a film, CD, disk, and so forth, is capable of being copyrighted.

Example: A retailer wants to market his products online. He has an artist create a specially designed web page for this purpose. Because it can be printed out, the web page may be copyrighted.

To establish a copyright, the creator must register the creative work with the **U.S. Copyright Office** in Washington, D.C. If the submitted work meets the basic requirements to be copyrighted, the Copyright Office will issue a **certificate of registration** to the creator that acts as proof of the copyright. To obtain this registration the registration must demonstrate that

- the work submitted is an original work that is not derived from any other work
- the work is the result of the independent creative process of the creator, and
- the work is submitted in a fixed format (photograph, CD, disk, printed copy, and so forth).

Once the Certificate of Registration is issued, the holder may license the use of the work to others. A **license** is an agreement whereby the copyright holder agrees to permit another to use or disseminate the work in consideration of that payment, known as a **royalty**, to the holder. In this manner the inchoate property right transforms into a direct economic benefit.

Example: A sculptor has registered a work with the U.S. Copyright Office and has been issued a Certificate of Registration. A few weeks later a company approaches the sculptor and asks him for permission to use an image of the sculpture for the design of its home page website. The sculptor and the company enter into a licensing agreement whereby the sculptor permits the company to use an image of the work for its web page and the company agrees to pay the sculptor a set amount of money for every hit of the page for the duration of the licensing agreement.

The transfer of a copyright can be filed in the Copyright Office in order to record the transfer so as to avoid later conflicts among several persons each claiming the right. This filing with the Copyright Office creates a **constructive notice** to all subsequent transferees of the right that such transfer may be ineffective or limited. The transfer could be ineffective if the transferor no longer has a transferable right at the time of the transfer. The transfer will be limited if the right was subject to a **nonexclusive license**, meaning that the transferor retained the ability to transfer the right to several persons concurrently.

Example: The sculptor from the previous example has licensed his work to the company only for use on its web page. The license is filed with the Copyright Office. Later, the sculptor grants the right to reproduce his work as the cover for a textbook to be distributed only in Europe, and such license is also filed. In these licenses each transferee has a limited nonexclusive right to use the work. The company may only use the image on its web page, and the publisher may only use the image on its texts distributed in Europe. The filing of these licenses has put each transferee on notice of the other licensee's rights.

To protect the copyright, the fixed format of the work must include a copyright mark that alerts the public that the work is copyrighted. The notice must indicate the following:

- a word or symbol that indicates a copyright
- the year of the first publication
- the name of the copyright holder.

Example: © 2004
            Jeffrey A. Helewitz
            All Rights Reserved.

Whenever a copyrighted work is used by someone not so authorized by the copyright holder, and such use does not fall into the fair use exception, such copyright violation is called a copyright **infringement**.

An infringement is considered to be a **direct infringement** if the unauthorized user specifically intended to make such unauthorized use. However, problems may arise if a direct infringer puts the work on an Internet bulletin board. Under traditional theory of copyright infringement, the bulletin board operator would be considered liable for economic injury to the copyright holder even though the unauthorized use occurred without his or her knowledge. In response to this problem, Congress enacted the **Digital Millennium Copyright Act of 1998 (DMCA)** which creates what are referred to as **safe harbors**, or exceptions, to protect innocent bulletin board operation. These safe harbors include:

- **system caching**: having the work placed on the bulletin board by someone other than the bulletin board operator
- **system storing**; boards used for storing, provided that the bulletin board operator has no direct knowledge of the infringement
- **routing**: temporary storage in the bulletin board for further transmission of the copyrighted work.

Note that these safe harbors only protect the bulletin board operators, not the direct infringer.

A person may also be held to have violated a copyright holder's rights by **contributory infringement** if he or she assists in the direct infringement of a copyright.

Example: An employee uses the company computer and e-mail to transmit copyrighted material in a manner that infringes on the rights of the copyright holder. The employee's manager is aware of this use but does nothing to stop the employee. In this instance the company may be held contributorily liable for permitting its employee to infringe on another's copyright.

Finally, if a person receives a direct economic benefit from a copyright infringement, even if the person is unaware of the infringement, this person may be considered to have **vicariously infringed** on the copyright.

If an infringement of a copyright can be proven, the copyright holder is entitled to the following remedies:

- **damages**: monetary relief to compensate him or her for the economic loss suffered, which could be **actual damages**, the amount proven to have been lost, or **statutory damages**, an amount set by the court of revenues lost because of the infringement would be difficult to prove

- **injunction**: a court order requiring the infringer to stop using the copyrighted work

- attorney's fees: the amount the copyright holder had to pay a lawyer to represent him or her in pursuing the infringer.

As discussed in earlier chapters, one of the major problems facing copyright protection and the Internet is the question of jurisdiction. Because the Internet is global in impact, a copyright infringement may arise anywhere in the world, and therefore a potential injury resulting from the infringement may be subject to conflicting laws. Recently, several countries have entered into the **Berne Convention for the Protection of Literary and Artistic Works** and the **World Intellectual Property Organization Copyright Treaty** to provide some uniformity for the enforcement of copyright protections. Unfortunately, not all countries belong, and these conventions only provide protocols rather than specific laws that can be uniformly enforced. (See Appendix C.)

Several solutions have been proffered to provide some protection for copyright holders against infringement on the Internet. Some of these solutions are:

- Imposing a fee for use to view a protected item on the web. This would provide the basis for a payment to the copyright holder, but may limit dissemination to persons who can afford such fees, which may not be in the best interests of the copyright holder or the public at large.

- Creating licensing societies that would be global in scope to provide copyright protection by hiring people to scan the Internet for unauthorized uses, in the same fashion that ASCAP (the American Society of Composers, Authors and Producers) protects copyrights for its members in traditional formats. However, because of the nature of the Internet, with virtually unlimited universal access, such monitoring may prove practically impossible.

- Using browsers to limit unauthorized use by limiting a user's ability to cut and paste certain copyrighted materials, as well as by using purging commands to counteract attempted unauthorized uses.

- Using traditional contract law to specify use, forum, choice of law, and available remedies to preclude challenges to jurisdiction or applicable law.

Copyright law has had particular cyberlaw application in three distinct areas: encryption, MP3 and deeplinking.

Encryption is the use of codes to secure material that is being transmitted by means of the Internet. Because encryption programs were considered more mechanical than intellectual, they were originally denied copyright protection. However, after many court cases, encryption was eventually determined to be an outgrowth of speech and the intellectual process and therefore such software may now be copyrighted and disseminated.

MP3 is a digital format that can store huge amounts of music in limited space. Using MP3 the stored music can be transmitted over the Internet, which can result in copyright infringement of the music so transmitted without the authorization of the copyright holder. To provide a remedy to this problem, in 1998 Congress enacted the **Digital Millennium Copyright Act (DMCA)** that makes it illegal to use any technology that circumvents copyright protections. This statute has also been used to enjoin making unauthorized copies by means of DVDs.

Deeplinking permits one website to link onto (access) another website by by-passing the second site's home page. If the second website home page requires an access fee to view copyrighted material, this deeplinking can operate as a copyright infringement. Also related to deeplinking is **framing** whereby one website appears in a window of another site which could result in a copyright infringement by bypassing the homepage. At the current time deeplinking and framing are the subjects of multiple lawsuits, but no resolution as yet been reached.

Just as technology has enabled various types of creative works to be copyrighted by providing the means to reduce them to a tangible format, it has also created expanded opportunities for infringement of the copyright holders' rights.

Marks

A **mark** is a word, group of words, or a symbol that distinguishes a particular good or service from similar goods or services in the marketplace. Marks are registered pursuant to the Trademark Act of 1946, 15 U.S.C. sec. 1501 et seq. at the United States Patent and Trademark Office in Washington, D.C. Marks are categorized as **trademarks** if the mark identifies a good, or a **service mark** if the mark identifies a service.

Example: An organization that manufactures computers wants to mark its product to distinguish it from other computers being sold, and so it designs a graphic representation of a tree as its trademark. This symbol now identifies this particular company's computers in the marketplace.

The right to hold a mark arises automatically by use; however, in order to afford the mark holder greater protection most marks are registered. To register a mark with the Patent and Trademark Office, the mark must fall into one of the following categories:

1. arbitrary or fanciful: the name is not real but is created specifically for the product, such as KODAK
2. suggestive: the mark does not designate the good or service but suggests it, such as FINDLAW
3. generic: the mark is a common name such as "General Nutrition Center."

Closely associated with trademarks and service marks are **trade names**, which are the actual name of the company that it uses to identify a particular business. There are no specific provisions for registering trade names under the Trademark Act, but many businesses use their trademarks as their trade names so as to afford them some protection against unauthorized use.

Recently, the law of trademarks has added a new classification known as a **trade dress**. A trade dress is a design that incorporates a particular shape or color that is associated with the particular product. These trade dresses provide immediate product identification to the consumer. A well-known example is the multi-colored flag, which is the trade dress used to identify Microsoft products.

When a mark is submitted for registration, the mark is placed in one of two distinct registers. If the mark is **inherently distinctive**, meaning that it is unique and specifically associated with the particular goods or services, the mark is filed in the **principal register**. If the mark is not inherently distinctive, but its association with a good or service is secondary to its use, the mark is deemed to have a **secondary meaning** and is placed in the **supplemental register**. Marks that are usually considered to have a secondary meaning are typically composed of common words or a person's name. However, the association of the secondary word with a specific product may eventually cause the mark to become distinctive to the product. If a secondary meaning mark appears on the supplemental register for five years, it may then be considered for placement on the principal register.

Similar to copyrights, having a mark registered gives the holder the exclusive right to use that mark to identify the good or service. However, marks are granted only to products within a given industry, meaning that the same mark may appear for products in different industries. The mark, if registered, gives the holder the exclusive right to that mark for a ten-year period, but this period may be continually renewed for additional ten-year periods. However, the holder will lose this exclusive right if:

a.   the mark comes into common parlance

Example: *The mark "Xerox" can be lost if that term becomes generally used to mean photocopying.*

b.   the holder permits an unauthorized use of the mark for a period of time.

If the holder does not protect the mark by preventing unauthorized uses or letting it come into general speech, the mark may be lost.

Any unauthorized use of a valid mark is deemed to be an infringement, just as with copyrights discussed above, and the mark holder is entitled to the same remedies afforded the copyright holder under similar circumstances. However, the law of trademarks identifies several uses of a mark that differ from copyright infringement whereby a mark holder may suffer legal injuries by dilution of the mark.

Trademark **dilution** occurs whenever a famous and distinctive mark is used by someone other than the mark holder in a manner that tends to diminish its value as a mark to the holder over a period of time. In 1996 the United States Congress enacted the **Federal Trademark Dilution Act**, 15 U.S.C. sec. 1125, specifically to address this problem. To institute an action for trademark dilution, the mark holder must allege and prove the following:

- that the mark is owned and registered by the party asserting the right

- the mark is both distinctive and famous, meaning that the mark has become used extensively over a period of time and is usually recognized by a significant portion of the general public as referring to the particular product (the bitten apple of MacIntosh)

- the use of the mark is causing the mark to be diluted to the mark holder. **Dilution** indicates that the mark is now being associated with more than just one product. Further, the statute also recognizes a **dilution by tarnishment** if the unauthorized use causes the mark to be associated with inferior goods or services.

Example: *A software manufacturer has become aware of another software company using a very similar mark to sell its products, which are of an extremely poor quality when compared to the mark holder's product. This manufacturer may be able to support a claim of trademark dilution if it can be shown that this use of a similar mark has diminished the value of its mark, and its mark predated the other use.*

Another form of dilution of a trademark can occur if the mark is being used in another industry, which is permitted, but over a period of time the distinctiveness of the mark to the holder has been lost. This is known as **dilution by blurring**. Note that this is different from traditional infringement in which the use is unauthorized. With dilution by blurring, each company has rights for its industry but its distinctiveness is lost. The company being sued, to prevail, must be able to demonstrate that its use of the mark has precedence in the marketplace.

The traditional law of trademarks overlaps with cyberlaw in the use of domain names. A **domain name** is a unique name that is used to identify a specific Internet site. Domain names may, and currently are, trademarked, and so the person who marks the domain name is afforded the same protections as all other mark holders.

Assignment of domain names comes under the purview of the **Internet Corporation for Assigned Names & Numbers** which has the authority to assign unique domain names. Until 1999, these assignments came under the exclusive control of **Network Solutions, Inc.**, but at this point in time many organizations have the authority to assign domain names. In 1999, the **Uniform Domain Name Dispute Resolution Policy (UDRP)** and the **Anticybersquatting Consumer Protection Act (ACPA)** were enacted to provide specific domain name protections beyond the scope of traditional trademark legislation.

Cybersquatting refers to the registration of a domain name that establishes a name with the specific intent of selling the name to the holder of a mark with the same name or a third person for profit. Unless the name is registered as a domain name, it cannot be used as such on the Internet, even if the name is marked as a trademark or service mark. UDRP was enacted in order to provide further protection to the mark holder and to mandate that the mark holder and the alleged cybersquatter settle the dispute by arbitration. To initiate the arbitration process, the claimant must demonstrate the following:

- The domain name is identical or confusingly similar to the mark.
- The mark is registered to the claimant.
- The domain name holder has no right to the marked name.
- The domain name was registered in bad faith.

In order to prove the "bad faith" element, the claimant must show the following:

- The domain name was registered only for the purpose of selling or transferring it.
- The name was registered to prevent the mark holder from using the mark as its domain name.
- The name was registered to discredit the mark holder's business.
- The person who registered the name intended to confuse the public by implying that they were dealing with the mark holder.

If successful, the claimant can have the domain name cancelled or transferred to him or her.

Under the ACPA, several remedies are afforded the mark holder if it proves that the name was registered in bad faith and that the name is registered to the claimant as a mark. To determine "bad faith," the court uses a variety of factors similar to those indicated above, but also includes as factors the use of the name for pornographic purposes and **typopiracy**, the deliberate misspelling of the mark designed to confuse the public.

Example: COMPAK for CPMPAQ

However, it must be remembered that in order to assert rights under these statutes, the claimant must have the mark registered with the U.S. Patent and Trademark Office.

Patents

A **patent** is a governmental grant of exclusive use of a scientific invention or process given to the inventor for a nonrenewable 20-year period. The rationale behind patent law is to encourage scientific progress by allowing the inventor to reap the financial rewards for his or her work but permit the work to be publicly available to be used by other scientists to develop other inventions. Pursuant to the United States Constitution, patents are under the exclusive jurisdiction of the federal government and are registered at the U.S. Patent and Trademark Office in Washington, D.C.

To be patentable, the scientist must prove that the invention is both new and useful and is not merely a simple modification of an existing invention. With respect to cyberlaw, since all technology is the result of scientific invention, most technology is patentable, both the hardware and the software. Recently, the problems of certain e-businesses with respect to patents have come to the forefront of cyberlaw.

As discussed in the previous chapter, e-business has become one of the most desirable methods of conducting a modern business. If the method of business operation is unique and has been specifically invented for the business, it may be capable of being patented. To date various business methods developed for the Internet have been granted patents, including methods of creating online payment processes, systems for multi-person online interaction, and so forth.

Chapter Review

One of the most frequently litigated areas in the field of cyberlaw involves intellectual property. Intellectual property refers to governmental grants of exclusive use given to the creator of an artistic or literary work (copyright), the inventor of a scientific invention (patent), or the holder of a word or symbol designating a specific product (mark). The cyberlaw problem encountered with intellectual property involves the unauthorized use of such property right by means of computers and computer technology.

Any unauthorized use of an intellectual property right is deemed to be an infringement, which affords the holder of the right and the ability to seek judicial remedies. However, as with all other areas of cyberlaw, the question of determining the appropriate jurisdiction in which to litigate the claim, as well as the appropriate law to apply to the infringement, remains problematical.

However, copyrights, marks and patents are provided some international protection pursuant to the **Agreement on the Trade-Related Aspects of Intellectual Property (TRIP)** under the auspices of the World Trade Organization. As technology develops, the need for increased international protection becomes more acute, and provides one of the fasted-growing areas of concern for the cyberlaw professional.

Key Terms

Agreement on the Trade-Related Aspects of Intellectual Property (TRIP)—Agreement designed to afford some international protections for copyrights, marks and patents

Anticybersquatting Consumer Protection Act (ACPA)—Law that provides protection for the mark holder against persons who register that mark as a domain name

Berne Convention for the Protection of Literary and Artistic Works—Recent international protocol to protect copyrights

Certificate of Registration—Document given to show copyright was registered

Contributory Infringement—Assisting in the infringement of protected intellectual property

Constructive Notice—Legal doctrine that registration puts others on notice of the copyright holder's rights

Copyright—Governmental grant of exclusive use given to an author or artist for his or her registered work

Cybersquatting—Registering a mark as a domain name to resell it for a profit

Damages—Monetary remedy

Deeplinking—One website accessing another by by-passing the second site's home page

Digital Millennium Copyright Act of 1998 (DMCA)—Statute designed to extend copyright protection to the new technology

Dilution—Lessening the value of a mark by unauthorized use

Dilution by Blurring—Dilution of a mark when it is used in another industry

Direct Infringement—Unauthorized use of a mark or copyright

Domain Name—Unique name used to identify a website

Encryption—Program that scrambles electronic transmissions for privacy

Fair Use—Permitted use of a copyright without the need for authorization

Federal Trademark Dilution Act—Federal statute designed to provide protection against trademark dilution

Fixed Creative Work—Primary requirement to obtain a copyright

Framing—Having a second website appear on a portion of another site

Infringement—Unauthorized use of a protected intellectual property right

Inherently Distinctive—Unique trade dress

Injunction—Court order to stop doing something

Intangible Property—Property whose value is representative rather than intrinsic

Intellectual Property—Copyrights, patents and marks

Internet Corporation for Assigned Names & Numbers—Organization that assigns domain names

License—Agreement authorizing the use of a copyright, mark or patent

Mark—Word or symbol used to distinguish a product or service

MP3—Method of putting large amounts of music on a DVD

Nonexclusive License—Permitting several people to use a copyright or mark

Patent—Governmental grant of exclusive use given to the inventor of a scientific process or invention

Principal Register—Place where inherently distinctive marks are recorded

Public Domain—Intellectual property that is no longer protected

Royalty—Fee paid for a license

Safe Harbor—Exceptions to infringements under the DMCA

Secondary Meaning—Meaning that is not inherently distinctive

Service Mark—Mark used to identify a service

Sonny Bono Copyright Term Extension Act—Federal statute that determines limits for copyrights

Statutory Damages—Monetary relief specified by legal enactment

Supplemental Register—Place where marks that are not inherently distinctive are recorded

System Caching—Having items placed on a bulletin board by someone other than the bulletin board operator

System Storing—Placing items on a bulletin board

Trade Dress—Specific color and design used to identify a product

Trade Name—Business name used to identify a business

Typopiracy—Deliberate misspelling of a name to confuse the public

Uniform Domain Name Dispute Resolution Policy (UDRP)—Statute mandating arbitration for domain name disputes

United States Copyright Office—Government agency that oversees copyrights

United States Patent and Trademark Office—Office where patents and marks are registered

Vicarious Infringement—Receiving an economic benefit from an infringement when one is not the actual infringer

World Intellectual Property Organization Copyright Treaty—Most recent international response to Internet copyright problems

Edited Cases

The first of the edited cases discusses trademark and trade name infringement, and the second case discusses copyright infringement. They are presented to underscore the topics introduced in this chapter.

Aura Communications, Inc. v. Aura Networks, Inc.
148 F. Supp. 2d 91 D. Mass. 2001)

Plaintiff Aura Communications, Inc. sues Defendant Aura Networks, Inc. for trademark infringement, trade-name infringement, false designation of origin, dilution, and unfair competition. Aura Communications moves for a Preliminary Injunction to prohibit Aura Networks from using the word "Aura" as its trade name and logo. For the reasons state below, Aura Communications' Motion is ALLOWED.

Background

Plaintiff has used the names "Aura Communications, Inc."; "Aura Communications"; and "Aura" as corporate identifiers since 1995. The company's mark consists of a stylized "AURA" with a right-leaning arch and a large dot within the arch. The United States Patent and Trademark Office issued a trademark registration for the mark in 1998.

Aura Communications is a telecommunications-technology company located in Wilmington, Massachusetts. The company develops wireless-communications products, and currently sells a single product—the VoiceLink™ Wireless IC chipset. When incorporated into a wireless telephone headset, the VoiceLink™ chip allows telephone users to wirelessly operate landline telephones. The company soon will release its LibertyLink™ Wireless IC chip that allows for a completely wireless desktop system, including a wireless mouse and keyboard. Aura Communications also tries to attract and hire skilled employees by using recruiters and placing regular advertisements on its website and in *The Boston Globe*.

Defendant has used the names "Aura Networks, Inc."; "Aura Networks"; and "Aura" since October 2000, when the company changed its name from Lancast, Inc.—its corporate name since 1981. The company's mark includes the word "Aura" in large letters with "NETWORKS" below in small letters. The word "Aura" is partially surrounded by a right-leaning arch. Aura Networks applied to register its mark with the U.S. Patent and Trademark Office, but registration is pending.

Aura Networks is located in Nashua, New Hampshire—within approximately thirty miles of Aura Communications. The company sells computer-network-infrastructure hardware, such as hubs, switches and media converters, that directs high-speed data traffic over the Internet using fiber-optic technology. Like Aura Communications, Aura Networks' success depends on its ability to attract skilled employees. The company also places regular employment advertisements in *The Boston Globe*.

Discussion

Aura Communications moves for a Preliminary Injunction. For a Preliminary Injunction to issue, the movant must show: (1) the likelihood of success on the merits; (2) irreparable harm if an injunction does not issue; (3) that the threat of injury to the movant outweighs the harm the injunction may inflict on the nonmovant; and (4) that granting the preliminary injunction will not violate the public interest.

I. Likelihood of Success on the Merits

Aura Communications alleges, inter alia, trademark infringement and trade-name infringement.

A. Trademark Infringement

To prove trademark infringement, Aura Communications must show "(1) that [it] uses and thereby 'owns' a mark; (2) that the defendant is using a same or similar mark; and (3) that the defendant's use is likely to confuse the public, thereby harming plaintiff." Aura Networks does not contest that Aura Communications owns and uses a mark, but only that its mark is dissimilar and unlikely to confuse the public.

1. Similarity of the Marks

Aura Networks argues that the trademarks are dissimilar because Aura Communications uses the mark "AURA," while Aura Networks used the composite mark "Aura NETWORKS." Conflicting marks are to be compared by analyzing them as a whole rather than comparing them by their component parts.

Aura Communications' mark is the word "AURA" with a right-leaning arch and a large dot within the arch. The Aura Networks mark is virtually identical. It includes the word "Aura," partially surrounded by a right-leaning arch, with the word "NETWORKS" below in a comparatively minuscule font.

Although Aura Networks argues that its mark is distinguishable because it includes the "NETWORKS" immediately under "Aura," the most predominant, eye-catching feature of the mark is the word "Aura" with the right-leaning arch. Considering the marks as a whole, they are unquestionably similar.

II. Likelihood of Confusion

The likelihood of confusion is generally measured by eight factors: (1) similarity of the marks; (2) similarity of the goods; (3) relationship between the parties' channels of trade; (4) relationship between the parties' advertising; (5) classes of prospective purchasers; (6) evidence of actual confusion; (7) defendant's intent in adopting the mark; and (8) strength of the mark. As noted above, the marks are similar.

a. Similarity of the Goods

Aura Communications states that both Parties' products are similar because they involve communications applications. Aura Networks disagrees. It argues that Aura Communications only sells the VoiceLink™ chip that allows for wireless telephone use; whereas Aura Networks sells computer-network-infrastructure products, including hubs, switches, and media converters—all devices that allow information to be transmitted over the Internet via copper wire or fiber-optic cable. Because its products do not relate to wireless-telephone technology, Aura Networks argues that the Parties' products are dissimilar.

Aura Networks fails to recognize that Aura Communications' technological capability is not limited to the VoiceLink™ chip. The company will soon release its LibertyLink™ Wireless IC chip for digital voice, audio, and data transmissions. This new chip will enable a completely wireless desktop, including a wireless computer mouse, keyboards, etc. It will be used in desktop computers and computer-network-infrastructure devices.

Although Aura Networks does not sell wireless products, the company's products are used in environments that also contain wireless products like the one soon to be sold by Aura Communications. Because both companies sell communications products that enable data, voice, and other information to be transported across electronic channels, their products are similar.

b. Channels of Trade, Parties' Advertising, and Prospective Purchasers

Courts typically analyze together the overlap between the parties' trade channels, advertising, and prospective purchasers. Aura Communications claims that overlap exists because both sell products on the Internet, at the same trade shows, and to the same customers. Aura Networks argues that it does not sell its products over the Internet, but rather uses a thirty-person sales force. The company also notes that it does not attend the same trade shows as Aura Communications, and does not market to the same consumers.

There is evidence in the record that Aura Networks' products can be purchased over the Internet, even if not directly from the Aura Networks' website, and both companies advertise their products over the Internet. Moreover, both companies advertise for employees in the exact same newspaper; they both seek employees in the technology sector; and they seek employees from the same geographic area. There is little evidence, however, on whether their products are purchased by the same consumers. At minimum, the Parties' channels of trade and methods of advertising are related.

c. Evidence of Actual Confusion

There is more than sufficient evidence of actual confusion, most of which Aura Networks acknowledges. Such evidence includes testimony from numerous Aura Communications' employees and agents. Below is some of the evidence of the actual confusion.

Tim White, Director of Programs at Aura Communications, stated that he circulated an email to schedule an onsite meeting with a client. The client later called Mr. White to confirm the directions he printed from the company's website. Based on the directions given by the client, Mr. White determined that client had wrongly accessed the Aura Networks website.

Nora Leonard, Aura Communications' Administrator of Sales and Marketing, testified that she received numerous telephone calls from persons intending to call Aura Networks.

Christopher Bunszel, Aura Communications' Strategic Marketing Manager, testified that while running the Aura Communications booth at a consumer-electronics trade show in Las Vegas, Nevada, he was twice approached by people indicating that they thought Aura Communications was Aura Networks.

Confusion includes not only consumer confusion, but confusion by prospective employees. Nicole Jackson, Executive Assistant of Aura Communications, testified that she has received phone calls from persons calling to inquire about the Aura Networks recruitment ad. Ms. Jackson also spoke to a professional recruiter who saw an Aura Networks advertisement and thought the advertisement was incorrectly printed and should have stated Aura Communications.

Kristen Gelinas, a QoS Staffing, Inc. recruiter hired by Aura Communications, stated that she asked another recruiter to work with Aura Communications. That individual thought Gelinas was calling on behalf of Aura Networks, and told her that she could not work with the company because Aura Networks already had representation.

d. Intent

Aura Communications does not make any allegation as to Aura Networks' intent. But assuming Aura Networks acted in good faith, such a finding "may not outweigh other factors that suggest a likelihood of confusion." "Evidence of bad intent, however, while potentially probative of the likelihood of confusion, is simply not required in a trademark infringement case; moreover a finding of good faith is no answer if the likelihood of confusion is otherwise established."

e. Mark's Strength

Aura Networks argues that Aura Communications' mark is heavily diluted because the term is ubiquitous, especially in the technology sector. A mark's strength is "ordinarily measured by such factors as: the length of time a mark has been used; the plaintiff's relative renown in its field; the plaintiff's vigilance in promoting the mark; number of similar registered marks in the field; and the success of other firms in registering similar marks."

The relevant evidence here shows that Aura Communications has used its mark for over five years, and has expended resources in promoting its mark. Even assuming this evidence only slightly supports this factor, "the strength of the mark is but one of the eight factors to be considered in analyzing the likelihood of confusion issue and sufficient evidence of other factors will sustain a finding of likelihood of confusion."

Based on the similarity of the marks, similarity of the goods, overlap between the Parties' trade channels and advertising, and overwhelming evidence of actual confusion, Aura Communications has demonstrated that Aura Networks' use of its mark has created a likelihood of confusion.

B. Trade-Name Infringement

To prove trade-name infringement, the plaintiff generally must show that the defendant used "in commerce any word, term, name, symbol, or device," which is likely to cause confusion as to the affiliation, connection, or association of the plaintiff to the defendant. As stated above, Aura Communications has shown actual confusion resulting from Aura Networks' use of the word "Aura" in its trade name, and thus has shown a likelihood of success on its trade-name-infringement claim.

III. Irreparable Harm

Aura Communications argues that it will suffer irreparable harm if an injunction does not issue because it will lose control of its reputation and its trademark. It further claims that the reputation of its products in the marketplace and its ability to attract employees will be damaged. Aura Networks counters that Aura Communications only seeks to redress its inability to attract quality employees, and that this type of harm can never be irreparable.

Where a likelihood of success is established, irreparable harm is presumed. The damage to Aura Communications' reputation and that of its products, combined with the company's inability to attract employees, sufficiently shows irreparable harm, particularly where Aura Communications has shown a likelihood of success on the merits.

IV. Balance of the Hardships

Aura Networks states that should an injunction issue, the company will suffer financial injury. Because all of the company's products are stamped with the company's logo, Aura Networks could not make any shipments, and would have to retool its factory to purge the words "Aura Networks."

The court recognizes that entering an injunction would financially affect Aura Networks. But there is substantial evidence of ongoing confusion. Additionally, Aura Communications has a federally registered trademark, and it has used its trade name for over five years. Aura Networks, on the other hand, changed its name from Lancast, Inc. in October, just eight months ago, and the company has not yet received a federally registered mark. These facts, in light of the current confusion, tip the hardships in Aura Communications' favor.

V. Public Interest

Because Aura Networks' name change is causing confusion, the public interest will best be served if an injunction enters.

Conclusion

For the foregoing reasons, Plaintiff's Motion for Preliminary Injunction is ALLOWED. ORDER WILL ISSUE.

Case Questions

1. How does the plaintiff attempt to prove that its right to the mark was infringed upon?

2. Why does the court grant the injunction?

Random House, Inc. v. Rosetta Books LLC
150 F. Supp. 2d 613 (S.D.N.Y. 2001)

In this copyright infringement action, Random House, Inc. seeks to enjoin Rosetta Books LLC and its Chief Executive Officer from selling in digital format eight specific works on the grounds that the authors of the works had previously granted Random House—not Rosetta Books—the right to "print, publish and sell the work[s] in book form." Rosetta

Books, on the other hand, claims it is not infringing upon the rights those authors gave Random House because the licensing agreements between the publisher and the author do not include a grant of digital or electronic rights. Relying on the language of the contracts and basic principles of contract interpretation, this Court finds that the right to "print, publish and sell the work[s] in book form" in the contracts at issue does not include the right to publish the works in the format that has come to be known as the "ebook." Accordingly, Random House's motion for a preliminary injunction is denied.

Background

In the year 2000 and the beginning of 2001, Rosetta Books contracted with several authors to publish certain of their works—including *The Confessions of Nat Turner* and *Sophie's Choice* by William Styron; *Slaughterhouse-Five*, *Breakfast of Champions*, *The Sirens of Titan*, *Cat's Cradle*, and *Player Piano* by Kurt Vonnegut; and *Promised Land* by Robert B. Parker—in digital format over the Internet. (Def. Ex. 21-23; http://www.rosettabooks.com/pages/aboutus.html.) On February 26, 2001, Rosetta Books launched its ebook business, offering those titles and others for sale in digital format. (Cantos Aff. P 2, Ex. A; http://www.rosettabooks.com.) The next day, Random House filed this complaint accusing Rosetta Books of committing copyright infringement and tortiously interfering with the contracts Random House had with Messrs. Parker, Styron and Vonnegut by selling its ebooks. It simultaneously moved for a preliminary injunction prohibiting Rosetta from infringing plaintiff's copyrights.

A. Ebooks

Ebooks are "digital book[s] that you can read on a computer screen or an electronic device." (Hrg. at 13; http://www.rosettabooks.com/pages/aboutebooks.html.) Ebooks are created by converting digitized text into a format readable by computer software. The text can be viewed on a desktop or laptop computer, personal digital assistant or handheld dedicated ebook reading device. (Van Dam Decl. P 9.) Rosetta's ebooks can only be read after they are downloaded into a computer that contains either Microsoft Reader, Adobe Acrobat Reader, or Adobe Acrobat eBook Reader software. (Dwyer Decl. P 11; Hrg. at 15.)

Included in a Rosetta ebook is a book cover, title page, copyright page and "eforward" all created by Rosetta Books. Although the text of the ebook is exactly the same as the text of the original work, the ebook contains various features that take advantage of its digital format. For example, ebook users can search the work electronically to find specific words and phrases. They can electronically "highlight" and "bookmark" certain text, which can then be automatically indexed and accessed through hyperlinks. They can use hyperlinks in the table of contents to jump to specific chapters.

Users can also type electronic notes which are stored with the related text. These notes can be automatically indexed, sorted and filed. Users can also change the font size and style of the text to accommodate personal preferences; thus, an electronic screen of text may contain more words, fewer words, or the same number of words as a page of the original published book. In addition, users can have displayed the definition of any word in the text. (Dwyer Decl. PP 6(g), 7.) In one version of the software, the word can also be pronounced aloud. (Dwyer Decl. P 7.)

Rosetta's ebooks contain certain security features to prevent users from printing, emailing or otherwise distributing the text. Although it is technologically possible to foil these security features, anyone who does so would be violating the licensing agreement accompanying the software. (Hrg. At 12; Dwyer Decl. P 7.)

B. Random House's licensing agreements

While each agreement between the author and Random House differs in some respects, each uses the phrase "print, publish and sell the work in book form" to convey rights from the author to the publisher. (Sarnoff Aff. Ex. A P 1(a)(i), Ex. B, P 1(a)(i), Ex. C P 1(a), Ex. D P 1(a), Ex. E P 1(a).)

1. Styron Agreements

Forty years ago, in 1961, William Styron granted Random House the right to publish *The Confessions of Nat Turner*. Besides granting Random House an exclusive license to "print, publish and sell the work in book form," Styron also gave it the right to "license publication of the work by book clubs," "license publication of a reprint edition," "license after book publication the publication of the work, in whole or in part, in anthologies, school books," and other shortened forms, "license without charge publication of the work in Braille, or photographing, recording, and microfilming the work for the physically handicapped," and "publish or permit others to publish or broadcast by radio or television . . . selections from the work, for publicity purposes . . . ." (Sarnoff Aff. Ex. A P 1(a)(ii)-(vi).) Styron demonstrated that he was not granting Random House the rights to license publication in the British Commonwealth or in foreign languages by crossing out these clauses on the form contract supplied by Random House. (*Id.* P 1(b), (c); Hrg. at 44; Def. Mem. at 8.)

The publisher agreed in the contract to "publish the work at its own expense and in such style and manner and at such a price as it deems suitable." (Sarnoff Aff. Ex. A P 2.) The contract also contains a noncompete clause that provides, in relevant part, that "the Author agrees that during the term of this agreement he will not, without the written permission of the Publisher, publish or permit to be published any material in book or pamphlet form, based on the material in the work, or which is reasonably likely to injure its sale." (*Id.* at P 8.) Styron's contract with Random House for the right to publish *Sophie's Choice*, executed in 1977, is virtually identical to his 1961 contract to publish *The Confessions of Nat Turner*. (Sarnoff Aff. Ex. B.)

2. Vonnegut Agreements

Kurt Vonnegut's 1967 contract granting Random House's predecessor-in-interest Dell Publishing Co., Inc. the license to publish *Slaughterhouse-Five* and *Breakfast of Champions* follows a similar structure to the Styron agreements. Paragraph # 1 is captioned "grant of rights" and contains those rights the author is granting to the book publisher. Certain rights on the publisher's form contract are crossed out, indicating that the author reserved them for himself. (Sarnoff Aff. Ex C, P 1(b), (e); Hrg. At 44; Def. Mem. at 10.) One of the rights granted by the author includes the "exclusive right to publish and to license the Work for publication, after book publication . . . in anthologies, selections, digests, abridgments, magazine condensations, serialization, newspaper syndication, picture book versions, microfilming,
Xerox and other forms of copying, either now in use or hereafter developed." (Sarnoff. Aff. Ex. C, P 1(d).)

Vonnegut specifically reserved for himself the "dramatic . . . motion picture (silent and sound) . . . radio broadcasting (including mechanical renditions and /or recordings of the text) . . . [and] television" rights. (Sarnoff Aff. Ex. C P 5.) Unlike the Styron agreements, this contract does not contain a noncompete clause.

Vonnegut's 1970 contract granting Dell the license to publish *The Sirens of Titan*, *Cat's Cradle*, and *Player Piano* contains virtually identical grants and reservations of rights as his 1967 contract. However, it does contain a noncompete clause, which provides that "the Author . . . will not publish or permit to be published any edition, adaptation or abridgment of the Work by any party other than Dell without Dell's prior written consent." (Sarnoff Aff. Ex. D P 10(e).)

3. Parker Agreement

Robert B. Parker's 1982 contract granting Dell the license to publish *Promised Land* is similar to the 1970 Vonnegut contract. (Sarnoff Aff. Ex. E P 1; Hrg. at 44; Def. Mem. at 12.) Paragraph # 1 contains the "grant of rights," certain of which have been crossed out by the author. The contract does grant Random House the right to "Xerox and other forms of copying of the printed page, either now in use or hereafter developed." (Sarnoff Aff. Ex. E P 1(d).) Parker also reserved the rights to the "dramatic . . . motion picture (silent and sound) . . . radio broadcasting . . television . . . mechanical or electronic recordings of the text . . . ." (Sarnoff. Aff. Ex. E P 5.) There is also a noncompete clause that provides, in relevant part, that "the Author . . . will not, without the written permission of Dell, publish or permit to be published any material based on the material in the Work, or which is reasonably likely to injure its sale." (Sarnoff Aff. Ex. E P 18.)

Discussion

A. Preliminary Injunction Standard for Copyright Infringement

Random House seeks a preliminary injunction against Rosetta Book's alleged infringing activity pursuant to 17 U.S.C. sec. 502(a) of the Copyright Act. In order to obtain a preliminary injunction, Random House must demonstrate "(1) irreparable harm and (2) either (a) a likelihood of success on the merits or (b) sufficiently serious questions about the merits to make them a fair ground for litigation and a balance of hardships tipping decidedly toward the party requesting relief." *Abkco Music, Inc. v. Stellar Records, Inc.*, 96 F.3d 60, 64 (2d Cir. 1996); see also *Consumers Union of U.S., Inc. v. General Signal Corp.*, 724 F.2d 1044, 1048 (2d Cir. 1983); *Tienshan, Inc. v. C.A.A Int'l Inc.*, 895 F. Supp. 651, 655 (S.D.N.Y. 1995). In addition, if the moving party establishes a *prima facie* case of copyright infringement, then a presumption of irreparable harm arises. See *Abkco Music*, 96 F.3d at 64;[**11] *Wainwright Sec., Inc. v. Wall Street Transcript Corp.*, 558 F.2d 91, 94 (2d Cir.1977); *Dynamic Solutions, Inc. v. Planning & Control, Inc.*, 646 F. Supp. 1329, 1337 (S.D.N.Y. 1986).

B. Ownership of a Valid Copyright

Two elements must be proven in order to establish a *prima facie* case of infringement: "(1) ownership of a valid copyright, and (2) copying of constituent elements of the work that are original." *Feist Publications, Inc. v. Rural Tel. Serv.*

Co., 499 U.S. 340, 361, 113 L. Ed. 2d 358, 111 S. Ct. 1282 (1991); see also *Abkco Music*, 96 F.3d at 64; *Tienshan*, 895 F. Supp. at 655. In this case, only the first element—ownership of a valid copyright—is at issue, since all parties concede that the text of the ebook is identical to the text of the book published by Random House.

It is well settled that although the authors own the copyrights to their works, "the legal or beneficial owner of an exclusive right under a copyright is entitled . . . to institute an action for any infringement of that particular right committed while he or she is the owner of it." 17 U.S.C. P 501 (b); see also *Essex Music, Inc. v. Abkco Music & Record, Inc.*, 743 F. Supp. 237, 241 (S.D.N.Y. 1990) ("Plaintiff as an exclusive licensee has the right to institute an action for copyright infringement."); Melville B. Nimmer & David Nimmer, *Nimmer on Copyright* sec. 12.02[b] at 12-50-51 (May, 2000) ("An exclusive licensee may not sue for infringement of rights as to which he is not licensed, even if the subject matter of the infringement is the work as to which he is a licensee."). The question for resolution, therefore, is whether Random House is the beneficial owner of the right to publish these works as ebooks.

1.   Contract Interpretation of Licensing Agreements—Legal Standards

Random House claims to own the rights in question through its licensing agreements with the authors. Interpretation of an agreement purporting to grant a copyright license is a matter of state contract law. See *Flack v. Friends of Queen Catherine Inc.*, 139 F. Supp. 2d 526, 536 (S.D.N.Y. 2001) ; see also *Boosey & Hawkes Music Publishers, Ltd. v. Walt Disney Co.*, 145 F.3d 481, 487 (2d Cir. 1998); *Bourne v. Walt Disney Co.*, 68 F.3d 621, 628-29 (2d Cir. 1995); *Video Trip Corp. v. Lightning Video, Inc.*, 866 F.2d 50, 52 (2d Cir. 1989) ("The real question presented was whether the claimant had ownership which could only be resolved by determining the contractual obligations of the parties. Neither substantive nor procedural copyright law was involved in the resolution of the dispute."); *Bartsch v. Metro-Goldwyn-Mayer, Inc.*, 391 F.2d 150, 153 (2d Cir. 1968); *Bloom v. Hearst Entm't, Inc.*, 33 F.3d 518, 522 (5th Cir. 1994). All of the agreements state that they "shall be interpreted according to the law of the State of New York." (Sarnoff Aff. Ex. A P 21, Ex. B P 22; Sarnoff Aff. Ex. C P 16, Ex. D P 16, Ex. E P 16 ("in accordance with the laws of the State of New York").)

In New York, a written contract is to be interpreted so as to give effect to the intention of the parties as expressed in the contract's language. See *Terwilliger v. Terwilliger*, 206 F.3d 240, 245 (2d. Cir. 2000) (citing *Breed v. Insurance Co. of N. Am.*, 46 N.Y.2d 351, 355, 385 N.E.2d 1280, 1283, 413 N.Y.S.2d 352, 355 (1978)). The court must consider the entire contract and reconcile all parts, if possible, to avoid an inconsistency. See *Terwilliger*, 206 F.3d at 245*; Laba v. Carey*, 29 N.Y.2d 302, 308, 277 N.E.2d 641, 644, 327 N.Y.S.2d 613, 618 (1971).

Determining whether a contract provision is ambiguous is a question of law to be decided by the court. See *Morse/Diesel, Inc. v. Trinity Indus., Inc.*, 67 F.3d 435, 443 (2d Cir. 1995); *W.W.W. Assocs. Inc. v. Frank Giancontieri*, 77 N.Y.2d 157, 162, 566 N.E.2d 639, 642, 565 N.Y.S.2d 440, 443 (1990). Pursuant to New York law, "contract language is ambiguous if it is capable of more than one meaning when viewed objectively by a reasonably intelligent person who has examined the context of the entire integrated agreement and who is cognizant of the customs, practices, usages and terminology as generally understood in the particular trade or business." *Sayers v. Rochester Tel. Corp. Supplemental Management Pension Plan*, 7 F.3d 1091, 1095 (2d Cir. N.Y. 1993) (internal quotations and citation omitted); see also *Bloom*, 33 F.3d at 522 (citing N.Y.U.C.C. sec. 2-202, Official Comment 1). "No ambiguity exists when contract language has a 'definite and precise meaning, unattended by danger of misconception in the purport of the [contract] itself, and concerning which there is no reasonable basis for a difference of opinion.'" *Sayers*, 7 F.3d at 1095 (quoting *Breed*, 46 N.Y.2d at 355, 385 N.E.2d at 1283, 413 N.Y.S.2d at 355).

If the language of a contract is ambiguous, interpretation of the contract becomes a question of fact for the finder of fact and extrinsic evidence is admissible. See *Seiden Assocs., Inc. v. ANC Holdings, Inc.*, 959 F.2d 425, 428 (2d Cir. 1992); *Raine v. CBS Inc.*, 25 F. Supp. 2d 434, 444 (S.D.N.Y. 1998); *Hartford Accident & Indem. Co. v. Wesolowski*, 33 N.Y.2d 169, 172, 305 N.E.2d 907, 909, 350 N.Y.S.2d 895, 898 (1973).

These principles are in accord with the approach the U.S. Court of Appeals for the Second Circuit uses in analyzing contractual language in disputes, such as this one, "about whether licensees may exploit licensed works through new marketing channels made possible by technologies developed after the licensing contract—often called 'new use' problems." *Boosey & Hawkes Music Publishers, Ltd v. Walt Disney Co.*, 145 F.3d 481, 486 (2d Cir. 1998). The two leading cases in this Circuit on how to determine whether "new uses" come within prior grants of rights are *Boosey and Bartsch v. Metro-Goldwyn-Mayer, Inc.*, 391 F.2d 150 (2d Cir. 1968), decided three decades apart.

In Bartsch, the author of the play "Maytime" granted Harry Bartsch in 1930 "the motion picture rights [to 'Maytime'] throughout the world," including the right to "copyright, vend, license and exhibit such motion picture photoplays throughout the world; together with the further sole and exclusive rights by mechanical and/or electrical means to record, reproduce and transmit sound, including spoken words . . . ." 391 F.2d at 150. He in turn assigned those rights to Warner Bros. Pictures, which transferred them to MGM. In 1958 MGM licensed its motion picture "Maytime" for viewing on television. Bartsch sued, claiming the right to transmit the play over television had not been given to MGM.

Judge Henry Friendly, for the Second Circuit, wrote in 1968 that "any effort to reconstruct what the parties actually intended nearly forty years ago is doomed to failure." *Id.* at 155. He added that the words of the grant by Bartsch "were well designed to give the assignee [i.e., MGM] the broadest rights with respect to its copyrighted property." *Id.* at 154. The words of the grant were broad enough to cover the new use—*i.e.*, viewing on television—and Judge Friendly interpreted them to do so. This interpretation, he wrote, permitted the licensee to "properly pursue any uses which may reasonably be said to fall within the medium as described in the license." *Id.* at 155. That interpretation also avoided the risk "that a deadlock between the grantor and the grantee might prevent the work's being shown over the new medium at all." *Id.*

In *Boosey*, the plaintiff was the assignee of Igor Stravinsky's copyrights in the musical composition, "The Rite of Spring." In 1939, Stravinsky had licensed Disney's use of "The Rite of Spring" in the motion picture "Fantasia." Fifty-two years later, in 1991, Disney released "Fantasia" in video format and Boosey brought an action seeking, among other relief, a declaration that the grant of rights did not include the right to use the Stravinsky work in video format. In *Boosey*, just as in *Bartsch*, the language of the grant was broad, enabling the licensee "to record in any manner, medium or form, and to license the performance of, the musical composition [for use] in a motion picture." 145 F.3d at 484.

At the Second Circuit, a unanimous panel focused on "neutral principles of contract interpretation rather than solicitude for either party." *Id.* at 487. "What governs," Judge Pierre Leval wrote, "is the language of the contract. If the contract is more reasonably read to convey one meaning, the party benefited by that reading should be able to rely on it; the party seeking exception or deviation from the meaning reasonably conveyed by the words of the contract should bear the burden of negotiating for language that would express the limitation or deviation. This principle favors neither licensors nor licensees. It follows simply from the words of the contract." *Id.*

The Second Circuit's neutral approach was specifically influenced by policy considerations on both sides. On the one hand, the approach seeks to encourage licensees—here, the publishers—to develop new technologies that will enable all to enjoy the creative work in a new way. On the other hand, it seeks to fulfill the purpose underlying federal copyright law—to encourage authors to create literary works. See *Boosey*, 145 F.3d at 487, 488 n.4.

2.   Application of Legal Standards

Relying on "the language of the license contract and basic principles of interpretation," *Boosey*, 145 F.3d at 487 n.3, as instructed to do so by *Boosey* and *Bartsch*, this Court finds that the most reasonable interpretation of the grant in the contracts at issue to "print, publish and sell the work in book form" does not include the right to publish the work as an ebook. At the outset, the phrase itself distinguishes between the pure content—*i.e.*, "the work"—and the format of display—"in book form." The Random House Webster's Unabridged Dictionary defines a "book" as "a written or printed work of fictionor nonfiction, usually on sheets of paper fastened or bound together within covers" and defines "form" as "external appearance of a clearly defined area, as distinguished from color or material; the shape of a thing or person." Random House *Webster's Unabridged Dictionary* (2001), available in searchable form at http://www.allwords.com.

Manifestly, paragraph # 1 of each contract—entitled either "grant of rights" or "exclusive publication right"—conveys certain rights from the author to the publisher. (Sarnoff Aff. Ex. A P 1, Ex. B, P 1, Ex. C P 1, Ex. D P 1, Ex. E P 1.) In that paragraph, separate grant language is used to convey the rights to publish book club editions, reprint editions, abridged forms, and editions in Braille. This language would not be necessary if the phrase "in book form" encompassed all types of books. That paragraph specifies exactly which rights were being granted by the author to the publisher. Indeed, many of the rights set forth in the publisher's form contracts were in fact not granted to the publisher, but rather were reserved by the authors to themselves. For example, each of the authors specifically reserved certain rights for themselves by striking out phrases, sentences, and paragraphs of the publisher's form contract. This evidences an intent by these authors not to grant the publisher the broadest rights in their works.

Random House contends that the phrase "in book form" means to faithfully reproduce the author's text in its complete form as a reading experience and that, since ebooks concededly contain the complete text of the work, Rosetta cannot also possess those rights. (Hrg. at 39; Green Aff. P 5; Miller Aff. P 15.) While Random House's definition distinguishes "book form" from other formats that require separate contractual language—such as audio books and serialization rights—it does not distinguish other formats specifically mentioned in paragraph # 1 of the contracts, such as book club editions and reprint editions. Because the Court must, if possible, give effect to all contractual language in order to "safeguard against adopting an interpretation that would render any individual provision superfluous," *Sayers*, 7 F.3d at 1095, Random House's definition cannot be adopted.

Random House points specifically to the clause requiring it to "publish the work at its own expense and in such a style and manner and at such a price as [Random House] deems suitable" as support for its position. (Sarnoff Aff. Ex. A P 2.) However, plaintiff takes this clause out of context. It appears in paragraph # 2, captioned "Style, Price and Date of Publication," not paragraph #1, which includes all the grants of rights. In context, the phrase simply means that Random House has control over the appearance of the formats granted to Random House in the first paragraph; *i.e.*, control over the style of the book.

Random House also cites the noncompete clauses as evidence that the authors granted it broad, exclusive rights in their work. Random House reasons that because the authors could not permit any material that would injure the sale of the work to be published without Random House's consent, the authors must have granted the right to publish ebooks to Random House. This reasoning turns the analysis on its head. First, the grant of rights follows from the grant language alone. See *Boosey*, 145 F.3d at 488. Second, noncompete clauses must be limited in scope in order to be enforceable in New York. See *American Broad. Cos. v. Wolf*, 52 N.Y.2d 394, 403-04, 420 N.E.2d 363, 367-68, 438 N.Y.S.2d 482, 486-87 (1981); *Columbia Ribbon & Carbon Mfg. Co., Inc. v. A-1-A Corp.*, 42 N.Y.2d 496, 500, 369 N.E.2d 4, 6, 398 N.Y.S.2d 1004, 1007 (1977). Third, even if the authors did violate this provision of their Random House agreements by contracting with Rosetta Books—a point on which this Court does not opine—the remedy is a breach of contract action against the authors, not a copyright infringement action against Rosetta Books. See, e.g., *Harlequin Enter. Ltd. v. Warner Books, Inc.*, 639 F. Supp. 1081 (S.D.N.Y. 1986).

The photocopy clause—giving Random House the right to "Xerox and other forms of copying, either now in use or hereafter developed"—similarly does not bolster Random House's position. Although the clause does appear in the grant language paragraph, taken in context, it clearly refers only to new developments in xerography and other forms of photocopying. Stretching it to include new forms of publishing, such as ebooks, would make the rest of the contract superfluous because there would be no reason for authors to reserve rights to forms of publishing "now in use." This interpretation also comports with the publishing industry's trade usage of the phrase. (See, e.g., *Fowler* Decl. PP 12, 20, Congdon Decl. P 27, Borchardt Decl. P 23).

Not only does the language of the contract itself lead almost ineluctably to the conclusion that Random House does not own the right to publish the works as ebooks, but also a reasonable person "cognizant of the customs, practices, usages and terminology as generally understood in the particular trade or business," *Sayers*, 7 F.3d at 1095, would conclude that the grant language does not include ebooks. "To print, publish and sell the work in book form" is understood in the publishing industry to be a "limited" grant. See *Field v. True Comics*, 89 F. Supp. 611, 613-14 (S.D.N.Y. 1950); see also Melville B. Nimmer & David Nimmer, *Nimmer on Copyright*, sec. 10.14[C] (2001) (citing Field).

In *Field v. True Comics*, the court held that "the sole and exclusive right to publish, print and market in book form"—especially when the author had specifically reserved rights for himself—was "much more limited" than "the sole and exclusive right to publish, print and market the book." 89 F. Supp. at 612 (emphasis added). In fact, the publishing industry generally interprets the phrase "in book form" as granting the publisher "the exclusive right to publish a hardcover trade book in English for distribution in North America." 1 *Lindey on Entertainment, Publishing and the Arts Form* 1.01-1 (2d ed.2000) (using the Random House form contract to explain the meaning of each clause); see also Borchardt Decl. PP 9-13, Brann Decl. PP 5-9, Congdon Decl. PP 9-17, Donald Farber Decl. PP 7-17, Fowler Decl. PP 10, 20-24, Friedman Decl. P 7, Levine Decl. PP 9-14, Maass Decl. PP 8-14. But see Klebanoff Dep. at 153-54 (acknowledging that the phrase, on its own, outside the context of a specific contract may include other forms of books such as book club editions, large print editions, leather bound editions, trade and mass market paperbacks); Levine Dep. at 37-38; Bloom Decl. Ex. K.

3.   Comparison to Prior "New Use" Caselaw

The finding that the five licensing agreements at issue do not convey the right to publish the works as ebooks accords with Second Circuit and New York case law. Indeed, the two leading cases lined above that found that a particular new use was included within the grant language—*Boosey*, 145 F.3d 481 (2d Cir. 1998), and *Bartsch*, 391 F.2d 150 (2d Cir. 1968)—can be distinguished from this case on four grounds.

First, the language conveying the rights in *Boosey* and *Bartsch* was far broader than here. See *Boosey*, 145 F.3d at 486; *Bartsch*, 391 F.2d at 153. Second, the "new use" in those cases—*i.e.* display of a motion picture on television or videocassette—fell squarely within the same medium as the original grant. See *Boosey*, 145 F.3d at 486 (describing videocassettes and laser discs as "subsequently developed methods of distribution of a motion picture"); *Bourne*, 68 F.3d at 630 ("The term 'motion picture' reasonably can be understood to refer to 'a broad genus whose fundamental characteristic is a series of related images that impart an impression of motion when shown in succession . . . . Under this concept the physical form in which the motion picture is fixed—film, tape, discs, and so forth—is irrelevant.'") (quoting S. Rep. No. 92-72, at 5 (1971)); see also *Bloom*, 33 F.3d at 523.

In this case, the "new use"—electronic digital signals sent over the Internet—is a separate medium from the original use—printed words on paper. Random House's own expert concludes that the media are distinct because information stored digitally can be manipulated in ways that analog information cannot. (Van Dam Dep. at 29-30, 36, 42.) Ebooks take advantage of the digital medium's ability to manipulate data by allowing ebook users to electronically search the text for specific words and phrases, change the font size and style, type notes into the text and electronically organize them, highlight and bookmark, hyperlink to specific parts of the text, and, in the future, to other sites on related topics as well, and access a dictionary that pronounces words in the ebook aloud. The need for a software program to interact with the data in order to make it usable, as well as the need for a piece of hardware to enable the reader to view the text, also distinguishes analog formats from digital formats. See *Greenberg v. National Geographic Soc'y*, 244 F.3d 1267, 1273 n.12 (11th Cir. 2001) (Digital format is not analogous to reproducing the magazine in microfilm or microfiche because it "requires the interaction of a computer program in order to accomplish the useful reproduction involved with the new medium.").

Therefore, *Boosey* and *Bartsch*, which apply to new uses within the same medium, do not control this case. See, e.g., *Raine*, 25 F. Supp. 2d 434, 445 (S.D.N.Y. 1998) (finding that the right to "television broadcasts" did not include broadcasts on cable television or videocassettes); *General Mills, Inc. v. Filmtel Int'l Corp.*, 195 A.D.2d 251, 252, 599 N.Y.S.2d 820, 821-22 (1st Dep't 1993); *Tele-Pac, Inc. v. Grainger*, 168 A.D.2d 11, 570 N.Y.S.2d 521 (1st Dep't 1991) (distinguishing Second Circuit "new use" doctrine by holding that right to "broadcast by television or any other similar device now known or hereafter to be made known" was so dissimilar from display on videocassette and videodisc "as to preclude consideration of video rights as even falling within the 'ambiguous penumbra' of the terms used in the agreement").

The third significant difference between the licensee in the motion picture cases cited above and the book publisher in this action is that the licensees in the motion picture cases have actually created a new work based on the material from the licensor. Therefore, the right to display that new work—whether on television or video—is derivative of the right to create that work. In the book publishing context, the publishers, although they participate in the editorial process, display the words written by the author, not themselves.

Fourth, the courts in *Boosey* and *Bartsch* were concerned that any approach to new use problems that "tilts against licensees [here, Random House] gives rise to antiprogressive incentives" insofar as licensees "would be reluctant to explore and utilize innovative technologies." *Boosey*, 145 F.3d at 488, n.4; see also *Bartsch*, 391 F.2d at 155. However, in this action, the policy rationale of encouraging development in new technology is at least as well served by finding that the licensors—*i.e.*, the authors—retain these rights to their works. In the 21st century, it cannot be said that licensees such as book publishers and movie producers are *ipso facto* more likely to make advances in digital technology than start-up companies.

Other case law interpreting the scope of book publishing licensing agreements is similarly unhelpful to Random House. In *Dolch v. Garrard Publ'g Co.*, 289 F. Supp. 687 (S.D.N.Y. 1968), the district court found that a license granting the publisher "the exclusive right of publication of the books" included the right to publish the books in paperback. Besides the obvious distinction that the grant language in *Dolch* is far broader—there is no distinction between "book" and "work"—the Dolch Court was applying Illinois contract law—not New York—which is far stricter about the use of parol evidence. See *id*. at 695.

In *Dresser v. William Morrow & Co.*, 278 A.D. 931, 105 N.Y.S.2d 706 (1st Dep't 1951), aff'd 304 N.Y. 603, 107 N.E.2d 89 (N.Y. 1952), the issue was whether an author could receive additional payments for reprint editions of his book when his publishing contract only provided for an "outright fixed payment." The *Dresser* court found that, under the terms of the contract, he could not. *Id*. at 932, 105 N.Y.S.2d at 707. The court relied on the fact that the contract was "at variance with the usual pattern of contracts between author and publisher." *Id*., 105 N.Y.S.2d at 707. Here, although each contract is slightly different, none varies greatly from the usual pattern of contracts between author and publisher; therefore, there is no reason to depart from the usual meaning of such contracts.

In contrast to Dresser and Dolch, other federal courts applying New York law have interpreted publishing licensing agreements more narrowly. See *Werbungs und Commerz Union Austalt v. Collectors' Guild, Ltd.*, 930 F.2d 1021, 1026 (2d Cir. 1991) (finding contract which conveys "right, title and interest in said two editions and all earnings therefrom" ambiguous as to whether it conveyed rights in the illustrations contained in those editions as well); *Field*, 89 F. Supp. at 613 (finding right to "publish, print and market in book form . . . the work" is a limited right and does not include publication of cartoon strip in a magazine).

C. Balance of Hardships

Because Random House cannot establish a *prima facie* case of copyright infringement, it is not likely to succeed on the merits and is not entitled to a presumption of irreparable harm. Random House has made no showing of irreparable harm; therefore, it cannot meet the test for obtaining a preliminary injunction. Even if it could show such harm, and could be considered to have presented sufficiently serious questions about the merits to make them a fair ground for litigation, the balance of hardships does not tip decidedly in Random House's favor. Random House fears that Rosetta's ebooks will harm its goodwill with its customers and cause direct competition in Random House's own efforts to establish its ebook business. Rosetta worries that a preliminary injunction will effectively put its new company out of business because it will impede its ability to publish any works previously licensed to other publishers. While both parties present valid concerns, Random House has not demonstrated that its concerns decidedly outweigh Rosetta's.

Conclusion

Employing the most important tool in the armamentarium of contract interpretation—the language of the contract itself —this Court has concluded that Random House is not the beneficial owner of the right to publish the eight works at issue as ebooks. This is neither a victory for technophiles nor a defeat for Luddites. It is merely a determination, relying on neutral principles of contract interpretation, that because Random House is not likely to succeed on the merits of its copyright infringement claim and cannot demonstrate irreparable harm, its motion for a preliminary injunction should be denied.

Case Questions

1. What does the court say is the standard for ordering a preliminary injunction?

2. What are the legal standards used to interpret licensing agreements?

Exercises

1. List 10 domain names that you commonly use.

2. Using the Internet find and download the documents used to register a copyright and a trademark.

3. Discuss several factors that would indicate a "fair use" of a copyrighted work.

4. Briefly discuss some problems that an intellectual property right holder might encounter in attempting to protect those rights being infringed on the Internet.

5.   Discuss the importance of domain names to the furthering of e-commerce.

6.   Indicate the different types of safe harbors.

7.   What are the different types of copyright infringement recognized by law?

8.   Differentiate between a mark and a copyright.

9.   Relate the concept of patents to the development of the Internet.

10. Use the Internet to find a sample licensing agreement.

Related Websites

Wipo.org
Itv.org

Appendix C

World Intellectual Property Organization Copyright Treaty

Chapter Six

CYBERCRIMES

Chapter Overview

The increased use of computer technology in many aspects of everyday life has caused a correspondingly increased use of the computer to commit crimes. Generally speaking, **cybercrime** is any criminal activity that uses a computer, its applications, or its technology, and includes such activities as credit card fraud, pornography, cyberspying and cyberstalking. Since the end of the twentieth century, government statistics indicate that cybercrime has become a major concern of law enforcement agencies, and yet the iniquity of cybercrimes typically goes unpunished because of the difficulty in locating the offenders and asserting jurisdiction over them and their acts.

Since the terrorist attacks on the World Trade Center and the Pentagon on September 11, 2001 (9-11), governments and private citizen groups have also been focusing on computers as the instrument of international terrorism. Congress has reacted by enacting statutes to combat terrorism that directly impact computer technology as well as having implications for potential infringement of personal constitutional rights (Chapter Three). However, with the changing world in which we live, law, technology and security are overlapping in a fashion never before seen or identified in human history.

This chapter will explore various areas of criminal activity that are directly attributable to computer technology. First, the basis of criminal law will be discussed, indicating how such crimes are now applicable to cyberspace. Then the new types of criminal activities that are direct outgrowths of technology will be examined.

Elements of Crimes

Criminal law refers to any activity that injures society as a whole rather than just a particular individual. Criminal law consists of acts that are specifically prohibited by state or federal statutes, and persons who are found to have violated these statutes are deemed to be **guilty** of committing a crime as opposed to being held **liable**, or legally responsible, for private injuries.

In order for a person to be found guilty of a crime, the government must prove the following elements:

- The person performed an act that is statutorily prohibited.
- The person had the requisite mental state to perform the act.
- There was a convergence of the mental state with the physical act.

The first element is satisfied if it can be shown that the individual, referred to as the **defendant**, actually performed the prohibited act. The second element dealing with the defendant's mental state depends upon the nature of the act in question. Certain crimes are considered to carry **strict liability**, meaning that as long as the defendant intended to perform the physical act, even if he or she did not intend the act to cause harm, the defendant will be found guilty. Other crimes require that the defendant have the mental intent to cause the injury by the commission of the physical act, and so a specific mental state must be proven.

The mental state of the defendant is referred to as **mens rea**, and the physical act is the **actus reus**. When the mens rea and the actus reus converge, the crime has been committed.

Crimes fall in to five broad categories, each of which will be discussed in turn:

1. inchoate crimes
2. crimes against the person
3. crimes against property
4. crimes against habitation
5. crimes against the judicial process.

Inchoate Crimes. An **inchoate crime** is one that is punishable under law even though no actual injury has occurred. The law recognizes three inchoate crimes:

a. **solicitation**, which is the inciting, convincing or conniving another to commit a crime with the intent that the person so solicited will commit the crime. To be found guilty of solicitation it is not necessary that the person solicited actually commit the offense.

Example: A woman e-mails her accountant asking him to inflate her expenses and not report all of her income when he prepares her taxes. The woman may be guilty of soliciting the accountant to commit tax fraud, regardless of whether or not the accountant agrees.

b. **conspiracy**, which is an agreement between two or more persons with the intent to enter into the agreement for the purpose of committing a crime. To be found guilty of conspiracy, the parties must agree *plus* perform any act in furtherance of the agreement.

*Example: Two students agree to hack into their school's computer in order to change their grades. The students start to try various passwords to enter the school's data bank. The students may be guilty of conspiracy even if they never discover the school's password. Such infiltration of a database is called **diddling**.*

c. **attempt**, which is any act performed with the intent to commit a crime that falls short of actually committing the crime. This act must consist of something other than mere preparation.

Example: When the students from the previous example start to try to break into the school's system, even if they are unsuccessful or decide to abandon the scheme before they actually change any grade, they may be found guilty of an attempt.

Crimes Against the Person. Most crimes against persons are also private injuries to individuals which are called **torts**, and the defendant may be sued civilly as well as prosecuted criminally. However, because most crimes against persons require some physical contact with the individual, only a few of these crimes have direct applicability to cyberlaw.

a. **homicide**, which is the unlawful taking of human life, may be difficult to accomplish exclusively by means of a computer. However, a person may threaten another with death by means of computer technology, and those threats may be deemed a crime against the person.

Example: A disgruntled ex-spouse sends constant death threats to the former spouse by means of e-mail. The disgruntled spouse may be convicted of attempted murder if the spouse coupled those threats with some action towards the commission of the crime.

b. drug and controlled substance related crimes. The selling of controlled substances is an illegal act. If someone sells controlled substances over the Internet, the person may be found guilty of a crime. Note that this would apply to all sales of controlled items, not just drugs.

Example: Over the Internet a person finds a website that advertises official New York City police badges for sale. These items may only be lawfully sold to active members of the New York City Police Department. If the seller can be found, he or she is guilty of the sale of a controlled item.

c. **fraud**, which is defined as the misrepresentation of a material fact made with the intent to deceive that is relied upon by a person to his or her detriment. This crime falls into the category of computer fraud, frequently encountered with the use of credit cards and the sale of bogus securities. Any time a person has been induced to materially change his or her position based on deliberately fraudulently information received over the Internet, the person who perpetrated such false information may be guilty of fraud.

Example: A man finds someone's credit card and uses it to make some purchases over the Internet without authorization. This man has committed credit card fraud by means of the computer when he stated that he was lawfully entitled to use the card and the vendor sent him the purchases so made.

d. **cyberstalking**, a new term derived directly from cyberlaw that makes it a crime to use a computer or computer technology to stalk another person. This crime involves a defendant acquiring information from the Internet about another, thus enabling the defendant to discover personal details about the victim's life and use that information to stalk the victim.

e. **spamming**, which is the sending of junk e-mail. The practice is annoying to the recipient but is only considered a crime in a few jurisdictions, and there is no federal statute addressing this issue. However, it is anticipated that more and more states will attempt to prohibit spamming by statutory enactments.

f. **hate crimes**, which are crimes directed against a particular group merely because of the group's common identity, have recently been given special sanctions under many state criminal laws. If the defendant uses the computer as an instrument of a hate crime, the defendant may be prosecuted under these more stringent statutes.

Example: A hate group singles out several individuals who belong to a community that is the object of the group's hatred. The group sends threats and pornographic material about the individuals over the Internet. The members of the group who sent the messages may be guilty of a cyberspace hate crime.

Crimes Against Property. Property crimes involve the injury or theft of another person's property and would include such offenses as:

a. **larceny**, which is defined as the taking and carrying away of the tangible personal property of another by trespass with the intent to deprive that person of the property permanently. The larceny could involve either the theft of a computer, computer equipment or computer software directly, or when the defendant **hacks** into another computer system (enters the system without authorization) and misappropriates the data contained therein. Recently a new computer scam has emerged that involves a crime against property known as **modem hijacking**. This involves software that automatically downloads onto a consumer's computer when the consumer accesses a website. This software downloads onto the hard drive and redirects the consumer's telephone line so that other person's telephone and computer uses are charged to the victim.

    b.   **embezzlement**, which is the fraudulent conversion of the personal property of another by a person who is in lawful possession of the property. Embezzlement differs from larceny in the fact that the embezzler has lawful possession of the property when he or she decides to deprive the owner of that property.

Example: A company bookkeeper uses the company computer to make all financial entries and to pay company obligations. If the bookkeeper decides to transfer a company car to her own name by making the transfer on the computer, she may be guilty of embezzlement and has used the computer as the tool of her crime.

    c.   **false pretenses**, which is obtaining title to another person's personal property by making a false statement with the intent to deceive the owner. False pretenses differ from embezzlement in that the defendant obtains title to the property rather than just possession.

Example: If the bookkeeper from the previous example transfers funds instead of a car, the crime would be false pretenses because obtaining cash is considered obtaining title and not just possession.

    d.   **forgery**, which is the making or altering of a writing with legal significance so that it is false and made with the intent to deceive. As discussed in Chapter Four, this crime has cyberlaw application in the area of electronic signatures.

    e.   **extortion**, which is using threats to intimidate another into transferring property to the person who is making the threats. If such threats are made over the Internet, the crime concerns cyberlaw.

Example: A man e-mails a politician threatening to expose a disreputable incident from the politician's past unless the politician gives him $10,000. The politician electronically transfers $10,000 to the man's account. This would be an example of extortion committed over the Internet.

    f.   **hacking**, obtaining unauthorized access to another's computer system, gives the hacker possession of the other person's property (the data). If the hacking is committed with a malicious intent, such as the intent to insert a virus on that system, it is referred to as **cracking**.

    g.   **cyberpiracy** involves the infringement of protected intellectual property. This concept has been discussed in the previous chapter.

    h.   **money laundering** is the process of hiding funds received from illegal activity by funneling them through legitimate businesses to obscure their source. With modern computer technology, complicated fund transfers are more easily accomplished than ever before.

Crimes Against Habitation. These offenses apply to any physical structure. Cyberlaw application of such crimes would involve the use of the computer to gain information about the structure so as to facilitate entry, or the theft of computers, computer equipment or computer technology from a structure belonging to another and injuring the structure itself during the process.

Crimes Against the Judicial Process. These offenses involve actions that hinder the judicial process. As more and more courts and government agencies utilize computer technology to assist in the judicial process, these offenses have greater potential application to cyberlaw.

   a. **perjury**, the intentional making of a false statement under oath may now be committed electronically with the advent of electronic signatures and notarizations.

   b. **subornation of perjury**, which is the inducement of another to commit perjury, can be applied to a computer if the suborner uses the Internet to send messages designed to induce another to commit perjury.

   c. **bribery**, which is the offering of something of value to a government official to induce the official to exert his or her office in a particular manner. The Internet could be used both as the means of communicating the request and the transferring of the item of value to secure the official's actions.

Terrorism and the Internet

One of the constitutional guarantees discussed in Chapter Three concerned the concept of a citizen being free from unreasonable searches and seizures by the government. One area of law that concerns this constitutional right is the ability of the police and other government officers to **wiretap**, or use technology to eavesdrop on private conversations, in order to gain evidence of criminal activity. In order for the government to wiretap, the agency must first obtain a **warrant**, or court authorization, from a judge after convincing the judge that there is probable cause to believe that illegal activity is being conducted by means of the telephone or other electronic device that is the subject of the warrant. After 9-11 there has been greater emphasis on providing the government with authority to have electronic surveillance to gain information about potential terrorist activity.

Because of a greater willingness on the part of the public to permit government surveillance of potential terrorism, on October 26, 2001, President Bush signed into law the so-called **USA Patriot Act**, Pub. L.No.107-56 (2001). The purpose of this statute is to provide law enforcement agencies with increased ability to intercept potential terrorist communication, including communication occurring over the Internet. (See Appendix D.) Prior to the Patriot Act, the government was permitted to intercept Internet communications pursuant to the Electronic Communication Privacy Act of 1986 previously discussed, which expanded wiretapping to include the new technology while still assuring the private rights of citizens as guaranteed by the Constitution.

The Patriot Act greatly expanded the government's ability to tap into electronic communication. Under section 216 of the Act, the government is allowed to tap into and access computer information. However, whereas the law does not automatically permit the tap of a computer without the constitutional guarantee of a warrant, it does give nationwide effect to any access permitted pursuant to its provisions.

The Patriot Act expands the type of information that the government can gather by means of a wiretap to include the names of subscribers of Internet service providers, including the source of all funds used for the payment of such services. Also, the Patriot Act grants the government access to information about cable subscribers who use cable services to access the Internet. The Act further permits a service provider to allow the government greater access to its records and information about subscribers than was permitted under prior law.

The purpose of the Patriot Act is to provide the government with greater tools to intercept espionage, terrorism and threats to essential government services that could be effectuated by means of computer technology. As of this writing, the Patriot Act is only the most recent of the various federal responses to cybercrime.

Federal Law and Cybercrime

Prior to the enactment of the Patriot Act, the federal government responded to growing concerns over cybercrime by enacting several statutes, most passing into law in 1999. The most significant of these statutes are:

- **The Computer Fraud and Abuse Act of 1986**, which enumerated several activities as being cybercrimes:
  a. committing espionage by accessing computer information
  b. accessing computer information without authorization
  c. accessing any nonpublic government computer database for any purpose
  d. accessing any computer with the intent to commit a crime
  e. intentionally damaging a computer
  f. trafficking in passwords (selling passwords without authorization)
  g. using the computer to extort money or other items of value.

- **The Child Online Protection Act of 1998**

- **The Federal Obscenity Law of 1999**

- **The Electronic Communication Privacy Act of 1998**

- **The Child Pornography Prevention Act of 1999**

Each of these last four statutes has been discussed in previous chapters.

> **The Economic Espionage Act of 1996**. This act was passed to protect trade secrets from being stolen by means of computer technology. This act covers such espionage that is intended to benefit foreign governments as well as other private persons and organizations. However, before anyone can be prosecuted under this statute, such prosecution must be authorized at the upper levels of the U.S. Department of Justice.

However, it must be borne in mind that the majority of criminal statues are enacted by state legislatures, and so most cybercrimes are prosecuted according to individual state law.

Jurisdiction Over Cybercrimes

Every state has statutes that define specific activities that are deemed to be criminal. However, all of these statutes were conceived centuries before the introduction of computers and the Internet. In order to address modern concerns, every state has enacted some form of legislation to address the application of traditional criminal law to cybercrimes. However, enforcement of these statutes has proven to be problematic.

As discussed in Chapter Two, one of the primary legal problems associated with cyberlaw is the question of asserting jurisdiction. Because the Internet is global in nature, it may be difficult or impossible to bring to justice a defendant whose activities emanate outside the state or country where the victim resides. In most situations the victim's place of residence will determine jurisdiction, but enforcement of criminal penalties on a nonresident may be impractical.

Recently, several proposals have been posited to make cybercrime jurisdiction nationwide, which would have the effect of at least bringing to justice criminals who are resident within the borders of the United States. However, this still leaves open the problem of prosecuting international cybercriminals. To date, however, all of the international conventions addressing this issue have dealt with intellectual property crimes as discussed in the previous chapter. More international cooperation will be necessary to resolve the problem of global cybercrime.

Chapter Review

Cybercrime involves any criminal activity that occurs on, by or to computer technology, and in the past decade it has become pandemic. However, despite this expansion of criminal activity over the Internet, the ability of law enforcement officials to punish the wrongdoer is almost impossible, and for this reason most perpetrators of cybercrimes go unpunished. In fact, there are only a limited number of judicial decisions dealing with cybercrimes.

Cybercrime involves all traditional criminal activity that is perpetrated by means of computer technology. This includes inchoate crimes, crimes against persons, property and habitation, and crimes that hinder the judicial process. Since the attacks on the United States on September 11, 2001, terrorist criminal activities that are furthered or perpetrated by means of the Internet have also received greater media attention as well as congressional response in the enactment of the Patriot Act of 2001. However, the primary problem associated with cybercrime is not in defining it but in prosecuting it.

Most activity that is deemed to be criminal is so defined by state statute, and a state's jurisdiction to enforce those statutes terminates at the state's geographic boundary. Most Internet crimes are global in nature because of the worldwide access of the Internet. Consequently, except for the few federal statutes dealing with computer crimes, it is difficult for government agencies to prosecute and punish cybercriminals.

Every state has enacted legislation that applies criminal law to cyberspace, but many jurists believe that a more national and global approach to jurisdiction is necessary to resolve jurisdictional problems. To date, most international protocols deal almost exclusively with crimes involving intellectual property. However, as citizens of more and more countries become victims of cybercrimes it can be expected that there will be a greater international response to this ever-increasing problem.

Key Terms

Actus Reus—The physical act of a crime

Attempt—Act of criminal activity that falls short of the actual crime

Bribery—Offering something of value to have a government official exert his authority in a particular manner

Child Online Protection Act of 1998—Federal law designed to protect children from cybercrime

Child Pornography Prevention Act of 1999—Federal statute making it a crime to use children for pornographic purposes online

Computer Fraud and Abuse Act of 1986—Federal law making the use of computer for fraud a crime

Conspiracy—Agreement of two or more people to commit a crime

Cracking—Hacking to insert a virus

Criminal Law—Offense against society as a whole

Cybercrime—Criminal activity involving the use of computer technology

Cyberpiracy—Using the computer to appropriate protected intellectual property

Cyberstalking—Using computer technology to stalk someone

Defendant—Person accused of committing a crime

Diddling—Hacking to change data

Economic Espionage Act of 1996—Federal law making it a crime to access nonpublic government databases

Electronic Communication Privacy Act of 1998—Federal law guaranteeing privacy rights with respect to computer use

Embezzlement—Taking of personal property of another by one in lawful possession of the property

Extortion—Threatening someone to have that person give the extorter something of value

False Pretenses—Obtaining title to another's personal property by fraudulent statements

Federal Obscenity Law of 1999—Federal law making it a crime to use computer technology for pornography

Forgery—Altering a writing with legal significance

Fraud—The misrepresentation of a material fact made with the intent to deceive relied upon by another to his or her detriment

Guilty—Having committed a crime

Hacking—Unauthorized access of another's computer system

Hate Crimes—Crimes perpetrated against a particular group

Homicide—The unlawful taking of a human life

Inchoate Crime—Solicitation, conspiracy and attempt

Larceny—The trespatory taking and carrying away of the personal property of another with the intent to permanently deprive them of that property

Liable—Having committed a civil wrong

Mens Rea—Mental element of a crime

Modem Hijacking—Property crime in which a consumer's modem is redirected so that the other person's telephone and computer use are charged to the victim

Money Laundering—Hiding the source of funds acquired from illegal activity

Perjury—Intentionally making a false statement under oath

Solicitation—Cajoling a person to commit a crime

Spamming—Sending unauthorized junk e-mail

Strict Liability—Criminal activity that does not require intent to cause harm

Subornation of Perjury—Convincing someone to commit perjury

Tort—Civil wrong

USA Patriot Act—Federal law enacted to combat terrorism by permitting government access to private Internet communication

Warrant—Judicial document needed prior to a wiretap

Wiretap—Government interception of private telephonic and electronic communications

Edited Cases

The following cases are included to highlight some of the topics discussed in this chapter. Both *United States of America v. Kennedy* and *United States v. Hilton* discuss child pornography on the Internet.

United States of America v. Kennedy
81 F. Supp. 2d 1103 (D. Kan. 2000)

On August 25, 1999, Defendant Michael R. Kennedy was indicted for the intentional receipt of child pornography in violation of 18 U.S.C. sec. 2252(a)(2) (Doc. 1) and forfeiture under 18 U.S.C. sec. 2253. Before the court for its consideration are:

1. Defendant's motion to suppress evidence (Doc. 13);

2. Defendant's memorandum in support of his motion to suppress (Doc. 14);

3. The government's response (Doc. 20);

4. The government's memorandum in support of its response (Doc. 21); and

5. Defendant's reply (Doc. 22).

An evidentiary hearing was held December 2, 1999. For the following reasons, defendant's motion to suppress is denied.

Facts

On July 2, 1999, Steven Idelman was working as a customer support specialist for Road Runner, a high speed Internet service provider. At approximately 9:00 p.m., Idelman received an anonymous phone call from a still-unidentified male ("the caller"). The caller told Idelman that he was at a friend's house, scanning other computers through the Internet and had viewed images of child pornography on a computer the caller believed to be serviced by Road Runner. The caller told Idelman the IP address of the computer from which the images were viewed, 24.94.200.54, and the directory and file names in which the images were located. The caller did not say that he was a law enforcement officer or that he was directed to view the computer's files by any law enforcement officer. The caller did not ask Idelman to call the police.

Shortly after the anonymous call, Idelman went to a computer and accessed the IP address given to him by the caller. His purpose was to determine if what the caller told him was correct. He located the computer with the IP address 24.94.200.54 and the directory tree and files mentioned by the caller. Idelman viewed two images located within those files. One of the images depicted two boys, whom Idelman estimated to be approximately eight or nine years old, posed in a sexual nature. Idelman then sent an e-mail to his supervisor, Anna Madden, describing the anonymous phone call and the results of his search of the computer with IP address 24.94.200.54.

On July 6, 1999, Kerry Jones, a network engineer for Road Runner, received an e-mail from Anna Madden asking him to research the owner of the Road Runner account connecting to the computer with the IP address 24.94.200.54. Jones was able to determine that the account was assigned to Rosemary D. Kennedy. Mr. Jones was able to determine that the account was assigned to the same IP address on July 2, 1999. Believing that the customer service agreement between Road Runner and the account holder authorized him to search a computer's files for offensive material, Jones then viewed the files on the computer's hard drive. The files depicted images of boys, whom Jones estimated to be approximately 10 to 13 years old, engaged in sexual activity. Jones then printed out an image of the computer's directory tree in which the files with offensive material were located.

That same day, after consulting with Road Runner's corporate attorney, Scott Petrie, the manager of Road Runner, made the decision to contact law enforcement authorities. Kerry Jones contacted the Exploited Children's Unit of the Wichita Police Department, but his phone call was not returned. Road Runner then contacted Special Agent Leslie Earl of the FBI. Special Agent Earl was informed by Road Runner that the FBI would need to obtain a court order for it to be able to supply the FBI with any subscriber information.

The United States Attorney's Office then applied to a United States magistrate judge for an order directing Road Runner to disclose subscriber information related to IP address 24.94.200.54. In the application, the Assistant United States Attorney stated that:

> The Federal Bureau of Investigation is conducting a criminal investigation in connection with possible violation(s) of Title 18, United States Code, Sections 2252 and 2252A; it is believed that the subject of the investigation used Road Runner's IP address 24.94.200.54 on July 2, 1999, at 11:48 p.m. in furtherance of the subject offenses; and that the information sought to be

obtained is relevant to a legitimate law enforcement inquiry in that it is believed that this information will assist in the investigation relating to the aforementioned offenses.

The magistrate judge issued an order, which was presented to Road Runner personnel, who provided the FBI with the following information:

The subscriber whose computer used I.P. address 24.94.200.54 on July 2, 1999, at 11:48 p.m. was Rosemay [sic] D. Kennedy of 9120 Harvest Court, Wichita, Kansas, telephone 316-722-6593. Two users were listed for that account: RKENNEDYsec.KSCable.COM and KENNEDYMsec.KSCable.Com. The account had been active since June 7, 1999.

Special Agent Earl next went to the house located at 9120 Harvest Court in Wichita, Kansas. He observed a Chrysler Sebring parked in the driveway. A records check with the Kansas Department of Motor Vehicles revealed that the car was registered to Michael R. Kennedy. Special Agent Earl then called the phone number given to the government by Road Runner. A person identifying himself as Michael Kennedy answered the phone.

In initiating the phone call, Special Agent Earl asked Kennedy if he was satisfied with his Road Runner cable modem Internet service.

Kennedy confirmed that his address was 9120 Harvest Court, Wichita, Kansas, and he confirmed that he was the primary user of the Road Runner cable modem Internet service. Kennedy said he was satisfied with the service and especially liked the speed and quality of the e-mail service. Kennedy estimated he spent an average of two to three hours per night online. Kennedy noted that he always left his system on and connected to the Internet. Kennedy said he used his Internet access only for pleasure and his computer and modem were located in his home.

Kennedy said his computer system was a Gateway 450 megahertz Pentium II with a 17-gigabyte hard drive. When asked if he had any concerns about the Road Runner service Kennedy said he thought the company should warn customers about the possibility of someone else trying to enter their computers through the Internet. Kennedy said he held Internet accounts through Netcom and AOL in the past. Kennedy left those services because they were too slow and he could not use e-mail and Usenet news groups the way he wanted to. Kennedy noted that it took too long for him to download mail with pictures attached on those other services.

(Affidavit in Support of Search Warrant at 14-15, Doc. 14, Ex. A). The government applied for and obtained a search warrant for property and evidence located at 9120 Harvest Court.

On August 10, 1999, Special Agents John Sullivan and Leslie Earl went to defendant's home to interview him and execute the search warrant. When defendant came to the door, the agents identified themselves. Defendant invited them in and the three men sat down in the kitchen. During the interview, defendant's mother and brother were in the living room, watching television.

Special Agent Sullivan told defendant why they were interviewing him. Defendant was informed that he was not under arrest and that he would not be arrested at the end of the interview. After providing the agents with some identifying information, defendant stated that he was 46 years old, did not have any drug or alcohol addiction problems, that he was not at that time under the influence of drugs or alcohol, and that he was not being treated for any physical or psychological problems. Defendant told the agents that he had spent one year in college.

Defendant stated that he owned three computers and used Multimedia Cablevision as his Internet service provider. Defendant acknowledged that he had downloaded pictures of young boys engaged in sexual acts from the Internet onto his hard drive. Defendant told the agents that he did not pay for any of the pictures, he did not know the identity of the person who posted the pictures on the Internet, he never discussed the pictures with anyone, nor had he ever transferred the pictures to anyone else. Defendant denied ever using an Internet chat room and claimed he never had any sexual contact with anyone under the age of 18. Although defendant admitted hearing that the possession of sexually explicit pictures of children was illegal, he was not really sure about the legality. Defendant stated that he did not think that anyone would ever find out that he had downloaded the pictures.

Defendant then showed the agents four sexually graphic pictures of young boys that he had printed out. These pictures were in defendant's bedroom. Defendant showed the agents his computers in the basement.

The interview lasted twenty to thirty minutes. Defendant never raised the issue of an attorney. Defendant never refused to answer a question. The agents never promised defendant anything in return for his statements. Defendant was not arrested at the conclusion of the interview and was allowed to turn himself in after the return of the indictment.

Analysis

A. SUBSCRIBER INFORMATION RECEIVED FROM ROAD RUNNER

Defendant first argues the subscriber information the FBI received from Road Runner should be suppressed. Defendant argues that the information was received in violation of the Electronic Communication Privacy Act and the Cable Communications Policy Act. Defendant further argues that all evidence obtained as a result of the illegal attainment of defendant's subscriber information should be suppressed as fruit of the poisonous tree. Although the court finds that the ECPA was violated, suppression of the evidence is not a remedy for such a violation. Because suppression is likewise not a remedy provided for under the CCPA, the court need not determine whether or not that statute was implicated.

1. The Electronic Communication Privacy Act

    18 U.S.C. sec.sec. 2701 et seq. regulates the disclosure of electronic communications and subscriber information. Section 2703(c)(1)(B) states that "[a] provider of electronic communication service . . . shall disclose a record or other information pertaining to a subscriber to or customer of such service . . . to a governmental entity only when the governmental entity . . . (ii) obtains a court order for such disclosure under subsection (d) of this section." Subsection (d) sets forth the requirements of such a court order:

    > (d) Requirements for court order—A court order for disclosure under subsection (b) or (c) . . . shall issue only if the governmental entity offers specific and articulable facts showing that there are reasonable grounds to believe that the contents of a wire or electronic communication, or the records or other information sought, are relevant and material to an ongoing criminal investigation.

    Defendant argues the government's application did not state specific and articulable facts, but mere conclusions. The government responds that at the time of the application, it did not know the identity of the subscriber, whether the subscriber was the person using the computer to store illegal material and how much child pornography was held by the computer. The government argues that the information it had at the time was minimal and the purpose of obtaining the order was to investigate the subscriber information completely.

The government's argument does not address the issue as to conclusory versus specific and articulable facts in regard to the information it did have. The government's application merely listed that the subscriber information connected to IP address 24.94.200.54 would possibly relate to an on-going criminal investigation. In accordance with 18 U.S.C. sec. 2703(d), the government should have articulated more specific facts such as how the government obtained the information it did have at the time and how this information lead the agents to believe that the attainment of the subscriber information of this particular IP address would assist in the investigation. The government's application for a section 2703(d) order did not meet the requirements of the statute.

Nonetheless, the government correctly points out that even if Road Runner divulged defendant's subscriber information pursuant to a court order based on an inadequate government application, suppression is not a remedy contemplated under the ECPA. The statute specifically allows for civil damages and criminal punishment for violations of the ECPA, see 18 U.S.C. secs. 2707, 2701(b), but speaks nothing about the suppression of information in a court proceeding. Compare 18 U.S.C. sec. 2515 (prohibiting the use of communications intercepted in violation of Title III of the Omnibus Crime Control and Safe Streets Act as evidence in any trial). Instead, Congress clearly intended for suppression not to be an option for a defendant whose electronic communications have been intercepted in violation of the ECPA. The statute specifically states that "the remedies and sanctions described in this chapter are the only judicial remedies and sanctions for nonconstitutional violations of this chapter." 18 U.S.C. sec. 2708.

Defendant's constitutional rights were not violated when Road Runner divulged his subscriber information to the government. Defendant has not demonstrated an objectively reasonable legitimate expectation of privacy in his subscriber information. On the contrary, the evidence is that defendant's computer had its sharing mechanism turned on. The only reasonable inference is that defendant had done so. See *California v. Greenwood*, 486 U.S. 35, 39, 108 S. Ct. 1625, 1628, 100 L. Ed. 2d 30 (1988). "What a person knowingly exposes to the public, even in his home or office, is not a subject of Fourth Amendment protection." *Katz v. United States*, 389 U.S. 347, 351, 88 S. Ct. 507, 511, 19 L. Ed. 2d 576 (1967). "[A] person has no legitimate expectation of privacy in information he voluntarily turns over to third parties." *Smith v. Maryland*, 442 U.S. 735, 743-44, 99 S. Ct. 2577, 2582, 61 L. Ed. 2d 220 (1979). When defendant entered into an agreement with Road Runner for Internet service, he knowingly revealed all information connected to the IP address 24.94.200.54. He cannot now claim to have a Fourth Amendment privacy interest in his subscriber information.

2.   The Cable Communications Policy Act

Defendant argues that the Cable Communications Policy Act, not the Electronic Communication Privacy Act, is the controlling statute which establishes the procedures for an Internet service provider, such as Road Runner, to disclose to the government a subscriber's information. The CCPA mandates the service provider notify the subscriber before divulging information to the government. Defendant contends that the government's attainment of the information was in violation of the CCPA and should be suppressed. The government responds that the CCPA does not apply.

In 1984, Congress enacted the CCPA to establish guidelines for the cable industry and set forth "a nationwide standard for the privacy protection of cable subscribers." H.R. Rep. No. 98-934, pt. IV, at 76 (1984) reprinted in 1984 U.S.C.C.A.N. 4655, 4713. The Act is codified at 47 U.S.C. secs. 521 et seq. Section 551 provides a privately enforceable scheme designed to protect cable subscriber privacy. This section regulates the disbursement of "personally identifiable information." The Act specifically states that, before obtaining information about a cable subscriber from a cable operator, the government must apply for a court order and offer clear and convincing evidence that the subscriber is suspected of engaging in criminal activity and that the information sought would be material evidence in the case. See 47 U.S.C. sec. 551(h). Furthermore, the CCPA requires that the subject of the information sought by the government must be notified and given the opportunity to contest the government's claim. See sec. 551(h)(2).

Traditionally, Internet providers have considered themselves subject to the regulations and prohibitions set forth in the Electronic Communication Privacy Act. See, *e.g.*, *United States v. Hambrick*, 55 F. Supp. 2d 504, 507 (W.D.Va. 1999) (analyzing Internet service's providing of customer's information under the ECPA). Cable operators, however, are subject to the Cable Communications Policy Act. So where does a cable operator, providing Internet services, look for its regulatory scheme? In this case, did Road Runner, a provider of high speed Internet services over cable wires, by complying with the Electronic Communication Privacy Act, completely identify and comply with its statutory duties?

The issue of whether the CCPA applies to a company such as Road Runner is one of first impression. Only one district court has discussed the issue. See *In re United States of America*, 36 F. Supp. 2d 430 (D. Mass. 1999). In *In re United States*, the issue was raised in an application for an order under the Electronic Communication Privacy Act. See *Id.* at 431. The district court was able to avoid deciding the statutory conflict by concluding it lacked jurisdiction because the issue was not ripe for adjudication. See *id.* at 433.

This court need not decide whether the CCPA was violated in the instant action because even if it were, defendant still would not be entitled to suppression of the evidence as a remedy for the violation. As with the ECPA, the CCPA speaks nothing of an exclusionary remedy, only a civil remedy. See 47 U.S.C. sec. 551(f). Furthermore, for the same reasons defendant did not have a Fourth Amendment interest under the ECPA, he has no such interest under the CCPA. See also, *Scofield v. Telecable of Overland Park, Inc.*, 973 F.2d 874, 876-77 (10th Cir. 1992) ("[The notice requirements of section 551] do not themselves create a class of protected privacy interests. That is, subscribers have no privacy interest in receiving a notice itself."). Therefore, even if the government's attainment of defendant's subscriber information from Road Runner violated the Cable Communications Policy Act, the statute affords him no suppression remedy.

B. INITIAL SEARCHES OF DEFENDANT'S COMPUTER FILES

Defendant argues that the initial warrantless searches of his computer files were done by government actors and were therefore in violation of his Fourth Amendment rights. The searches he refers to are those performed by the anonymous caller and Road Runner personnel. He asks this court to suppress all evidence as fruit of this poisonous tree. Because the court finds that these searches were done entirely by private individuals, the searches were not within the purview of the Fourth Amendment.

The Fourth Amendment's protection against unreasonable searches and seizures "proscribes only governmental action; it is wholly inapplicable 'to a search or seizure, even an unreasonable one, effected by a private individual not acting as an agent of the Government or with the participation or knowledge of any governmental official.'" *United States v. Jacobsen*, 466 U.S. 109, 113, 104 S. Ct. 1652, 1656, 80 L. Ed. 2d 85 (1984) (quoting *Walter v. United States*, 447 U.S. 649, 662, 100 S. Ct. 2395, 2404, 65 L. Ed. 2d 410 (1980) (Blackmun, J., dissenting)). The Tenth Circuit applies a two part test in determining when a search by a private individual becomes government action: "1) whether the government knew of and acquiesced in the intrusive conduct, and 2) whether the party performing the search intended to assist law enforcement efforts or to further his own ends." *Pleasant v. Lovell*, 876 F.2d 787, 797 (10th Cir. 1989). Both inquiries must be answered in the affirmative before an otherwise private search will be deemed governmental for Fourth Amendment purposes. See *United States v. Leffall*, 82 F.3d 343, 347 (10th Cir. 1996).

In this case, the first requirement is not met. There is no evidence to support defendant's allegation that the government either knew of or acquiesced in either the caller's or the Road Runner personnel's search of defendant's computer. "The proponent of a motion to suppress bears the burden of proof." *United States v. Madrid*, 30 F.3d 1269, 1275 (10th Cir. 1994). Defendant bears the burden of establishing that the government involvement of the initial searches was significant enough to change them into governmental searches.

Defendant has not met his burden.

C.   AFFIDAVIT IN SUPPORT OF THE SEARCH WARRANT [Omitted]

D.   DEFENDANT'S STATEMENTS ON AUGUST 10TH [Omitted]

Conclusion

IT IS THEREFORE ORDERED BY THE COURT that defendant's motion to suppress (Doc. 13) is DENIED.

Case Questions

1.   Why does the defendant contend that certain items of evidence should be suppressed?

2.   Which statute does the court find controlling in this case?

United States of America v. Hilton
167 F.3d 61 (1st Cir. 1999)

Congress enacted the Child Pornography Prevention Act (the "CPPA"), 18 U.S.C. sec. 2252A, to attack the rise of computerized or "virtual" child pornography. These images may take many forms—a photograph of a real child may be scanned and replicated, an innocent picture of a child may be manipulated by computer to create a sexually-oriented photo, or a fake child (ranging from a simple cartoon character to a high-resolution image resembling a real child) can be generated wholly by computer graphics.

The law prohibits, *inter alia*, knowing possession of visual images depicting minors or those who "appear to be" minors engaging in sexually explicit conduct. This case presents constitutional issues of first impression in this circuit: whether the CPPA's definition of child pornography is so overbroad as to contravene the First Amendment or so vague as to violate due process.

In resolving defendant David Hilton's motion to dismiss the indictment in his favor, the United States District Court for the District of Maine answered both questions in the affirmative. The court was troubled by a perceived difficulty in determining whether a depicted person appeared to be under 18 years old and by its belief that the statute impermissibly criminalizes possession of adult pornography.

We reverse. We hold that the law, properly construed, survives Hilton's facial constitutional challenge. It neither impinges substantially on protected expression nor is so vague as to offend due process.

I.   We assess the constitutionality of the CPPA *de novo*. See *United States v. DeLuca*, 137 F.3d 24, 40 n.19 (1st Cir. 1998). In doing so, we must carefully consider fundamental constitutional norms in light of recent technological advances to determine whether Congress's objectives and the statutory scheme it has established are in accord with our constitutional design.

We begin by providing an overview of the CPPA and by considering the underlying legislative purposes of the Act. Congress enacted the CPPA to modernize federal law by enhancing its ability to combat child pornography in the cyberspace era. See S. Rep. No. 104-358, at pt. I (1996) (declaring that statute addresses "problem of 'high-tech kiddie porn'"). Lawmakers wished to improve law enforcement tools to keep pace with technological improvements that have made it possible for child pornographers to use computers to "morph" or alter innocent images of actual children to create a composite image showing them in sexually explicit poses. Through readily available desktop computer programs, one can even create a realistic picture of an imaginary child engaged in sexual activity and pass off that creation as an image of a real child.

The statute's operative provisions, taken together, criminalize the reproduction, possession, sale, and distribution of child pornography. See 18 U.S.C. sec. 2252A(a). They also prohibit the pandering of material as child pornography by making it a crime to advertise, promote, or present material "in such a manner that it conveys the impression that the material is, or contains" child pornography. 18 U.S.C. sec. 2256(8)(D).

The statute defines child pornography as:

> any visual depiction, including any photograph, film, video, picture, or computer or computer-generated image or picture, whether made or produced by electronic, mechanical, or other means, of sexually explicit conduct, where—(A) the production of such visual depiction involves the use of a minor engaging in sexually explicit conduct; (B) such visual depiction is, or appears to be, of a minor engaging in sexually explicit conduct; (C) such visual depiction has been created, adapted, or modified to appear that an identifiable minor is engaging in sexually explicit conduct; or (D) such visual depiction is advertised, promoted, presented, described, or distributed in such a manner that conveys the impression

that the material is or contains a visual depiction of a minor engaging in sexually explicit conduct . . .

18 U.S.C. sec. 2256(8). A "visual depiction" includes—but is not necessarily limited to—"undeveloped film and videotape, and data stored on computer disk or by electronic means which is capable of conversion into a visual image." 18 U.S.C. sec. 2256(5). A "minor," in turn, means "any person under the age of eighteen years." 18 U.S.C. sec. 2256(1). Sexually explicit conduct is described as "actual or simulated—(A) sexual intercourse, including genital-genital, oral-genital, anal-genital, or oral-anal, whether between persons of the same sex or opposite sex; (B) bestiality; (C) masturbation; (D) sadistic or masochistic abuse; or (E) lascivious exhibition of the genitals or pubic area of any person." 18 U.S.C. sec. 2256(2).

There is some overlap in the definition of child pornography—material created by manipulating an image of an "identifiable minor" would typically, but not necessarily, appear to be of a minor; similarly, an image showing an actual minor would probably also "appear to be a minor." On the other hand, images of a purely fictional child might only satisfy the "appears to be a minor" test. Under the statutory framework established by Congress, a defendant charged with unlawful distribution or sale would be entitled to a complete defense by showing that the person depicted actually was an adult (provided that the material was not promoted or presented to give the impression that it depicts an actual minor). See 18 U.S.C. sec. 2252A(c). The affirmative defense is not made available, however, to those charged with unlawful possession of child pornography.

Congress broadened the scope of federal anti-child pornography statutes to address a set of related concerns aimed at the ultimate goal of destroying the underground supply of child pornography in all of its manifestations. First, the legislature desired to reduce the sheer volume of computerized child pornography that could be used by child molesters and pedophiles to "stimulate or whet their own sexual appetites." S. Rep. 104-358, at pt. IV(B).

Second, Congress sought to ban computer-generated images that are "virtually indistinguishable" from those of real children, but are made without live children. *Id.* These images can be created with very little expense, and often are bought, sold, or traded in the same manner as images created through the use of real children. They can be downloaded from Internet websites, viewed on computer screens, or stored on hard drives or floppy disks for later use. Until now, such materials were largely beyond the reach of federal law, which had focused on representations of actual minors.

Third, the new law was designed to protect the privacy of actual children whose innocuous images are altered to create sexually explicit pictures. Lawmakers hoped to deter the creation of such invasive material and encourage the destruction of that which currently exists. See *id.* at sec. 2(7).

Fourth, Congress wished to deprive child abusers of a "criminal tool" frequently used to facilitate the sexual abuse of children. After hearing from an array of experts, Congress specifically found that virtual pornography created without the involvement of real minors (often via computer technology alone) is increasingly used by pedophiles and child molesters to seduce or entice children into participating in sexual activity by breaking down their natural inhibitions. Congress determined that "a child who is reluctant to engage in sexual activity with an adult, or to pose for sexually explicit photographs, can sometimes be convinced by viewing depictions of other children 'having fun' participating in such activity." *Id.* at sec. 2(3). This material is routinely used to instruct children how to perform certain sexual acts. Images made by manipulating an innocent picture of a real child to show sexual conduct can also be used to blackmail that child into submitting to abuse and remaining in fearful silence about it. Congress deemed the threat of these forms of physical and emotional abuse to be as grave as when images of real children are used, for a child shown a computer-generated image cannot be expected to know whether the child portrayed in an image is that of a real child or merely a fanciful creation.

II. We recount the relatively short history of this case. On December 17, 1997, a federal grand jury indicted Hilton for criminal possession of computer disks containing three or more images of child pornography in violation of 18 U.S.C. sec. 2252A(a)(5)(B). Well before trial, Hilton moved to dismiss the indictment, mounting solely a facial attack on the CPPA. He argued that the statute, by its terms, was unconstitutionally vague and overbroad, and therefore unenforceable.

On March 26, 1998, the United States District Court for the District of Maine agreed. The court determined that [**11] the CPPA was a content-neutral regulation "designed to ameliorate significant harmful secondary effects of the protected speech rather than suppress the speech itself." *United States v. Hilton*, 999 F. Supp. 131, 134 (D. Me. 1998). Nevertheless, the court concluded that the statutory definition of "child pornography" was both vague and overbroad. It found the "appears to be a minor" language overly subjective, creating "substantial uncertainty for viewers presented with materials depicting post-pubescent individuals" because it may be difficult to distinguish between teenagers and young adults. *Id.* at 136. The court further found the definition unconstitutionally overbroad, impacting a "significant amount of adult pornography featuring adults who appear youthful." *Id.* at 137. Despite holding this portion of the CPPA's definition of child pornography unconstitutional, the district court made no effort to ascertain the impact of its ruling on the statute as a whole by examining and applying the statute's severability clause. Instead, it simply dismissed the indictment. The government now appeals.

III. The government attacks the district court's analysis in several critical respects. It first questions the lower court's conclusion that the statute is overbroad. In its view, the CPPA does not reach innocuous pictures of children or criminalize protected adult pornography. The government also takes issue with the district court's determination that the Act is too vague. The government urges us to hold that the statute allows persons of ordinary intelligence to determine what types of material are banned and to conform their conduct accordingly. To require further specificity, it insists, would be not only impractical, but unrealistic. Additionally, the government asks us to deem the "appears to be a minor" standard to be grounded in prosecutorial necessity because it is exceedingly difficult, if not impossible, for an expert to discern whether an image is one of a real child. The broadening of the definition of child pornography is critical, the government argues, because in more and more cases involving virtual child pornography, the prosecution is unable to prove that real children under a specified age are depicted.

We turn our attention to familiar constitutional terrain. The First Amendment declares that "Congress shall make no law . . . abridging freedom of speech." U.S. Const., amend. I. We offer a few words about the doctrines that have developed over time to give meaning to the protective force of the First Amendment. In general, laws that aim only to prescribe the conditions under which certain speech may be carried out may be upheld as neutral time, place or manner restrictions. See *United States v.*

Grace, 461 U.S. 171, 177, 75 L. Ed. 2d 736, 103 S. Ct. 1702 (1983) ("The government may enforce reasonable time, place, and manner regulations as long as the restrictions 'are content neutral, are narrowly tailored to serve a significant government interest, and leave open ample alternative channels of communication.'") (citation omitted). But a statute or regulation that discriminates based on the content of the speech itself typically must comport with the following standards to survive a constitutional challenge: it must be (1) animated by one or more compelling state interests; and (2) narrowly tailored toward fulfilling those concerns. Nevertheless, certain types of expression—chief among them fighting words, libel, and obscenity—are unprotected altogether. See *R.A.V. v. City of St. Paul*, 505 U.S. 377, 383-85, 120 L. Ed. 2d 305, 112 S. Ct. 2538 (1992). Child pornography falls into the category of unprotected speech. See *New York v. Ferber*, 458 U.S. 747, 764, 73 L. Ed. 2d 1113, 102 S. Ct. 3348 (1982). Finally, an otherwise valid law may be so overbroad that it encroaches on protected expression or so vague that prosecuting a person under the statute would effectively deprive that person of due process of law. See *Kolender v. Lawson*, 461 U.S. 352, 357-58, 75 L. Ed. 2d 903, 103 S. Ct. 1855 (1983).

For the sake of clarifying this area of law, we find it necessary to point out that the district court misapplied the time, place or manner doctrine by mistaking the CPPA for a content-neutral law. A distinct line of cases upholds reasonably-crafted regulations where the state acts not to suppress certain speech but to direct, in a content-neutral way, how or when that speech may be expressed in the public sphere. See, *e.g.*, *United States v. Kokinda*, 497 U.S. 720, 111 L. Ed. 2d 571, 110 S. Ct. 3115 (1990) (upholding federal regulation prohibiting solicitation on postal property). Still, "any restriction on speech, the application of which turns on the content of the speech, is a content-based restriction regardless of the motivation that lies behind it." *Boos v. Barry*, 485 U.S. 312, 335-36, 99 L. Ed. 2d 333, 108 S. Ct. 1157 (1988) (Brennan, J., concurring). Of course, if a law is directed at the impact of the speech on its viewers, it cannot be evaluated as a time, place or manner restriction. See *Reno v. American Civil Liberties Union*, 521 U.S. 844, 117 S. Ct. 2329, 2342-43, 138 L. Ed. 2d 874 (1997) (rejecting argument that Communications Decency Act, which banned online transmission of "obscene or indecent" messages, was time, place or manner regulation); *Forsyth County v. Nationalist Movement*, 505 U.S. 123, 134, 120 L. Ed. 2d 101, 112 S. Ct. 2395 (1992) ("Listeners' reaction to speech is not a content-neutral basis for regulation.").

The CPPA fails both tests for substantive neutrality: it expressly aims to curb a particular category of expression (child pornography) by singling out that type of expression based on its content and banning it. Blanket suppression of an entire type of speech is by its very nature a content-discriminating act. Furthermore, Congress has not kept secret that one of its motivating reasons for enacting the CPPA was to counter the primary effect child pornography has on those who view it. See S. Rep. 104-358, at pt. III, IV(A) (reflecting congressional concern that a "child molester or pedophile [may use] the material to whet his sexual appetites," that child pornography "poisons the minds and spirits of our youth," and that, if shown to children, the material may "make children more susceptible of acceding to sexual demands of would-be abusers"); *see also id.* at pt. IV(B) (observing that "a major part of the threat to children posed by child pornography is its effect on the viewers of such material"). For these related reasons, the child pornography law is plainly activated by a "content-based classification of speech." *Ferber*, 458 U.S. at 763.

Moreover, the statute makes no effort to permit alternative methods of disseminating or possessing the material in question. In this respect, the district court also erred in finding that adequate alternative avenues of expression exist. The CPPA is a quintessential content-specific statute, and therefore cannot be properly understood as a time, place or manner regulation.

But to say that the CPPA is content-based does not end the matter, for it is well settled that child pornography, an unprotected category of expression identified by its content, may be freely regulated. We are asked to determine: first, whether the statute's definition of child pornography, expanded in an effort to outlaw computerized child pornography, satisfies the First Amendment; and second, assuming its sweep is appropriate, whether the law is adequately precise as to provide fair warning.

To resolve these issues, we start by reviewing the Supreme Court's pronouncements on the government's power to regulate child pornography. In *Ferber*, the Supreme Court first upheld the constitutionality of a state law proscribing the distribution of material depicting sexual performances by children under the age of 16. See 458 U.S. 747, 102 S. Ct. 3348, 73 L. Ed. 2d 1113. In doing so, it carved out an entire category of speech "which, like obscenity, is unprotected by the First Amendment." *Id.* at 764. The Court likened child pornography to obscenity in that both kinds of expression may be banned, but explained that because of the state's "compelling interest in prosecuting those who promote the sexual exploitation of children," see *id.* at 761, a law regulating child pornography need not adhere mechanistically to the three-part test for obscenity originally enunciated in *Miller v. California*, 413 U.S. 15, 37 L. Ed. 2d 419, 93 S. Ct. 2607 (1973). One reason for allowing a departure from the obscenity rule and, as a result, somewhat greater authority to regulate child pornography is that "a work which . . . contains serious literary, artistic, political, or scientific value may nevertheless embody the hardest core of child pornography." *Id.*

The *Ferber* Court did not establish a single one-size-fits-all constitutional definition of child pornography (as the Court arguably has done for obscenity), but provided general guiding principles. Ultimately, to pass constitutional muster, a particular anti-child pornography statute must be adequately defined. 458 U.S. at 764. In *Ferber*, the Court pointed out that New York's prohibition was confined to works that "visually depict sexual conduct by children below a specified age." *Id.* (Emphasis in original). It was also persuaded that the law's definition of sexual activity was "suitably limited and described." *Id.*

The Court further developed the contours of its child pornography jurisprudence in *Osborne v. Ohio*, 495 U.S. 103, 109 L. Ed. 2d 98, 110 S. Ct. 691 (1990). There, the Court evaluated a state law prohibiting the possession and viewing of material depicting a nude minor "where such nudity constitutes a lewd exhibition or involves a graphic focus on the genitals." A defendant charged with unlawful possession attacked the statute as overbroad and vague. Rebuffing his twin challenges, the Court found that the statute was not aimed at controlling a person's private thoughts, but had been enacted to "protect victims of child pornography" and to "destroy a market for the exploitative use of children." 495 U.S. at 109. The *Osborne* Court explicitly approved the following legislative goals: stamping out child pornography because it often serves as a record of abuse of real children; and denying pedophiles and would-be child abusers access to child pornography, which would be used to seduce or coerce children into sexual activity. See *id.* at 10-11. The former remains intricately tied to the need to protect real children represented in the pictures, but the latter marks a subtle, yet crucial, extension of a state's legitimate interest to the protection of children not actually depicted in prohibited images.

As these cases demonstrate, the line between unprotected child pornography and otherwise protected expression (including possession of adult pornography, see *Stanley v. Georgia*, 394 U.S. 557, 22 L. Ed. 2d 542, 89 S. Ct. 1243 (1969)) is not entirely tangle-free. Nonetheless, four lessons can be drawn from the decisions.

First, sexually explicit material may be seen to fall along a constitutional continuum entitling it to varying degrees of protection. At one end of the spectrum, pictures of actual children in sexually compromising positions, deemed to have little or no social value, are entitled to no constitutional protection. At the opposite end of the spectrum, nonobscene images involving actual adults are entitled to full protection. Sexually explicit material created without the benefit of a live child model but which appears to depict an actual minor, or produced by having an adult pose as a minor and later presented or sold as if it depicted as an actual minor, arguably falls somewhere in between.

Second, considerations beyond preventing the direct abuse of actual children can qualify as compelling government objectives where child pornography is concerned. When child pornography is the target, government is justified in not only driving it from the marketplace through aggressive anti-trafficking laws, but forbidding the private possession or personal viewing of these products altogether. See *Osborne*, 495 U.S. at 110 (approving of state's efforts to "stamp out this vice at all levels in the distribution chain"). In this sense, concerns about how adults may use child pornography vis-a-vis children and how children might behave after viewing it legitimately inform legislators' collective decision to ban this material.

Third, in effecting such a prohibition, a criminal statute must engage government authority by "adequately defining" the type of image that is to be forbidden. The cases require not only that the term "minor" be defined, but also that the type of condemned sexual depiction be carefully described.

Fourth, wherever the constitutional demarcation is to be properly drawn, "greater leeway" ought to be afforded legislatures to regulate sexual depictions of children. *Ferber*, 458 U.S. at 756. The Court's instruction to federal courts to permit Congress slightly more room to operate in this area is bolstered by its view that "the value of permitting . . . photographic reproductions of children engaged in lewd sexual conduct is exceedingly modest, if not *de minimis.*" *Id.* at 762. As a result, some discretion has been given legislatures to set out the parameters of anti-pornography restrictions. For instance, the Court has repeatedly acknowledged that states have latitude to set the age at which an image is of a child rather than an adult. See, *e.g.*, *United States v. X-Citement Video, Inc.*, 513 U.S. 64, 67, 130 L. Ed. 2d 372, 115 S. Ct. 464 (1994)(upholding federal law that employs 18 as age of majority); Ferber, 458 U.S. at 749 (law set age of majority at 16). Congress and statehouses have some leeway in defining the kind of sexual depiction to be proscribed as well. See *X-Citement Video*, 513 U.S. at 78-79 (holding that it is constitutionally permissible to use either formulation—"lewd" or "lascivious" display of children's genitals).

With this analytic framework in mind, we turn to the task of assessing the constitutionality of the CPPA. The initial step is to ascertain the general scope of the statutory definition of child pornography, a task of pure statutory interpretation. Comparison of the law with prevailing constitutional precepts then follows.

IV. We first evaluate the district court's conclusion that the CPPA is unconstitutionally overbroad. Overbroad statutes by their nature present a host of difficulties for our system of ordered liberty, not the least of which is a chilling effect on the communication of lawful ideas. But a statute will not be invalidated as overbroad unless its overbreadth is "real, but substantial as well, judged in relation to the statute's plainly legitimate sweep." *Osborne*, 495 U.S. at 112 (citation omitted). As the Court has admonished, the overbreadth doctrine is "strong medicine" that should be utilized "only as a last resort." Ferber, 458 U.S. at 769 (quoting *Broadrick v. Oklahoma*, 413 U.S. 601, 613, 37 L. Ed. 2d 830, 93 S. Ct. 2908 (1973)).

Judicial disinclination to employ the overbreadth doctrine is rooted in several important considerations. The first is an appreciation for the "wide-reaching effects of striking down a statute on its face." *Id.* Another related reason is that it may be inefficient to do so: facial invalidation is unwarranted if the likely number of lawful applications of the challenged statute far outstrips the few arguably problematic prosecutions under the law. It makes little sense to strike down an entire statute in response to a facial attack when potential difficulties can be remedied in future cases through fact-specific as-applied challenges. A third reason to hesitate before invoking the overbreadth doctrine is that doing so may be unwise. Deciding constitutional questions in the abstract is a recipe for making bad law. See 458 U.S. at 781 (Stevens, J., concurring) ("Hypothetical rulings are inherently treacherous and prone to lead us into unforeseen efforts; they are qualitatively less reliable than the products of case-by-case adjudication.").

The key question, then, is whether the CPPA poses substantial problems of overbreadth sufficient to justify overturning the judgment of the lawmaking branches. We conclude that it does not. We begin with the language of the statute. To the extent the CPPA criminalizes the possession, reproduction or distribution of a visual representation of an actual minor engaged in sexual conduct, it falls easily within the parameters established by *Ferber* and *Osborne*. The government's interests in deterring the direct abuse of children and destroying the illicit child pornography trade amply justify these steps, and the CPPA's methods of eradicating such images are appropriate.

Whether or not the prohibition of material that "appears to be" of a minor comports with the First Amendment is more troublesome. At first blush, potential problems threaten to doom the law. First and foremost, "appears" to whom? The statute itself is silent as to whether the test is meant to be objective or subjective or some combination of the two. On its face, the statute might also reach depictions with political, artistic, scientific, or educational value. If so, it is unclear whether that would be constitutionally permissible. And if, as *Hilton* and *amici* insist, the phrase "appears to be a minor" criminalizes possession of adult pornography created with models over the age of majority who look youthful, this too might pose additional constitutional difficulties.

A correct interpretation of the "appears to be a minor" standard and a full understanding of the interplay between the legal protections afforded an individual, we believe, puts the bulk of these concerns to rest. As to the breadth of the material covered by the statute, Congress's statements provide us with a precise and limited understanding of the "appears to be" language. We are obligated to follow it. "Where a statute is susceptible of two constructions, by one of which grave and doubtful constitutional questions arise and by the other of which such questions are avoided, our duty is to adopt the latter." *Almendarez-Torres v. United States*, 523 U.S. 224, 140 L. Ed. 2d 350, 118 S. Ct. 1219, 1234 (1998)(Scalia, J., dissenting) (quoting *United States ex rel. Attorney General v. Delaware and Hudson Co.*, 213 U.S. 366, 408, 53 L. Ed. 836, 29 S. Ct. 527 (1909)); see also Ferber, 458 U.S. at 769 n.24 ("When a federal court is dealing with a federal statute challenged as overbroad, it should . . . construe the statute to avoid constitutional problems, if the statute is subject to such a limiting construction."); *Veiga v. McGee*, 26 F.3d 1206, 1212 (1st Cir. 1994) ("In the absence of clear legislative intent, we will not adopt an interpretation of a statute that would render it constitutionally suspect.").

We take our cue from the legislative record, which makes plain that the new language was intended to target only a narrow class of images—visual depictions "which are virtually indistinguishable to unsuspecting viewers from unretouched photographs of actual children engaging in identical sexual conduct." S. Rep. 104-358, at pt. I, IV(B). The Senate, in enacting S. 1237, explicitly stated that the "appears to be" language "applies to the same type of photographic images already prohibited, but which does not require the use of an actual minor in its production." *Id.* at pt. IV(C). The Senate clearly indicated that, by employing the phrase "appears to be," it was "extending [the prohibition against child pornography] from photographic depictions of actual minors engaging in sexually explicit conduct to the identical type of depiction, one of which is virtually indistinguishable from the banned photographic depiction," and no further. *Id.* (Emphasis added).

A few observations logically flow from this narrow construct. The primary one is that Congress meant only to extend federal authority in an important but limited fashion to a specific subset of visual images—those which are easily mistaken for that of real children.

It follows that drawings, cartoons, sculptures, and paintings depicting youthful persons in sexually explicit poses plainly lie beyond the reach of the Act. By definition, they would not be "virtually indistinguishable" from an image of an actual minor. The CPPA therefore does not pose a threat to the vast majority of everyday artistic expression, even to speech involving sexual themes.

Hilton (and assorted *amici*) nevertheless insists that the First Amendment allows regulation of sexually explicit material only where actual children are abused in its creation. They also contend that the statute is impermissibly expansive because it is very difficult to determine whether a person looks 17 or 18; they believe that the statute is bound to criminalize possession of protected adult pornography.

Their first argument amounts to an effort to draw a bright line in an area of law in which courts have resisted creating clear-cut categories. Relying on *Ferber's* discussion of the importance of protecting children from sexual exploitation, they argue that the Supreme Court has strictly limited regulation of child pornography to images manufactured with the use of live children. But we find no firm basis for this overly restrictive reading of precedent. We do not read the cases to say that Congress has power to remedy only the abuse of children during the process used to produce traditional forms of child pornography. While the Court certainly has been concerned with the "surpassing importance" of protecting the actual abuse of children who appear in pornographic material, it has not limited the government's authority to achieving that objective, and that objective alone. *Ferber*, 458 U.S. at 757. Rather, it has mandated that government be permitted a certain degree of flexibility in how it chooses to grapple with new problems presented by the evolving nature of the child pornography industry. See *Osborne*, 495 U.S. at 110. The cases do suggest, however, that an appropriate set of governmental goals (and the government's methods of fulfilling those goals) should be reasonably related to the primary aim of "safeguarding the physical and psychological well-being" of children, and, by extension, crippling the clandestine child pornography trade. *Id.* at 109 (citation omitted).

The laws in force when the Court decided *Ferber* and *Osborne* uniformly defined child pornography by focusing on material involving the use of actual children. The Court in those cases used, for purposes of its constitutional discussion, the statutory definition of child pornography then before it. The legal issues presented in this case, including Congress's justifications offered for extending child pornography statutes to stem the flow of virtual child pornography, have not been analyzed by this, or any other, court of appeals.

We think that it is a logical and permissible extension of the rationales in *Ferber* and *Osborne* to allow the regulation of sexual materials that appear to be of children but did not, in fact, involve the use of live children in their production. Like sexually explicit material produced with actual children, there is little, if any, social value in this type of expression. In constitutional terms, sexually explicit material produced without the benefit of a live child model but giving the appearance as if it had been is more akin to traditionally unprotected child pornography than adult pornography. The same is true of material created by having a youthful-looking adult pose as a minor that is sold or presented as though it contained a pornographic image of an actual minor. Such depictions can be readily used so as to further the child pornography trade or to facilitate the abuse of children.

The government's interest in safeguarding the welfare of children is compelling in these situations. Computer-created or enhanced material can be bought, sold, or traded like any other form of child pornography, adding further fuel to the underground child pornography industry. It can be used just as effectively as pictures of actual children to entice or blackmail children into cooperating with would-be abusers. Moreover, the material may have been created through the abuse of an actual minor but altered so that it may be impossible to show that a real child was ever involved in its creation. As technology improves and access to technology increases, efforts to eradicate the child pornography industry could be effectively frustrated if Congress were prevented from targeting sexually explicit material that "appears to be" of real children. The government's interest in addressing these forms of child pornography is no less powerful than in instances where an actual child is actually used and abused during the production process. We will not second-guess Congress's decision to address the social ills posed by the various types of virtual child pornography.

Hilton's and *amici's* next objection also misses the mark. They maintain that the inherent difficulty of determining whether a depicted person "appears to be" 17 or 18 renders the definition overly broad. They fear that persons will be convicted of possessing sexually explicit material of adults who look or dress in a youthful manner. We think this danger is overstated. The main flaw in the argument is its inordinate focus on the arguably fuzzy line between age 17 and 18, a line which, as with many laws, must be drawn somewhere. More importantly, we are satisfied that the vast majority of prosecutions under the "appears to be a minor" provision would involve images of pre-pubescent children or persons who otherwise clearly appear to be under the age of 18. Congress, relying on the opinion of experts, has determined that purveyors of child pornography usually cater to pedophiles, who by definition have a predilection for pre-pubertal children. See *S. Rep.* 104-358, at sec. 2, pts. IV(A), (C). The apparent age of a pre-pubescent child can easily be established through objective proof. While it is theoretically possible that there may be prosecutions of individuals selling or possessing images of youthful-looking adults, it is unlikely that they would comprise a substantial proportion of the prosecutions under the statute.

The existence of a few possibly impermissible applications of the Act does not warrant its condemnation. As the Court has repeatedly made plain, even if a statute at its margins infringes on protected activity, the solution is not invalidation of the entire scheme. See *Frisby v. Schultz*, 487 U.S. 474, 488, 101 L. Ed. 2d 420, 108 S. Ct. 2495 (1988) (declining to evaluate all "hypothetical applications" of ordinance in resolving facial challenge). Whatever overbreadth may exist at the edges is more appropriately cured through a more precise case-by-case evaluation of the facts in a given case. See *New York State Club Assoc., Inc. v. City of New York*, 487 U.S. 1, 14, 101 L. Ed. 2d 1, 108 S. Ct. 2225 (1988).

We recognize that the Court has said that adult models may be employed under certain circumstances to simulate minors posing in a sexually provocative manner for serious artistic, educational, or scientific purposes. Indeed, in *Ferber*, the Court observed that "if it were necessary for literary or artistic value, a person over the statutory age who perhaps looked younger could be utilized." 458 U.S. at 763; see also *X-Citement Video*, 513 U.S. at 72 ("Nonobscene, sexually explicit materials involving persons over the age of 17 are protected by the First Amendment.").

Take, for example, a film version of Nabokov's *Lolita*. A director might legitimately wish to employ a youthful-looking adult to portray, in a nonobscene manner, a sexual encounter between Lolita and Humbert. Similarly, use of an adult model to simulate the sexual behavior of a child might be necessary for scientific research. The social value of these works obviously could not be shrugged off as *de minimis*. They would be far from the "hardest core of child pornography." *Ferber*, 458 U.S. at 761. The First Amendment interest in permitting dissemination of such material would be sufficiently strong to warrant its protection. At the same time, the government's countervailing interest in protecting children "is likely to be far less compelling" when "the depiction is a serious contribution to art or science." *Id.* at 776 (Brennan, J., concurring). Should the government decide to prosecute someone for distributing or possessing such material, we believe there would be an affirmative First Amendment defense available to the accused, although we need not define now its precise dimensions. Recognizing such a defense is consistent with Congress's general view that the law generally "does not, and is not intended to, apply to a depiction produced using adults engaging in sexually explicit conduct, even where a depicted individual may appear to be a minor." S. Rep. 104-358, at pt. IV(C). It is also consonant with the Court's teachings in *Ferber*, where the Court assumed that even if in some rare instance the depiction of children performing sexual acts might be necessary for literary or artistic reasons, "a person over the statutory age who perhaps looked younger could be utilized." 458 U.S. at 763.

We need not fully explore the details of this exception today. Suffice it to say that the existence of a tiny fraction of material that could conceivably qualify for heightened protection but might nevertheless fall within the purview of the Act (*i.e.*, where youthful adults pose as children for sexually provocative images with redeeming social value) does not render the statute as a whole substantially overbroad. The appropriate remedy is reversal of an unconstitutional conviction should the circumstance arise, not invalidation of the statute in toto at this stage.

Once the phrase "appears to be a minor" is properly understood, the constitutional barriers fall away. The fear of a chilling effect on protected speech subsides. We conclude, therefore, that the CPPA is not unconstitutionally overbroad.

V. We next consider whether the district court erred in holding the CPPA unconstitutionally vague. The touchstone of our system of justice is the right to fair warning of criminal charges. An ambiguous law fails to provide the requisite notice and undermines public confidence that the laws are equally enforced.

The standard for overturning a law on vagueness grounds is a stringent one. A statute will not be held void for vagueness unless it fails to "define the criminal offense with sufficient definiteness that ordinary people can understand what conduct is prohibited and in a manner that does not encourage arbitrary or discriminatory enforcement." *Kolender*, 461 U.S. at 357; see also *United States v. Bohai Trading Co.*, 45 F.3d 577, 580 (1st Cir. 1995) (proper inquiry is whether statute "provides a constitutionally adequate warning to those whose activities are governed") (citation omitted). When a law directly impinges on freedom of expression, as the CPPA does here, we must scrutinize the law with an even more skeptical eye. We are obliged do so because the threat of severe criminal sanctions and the full force of social stigma, coupled with uncertain notice of criminal liability offered by a poorly worded statute, "may well cause speakers to remain silent rather than communicate even arguably unlawful words, ideas, and images." *Reno v. ACLU*, 521 U.S. at, 117 S. Ct. at 2345.

The district court found the CPPA unduly vague because it believed the "appears to be a minor" standard to be purely subjective in nature. To the contrary, we hold that the standard is an objective one. A jury must decide, based on the totality of the circumstances, whether a reasonable unsuspecting viewer would consider the depiction to be of an actual individual less than 18 engaged in sexual activity. See S. Rep. 104-358, at pt. IV(C).

Without limiting *a priori* the type of evidence that would be admissible on this question in a given case, the following proof could be offered to establish the apparent age of the person shown: the physical characteristics of the person; expert testimony as to the physical development of the depicted person; how the disk, file, or video was labeled or marked by the creator or the distributor of the image, or the defendant himself, see, *e.g.*, *United States v. Robinson*, 137 F.3d 652, 652 (1st Cir. 1998) (photographs labeled by names, dates taken, and ages of boys depicted); and the manner in which the image was described, displayed, or advertised. While this list is hardly exhaustive, it gives a flavor of the ways in which a depicted person's apparent age might be objectively proven.

The element of scienter also must be satisfied by the prosecution before a valid conviction may be obtained—for instance, the government must prove beyond a reasonable doubt that an individual "knowingly" possessed the child pornography. See 18 U.S.C. sec. 2252A(a)(5)(B). This statutory requirement serves as an additional safeguard, for the government must show not only that the individual purposefully acquired or distributed the material, but that he did so believing that the material was sexually explicit in nature and that it depicted a person who appeared to him to be (or that he anticipated would be) under 18 years old. See *X-Citement Video, Inc.*, 513 U.S. at 78 (holding that scienter requirement in related anti-child pornography statute "extends to both the sexually explicit nature of the material and to the age of the performers").

The CPPA offers an added measure of protection. It provides an affirmative defense if the person depicted actually was an adult at the time the image was created. When the defense is appropriate, the fact that the person depicted was a live model at least 18 years of age typically will lead to dismissal of the charge. Although Congress did not make the affirmative defense available to someone accused of unlawful possession (as opposed to any of the other offenses such as distribution), what an individual actually believed to be the age of the depicted person still goes to his state of mind in possessing the material. Thus, a defendant who honestly believes that the individual depicted in the image appears to be 18 years old or older (and is believed by a jury), or who can show that he knew the images were created by having youthful looking adults pose for them, must be acquitted, so long as the image was not presented or marketed as if it contained a real minor.

We believe, in short, that the statute's provisions "suitably limit" the reach of the Act so that a person of ordinary intelligence can easily discern likely unlawful conduct and conform his or her conduct appropriately. The statute carefully defines the term "minor." The scope of its prohibition, like the law evaluated in *Ferber*, is restricted to visual images. The statute describes, in painstaking detail, the types of sexually explicit depictions of children that are forbidden. As the Court said in *Osborne*, such limiting language "avoids penalizing persons for viewing or possessing innocuous photographs of naked children." 495 U.S. at 114.

We disagree with the district court's assumption that the use of a legal standard requiring an evaluation of the appearance of an image renders the test arbitrary or overly susceptible to manipulation. Reasonable objective assessments of the impression conveyed by a person's actions or how an image "appears" are routinely made by judges and juries. See, *e.g.*, *Liteky v. United States*, 510 U.S. 540, 553 n.2, 127 L. Ed. 2d 474, 114 S. Ct. 1147 (1994) (noting that recusal motions under 28 U.S.C. sec. 455(a) are governed by "objective appearance of partiality" test); *Ferber*, 458 U.S. at 751 (approved definition of child pornography banned "simulated" sexual conduct, which in ordinary usage means "to have or take on the appearance of"); *Miller*, 413 U.S. at 24 (obscenity depends in part on whether material appeals to prurient interest of average person).

Yet *Hilton* returns to a familiar refrain: that it is terribly difficult to distinguish between an apparent 17 year old and an apparent 18 year old. This problem, he argues, renders the statute unduly vague (as well as overbroad). We think not. As discussed earlier, any number of objective signs should be enough to warn an ordinary viewer of sexually explicit material of the apparent age of the person depicted, including his or her physical characteristics and how the image is labeled or marketed. And those involved in the production of lawful sexually explicit material can easily protect themselves by verifying the ages of the models they employ or by taking steps to visually demonstrate that a computer-generated image is meant to portray an adult.

There is another reason why *Hilton's* vagueness challenge fails: there are few equally efficacious alternatives. At oral argument, defense counsel suggested that a better approach would be to prohibit images of persons who are or appear to be "physically sexually immature." Such a test, had Congress selected it, might very well have been more precise than the one Congress chose to adopt, which turns on the age or apparent age of the person depicted. It is often said that because we are "condemned to the use of words, we can never expect mathematical certainty from our language." *Grayned v. City of Rockford*, 408 U.S. 104, 109, 33 L. Ed. 2d 222, 92 S. Ct. 2294 (1972). That lesson applies here.

But even if the proffered standard were more exact, there would still be a more fundamental problem—it would fail to reach a whole category of persons Congress intended to protect, namely, those youngsters who appear "physically sexually mature" but are under the age of consent. We reject the suggestion that Congress must be confined to addressing pornographic images of some children, but not others. Firmly satisfied that it is well within Congress's power to regulate virtual pornography of minors of all ages (infancy through age of majority as set by the legislature), we are aware of few other linguistic approaches that would achieve the same goals. Defendant's proposal does not fit the bill. The "appears to be a minor" test, by comparison, is sufficiently precise to pass constitutional muster and yet flexible enough to meet the challenges posed by computerized child pornography.

We see no reason to strike down the CPPA as unconstitutionally vague. The language of the statute affords an ordinary consumer of sexually explicit material adequate notice of the kinds of images to avoid. The interaction between the applicable legal standards, moreover, offers the average person additional protection. These safeguards, working in concert, minimize the danger that this law might be enforced in an arbitrary or discriminatory fashion by overzealous police officers or prosecutors.

The judgment of the district court is reversed.

Case Questions

1. What is the "time, place and manner" doctrine discussed by the court?

2. Why did the district court find the CPPA unconstitutionally overbroad?

Exercises

1. Locate a newspaper article that discusses a cybercrime.

2. How would you balance constitutional guarantees of privacy with the need to protect the populace from terrorism?

3. Why do you believe the international community has been so slow in addressing cybercrimes? Discuss.

4. Discuss why hacking is a crime against property.

5. How could computer technology be used to gather evidence of criminal activity? Discuss in detail.

6. What are the five categories of crimes into which all crimes fall?

7. Define "hacking."

8. What is your opinion of the Patriot Act?

9. What elements can be proven to find a person guilty of a crime?

10. Research your jurisdiction to ascertain whether it has enacted any statutes specifically addressing cybercrimes.

Related Websites

Econsumer.com
Nytimes.com
Jmls.edu/cyber/index/index.html

Appendix D

The Patriot Act

**CONVENTION
ON CYBERCRIME**

European Treaty Series - No. 185
Budapest, 23.XI.2001

Preamble

The member States of the Council of Europe and the other States signatory hereto,

Considering that the aim of the Council of Europe is to achieve a greater unity between its members;

Recognising the value of fostering co-operation with the other States parties to this Convention;

Convinced of the need to pursue, as a matter of priority, a common criminal policy aimed at the protection of society against cybercrime, *inter alia*, by adopting appropriate legislation and fostering international co-operation;

Conscious of the profound changes brought about by the digitalisation, convergence and continuing globalisation of computer networks;

Concerned by the risk that computer networks and electronic information may also be used for committing criminal offences and that evidence relating to such offences may be stored and transferred by these networks;

Recognising the need for co-operation between States and private industry in combating cybercrime and the need to protect legitimate interests in the use and development of information technologies;

Believing that an effective fight against cybercrime requires increased, rapid and well-functioning international co-operation in criminal matters;

Convinced that the present Convention is necessary to deter action directed against the confidentiality, integrity and availability of computer systems, networks and computer data as well as the misuse of such systems, networks and data by providing for the criminalisation of such conduct, as described in this Convention, and the adoption of powers sufficient for effectively combating such criminal offences, by facilitating their detection, investigation and prosecution at both the domestic and international levels and by providing arrangements for fast and reliable international co-operation;

Mindful of the need to ensure a proper balance between the interests of law enforcement and respect for fundamental human rights as enshrined in the 1950 Council of Europe Convention for the Protection of Human Rights and Fundamental Freedoms, the 1966 United Nations International Covenant on Civil and Political Rights and other applicable international human rights treaties, which reaffirm the right of everyone to hold opinions without interference, as well as the right to freedom of expression, including the freedom to seek, receive, and impart information and ideas of all kinds, regardless of frontiers, and the rights concerning the respect for privacy;

Mindful also of the right to the protection of personal data, as conferred, for example, by the 1981 Council of Europe Convention for the Protection of Individuals with regard to Automatic Processing of Personal Data;

Considering the 1989 United Nations Convention on the Rights of the Child and the 1999 International Labour Organization Worst Forms of Child Labour Convention;

Taking into account the existing Council of Europe conventions on co-operation in the penal field, as well as similar treaties which exist between Council of Europe member States and other States, and stressing that the present Convention is intended to supplement those conventions in order to make criminal investigations and proceedings concerning criminal offences related to computer systems and data more effective and to enable the collection of evidence in electronic form of a criminal offence;

Welcoming recent developments which further advance international understanding and co-operation in combating cybercrime, including action taken by the United Nations, the OECD, the European Union and the G8;

Recalling Committee of Ministers Recommendations No. R (85) 10 concerning the practical application of the European Convention on Mutual Assistance in Criminal Matters in respect of letters rogatory for the interception of telecommunications, No. R (88) 2 on piracy in the field of copyright and neighbouring rights, No. R (87) 15 regulating the use of personal data in the police sector, No. R (95) 4 on the protection of personal data in the area of telecommunication services, with particular reference to telephone services, as well as No. R (89) 9 on computer-related crime providing guidelines for national legislatures concerning the definition of certain computer crimes and No. R (95) 13 concerning problems of criminal procedural law connected with information technology;

Having regard to Resolution No. 1 adopted by the European Ministers of Justice at their 21st Conference (Prague, 10 and 11 June 1997), which recommended that the Committee of Ministers support the work on cybercrime carried out by the European Committee on Crime Problems (CDPC) in order to bring domestic criminal law provisions closer to each other and enable the use of effective means of investigation into such offences, as well as to Resolution No. 3 adopted at the 23rd Conference of the European Ministers of Justice (London, 8 and 9 June 2000), which encouraged the negotiating parties to pursue their efforts with a view to finding appropriate solutions to enable the largest possible number of States to become parties to the Convention and acknowledged the need for a swift and efficient system of international co-operation, which duly takes into account the specific requirements of the fight against cybercrime;

Having also regard to the Action Plan adopted by the Heads of State and Government of the Council of Europe on the occasion of their Second Summit (Strasbourg, 10 and 11 October 1997), to seek common responses to the development of the new information technologies based on the standards and values of the Council of Europe;

Have agreed as follows:

Chapter I—Use of terms

Article 1—Definitions

For the purposes of this Convention:

    a.   "computer system" means any device or a group of interconnected or related devices, one or more of which, pursuant to a program, performs automatic processing of data;

b. "computer data" means any representation of facts, information or concepts in a form suitable for processing in a computer system, including a program suitable to cause a computer system to perform a function;

c. "service provider" means:

    i. any public or private entity that provides to users of its service the ability to communicate by means of a computer system, and

    ii. any other entity that processes or stores computer data on behalf of such communication service or users of such service;

d. "traffic data" means any computer data relating to a communication by means of a computer system, generated by a computer system that formed a part in the chain of communication, indicating the communication's origin, destination, route, time, date, size, duration, or type of underlying service.

Chapter II—Measures to be taken at the national level

Section 1—Substantive criminal law

Title 1—Offences against the confidentiality, integrity and availability of computer data and systems

Article 2—Illegal access

Each Party shall adopt such legislative and other measures as may be necessary to establish as criminal offences under its domestic law, when committed intentionally, the access to the whole or any part of a computer system without right. A Party may require that the offence be committed by infringing security measures, with the intent of obtaining computer data or other dishonest intent, or in relation to a computer system that is connected to another computer system.

Article 3—Illegal interception

Each Party shall adopt such legislative and other measures as may be necessary to establish as criminal offences under its domestic law, when committed intentionally, the interception without right, made by technical means, of non-public transmissions of computer data to, from or within a computer system, including electromagnetic emissions from a computer system carrying such computer data. A Party may require that the offence be committed with dishonest intent, or in relation to a computer system that is connected to another computer system.

Article 4—Data interference

1   Each Party shall adopt such legislative and other measures as may be necessary to establish as criminal offences under its domestic law, when committed intentionally, the damaging, deletion, deterioration, alteration or suppression of computer data without right.

2   A Party may reserve the right to require that the conduct described in paragraph 1 result in serious harm.

Article 5—System interference

Each Party shall adopt such legislative and other measures as may be necessary to establish as criminal offences under its domestic law, when committed intentionally, the serious hindering without right of the functioning of a computer system by inputting, transmitting, damaging, deleting, deteriorating, altering or suppressing computer data.

Article 6—Misuse of devices

1. Each Party shall adopt such legislative and other measures as may be necessary to establish as criminal offences under its domestic law, when committed intentionally and without right:

    a. the production, sale, procurement for use, import, distribution or otherwise making available:

        i. a device, including a computer program, designed or adapted primarily for the purpose of committing any of the offences established in accordance with the above Articles 2 through 5;

        ii. a computer password, access code, or similar data by which the whole or any part of a computer system is capable of being accessed, with intent that it be used for the purpose of committing any of the offences established in Articles 2 through 5; and

    b. the possession of an item referred to in paragraphs a.i or ii above, with intent that it be used for the purpose of committing any of the offences established in Articles 2 through 5. A Party may require by law that a number of such items be possessed before criminal liability attaches.

2. This article shall not be interpreted as imposing criminal liability where the production, sale, procurement for use, import, distribution or otherwise making available or possession referred to in paragraph 1 of this article is not for the purpose of committing an offence established in accordance with Articles 2 through 5 of this Convention, such as for the authorised testing or protection of a computer system.

3. Each Party may reserve the right not to apply paragraph 1 of this article, provided that the reservation does not concern the sale, distribution or otherwise making available of the items referred to in paragraph 1 a.ii. of this article.

Title 2—Computer-related offences

Article 7—Computer-related forgery

Each Party shall adopt such legislative and other measures as may be necessary to establish as criminal offences under its domestic law, when committed intentionally and without right, the input, alteration, deletion, or suppression of computer data, resulting in inauthentic data with the intent that it be considered or acted upon for legal purposes as if it were authentic, regardless whether or not the data is directly readable and intelligible. A Party may require an intent to defraud, or similar dishonest intent, before criminal liability attaches.

Article 8—Computer-related fraud

Each Party shall adopt such legislative and other measures as may be necessary to establish as criminal offences under its domestic law, when committed intentionally and without right, the causing of a loss of property to another person by:

    a. any input, alteration, deletion or suppression of computer data;

    b. any interference with the functioning of a computer system, with fraudulent or dishonest intent of procuring, without right, an economic benefit for oneself or for another person.

Title 3—Content-related offences

Article 9—Offences related to child pornography

1. Each Party shall adopt such legislative and other measures as may be necessary to establish as criminal offences under its domestic law, when committed intentionally and without right, the following conduct:

    a. producing child pornography for the purpose of its distribution through a computer system;

    b. offering or making available child pornography through a computer system;

    c. distributing or transmitting child pornography through a computer system;

    d. procuring child pornography through a computer system for oneself or for another person;

    e. possessing child pornography in a computer system or on a computer-data storage medium.

2. For the purpose of paragraph 1 above, the term "child pornography" shall include pornographic material that visually depicts:

    a. a minor engaged in sexually explicit conduct;

    b. a person appearing to be a minor engaged in sexually explicit conduct;

    c. realistic images representing a minor engaged in sexually explicit conduct.

3. For the purpose of paragraph 2 above, the term "minor" shall include all persons under 18 years of age. A Party may, however, require a lower age-limit, which shall be not less than 16 years.

4. Each Party may reserve the right not to apply, in whole or in part, paragraphs 1, sub-paragraphs d. and e, and 2, sub-paragraphs b. and c.

Title 4—Offences related to infringements of copyright and related rights

Article 10—Offences related to infringements of copyright and related rights

1. Each Party shall adopt such legislative and other measures as may be necessary to establish as criminal offences under its domestic law the infringement of copyright, as defined under the law of that Party, pursuant to the obligations it has undertaken under the Paris Act of 24 July 1971 revising the Bern Convention for the Protection of Literary and Artistic Works, the Agreement on Trade-Related Aspects of Intellectual Property Rights and the WIPO Copyright Treaty, with the exception of any moral rights conferred by such conventions, where such acts are committed wilfully, on a commercial scale and by means of a computer system.

2. Each Party shall adopt such legislative and other measures as may be necessary to establish as criminal offences under its domestic law the infringement of related rights, as defined under the law of that Party, pursuant to the obligations it has undertaken under the International Convention for the Protection of Performers, Producers of Phonograms and Broadcasting Organisations (Rome Convention), the Agreement on Trade-Related Aspects of Intellectual Property Rights and the WIPO Performances and Phonograms Treaty, with the exception of any moral rights conferred by such conventions, where such acts are committed wilfully, on a commercial scale and by means of a computer system.

3. A Party may reserve the right not to impose criminal liability under paragraphs 1 and 2 of this article in limited circumstances, provided that other effective remedies are available and that such reservation does not derogate from the Party's international obligations set forth in the international instruments referred to in paragraphs 1 and 2 of this article.

Title 5—Ancillary liability and sanctions

Article 11—Attempt and aiding or abetting

1. Each Party shall adopt such legislative and other measures as may be necessary to establish as criminal offences under its domestic law, when committed intentionally, aiding or abetting the commission of any of the offences established in accordance with Articles 2 through 10 of the present Convention with intent that such offence be committed.

2. Each Party shall adopt such legislative and other measures as may be necessary to establish as criminal offences under its domestic law, when committed intentionally, an attempt to commit any of the offences established in accordance with Articles 3 through 5, 7, 8, and 9.1.a and c. of this Convention.

3. Each Party may reserve the right not to apply, in whole or in part, paragraph 2 of this article.

Article 12—Corporate liability

1. Each Party shall adopt such legislative and other measures as may be necessary to ensure that legal persons can be held liable for a criminal offence established in accordance with this Convention, committed for their benefit by any natural person, acting either individually or as part of an organ of the legal person, who has a leading position within it, based on:

   a. a power of representation of the legal person;

   b. an authority to take decisions on behalf of the legal person;

   c. an authority to exercise control within the legal person.

2. In addition to the cases already provided for in paragraph 1 of this article, each Party shall take the measures necessary to ensure that a legal person can be held liable where the lack of supervision or control by a natural person referred to in paragraph 1 has made possible the commission of a criminal offence established in accordance with this Convention for the benefit of that legal person by a natural person acting under its authority.

3. Subject to the legal principles of the Party, the liability of a legal person may be criminal, civil or administrative.

4. Such liability shall be without prejudice to the criminal liability of the natural persons who have committed the offence.

Article 13—Sanctions and measures

1. Each Party shall adopt such legislative and other measures as may be necessary to ensure that the criminal offences established in accordance with Articles 2 through 11 are punishable by effective, proportionate and dissuasive sanctions, which include deprivation of liberty.

2. Each Party shall ensure that legal persons held liable in accordance with Article 12 shall be subject to effective, proportionate and dissuasive criminal or non-criminal sanctions or measures, including monetary sanctions.

Section 2—Procedural law

Title 1—Common provisions

Article 14—Scope of procedural provisions

1. Each Party shall adopt such legislative and other measures as may be necessary to establish the powers and procedures provided for in this section for the purpose of specific criminal investigations or proceedings.

2. Except as specifically provided otherwise in Article 21, each Party shall apply the powers and procedures referred to in paragraph 1 of this article to:

   a. the criminal offences established in accordance with Articles 2 through 11 of this Convention;

   b. other criminal offences committed by means of a computer system; and

   c. the collection of evidence in electronic form of a criminal offence.

3. a. Each Party may reserve the right to apply the measures referred to in Article 20 only to offences or categories of offences specified in the reservation, provided that the range of such offences or categories of offences is not more restricted than the range of offences to which it applies the measures referred to in Article 21. Each Party shall consider restricting such a reservation to enable the broadest application of the measure referred to in Article 20.

   b. Where a Party, due to limitations in its legislation in force at the time of the adoption of the present Convention, is not able to apply the measures referred to in Articles 20 and 21 to communications being transmitted within a computer system of a service provider, which system:

   i. is being operated for the benefit of a closed group of users, and

   ii. does not employ public communications networks and is not connected with another computer system, whether public or private,

   that Party may reserve the right not to apply these measures to such communications. Each Party shall consider restricting such a reservation to enable the broadest application of the measures referred to in Articles 20 and 21.

Article 15—Conditions and safeguards

1. Each Party shall ensure that the establishment, implementation and application of the powers and procedures provided for in this Section are subject to conditions and safeguards provided for under its domestic law, which shall provide for the adequate protection of human rights and liberties, including rights arising pursuant to obligations it has undertaken under the 1950 Council of Europe Convention for the Protection of Human Rights and Fundamental Freedoms, the 1966 United Nations International Covenant on Civil and Political Rights, and other applicable international human rights instruments, and which shall incorporate the principle of proportionality.

2. Such conditions and safeguards shall, as appropriate in view of the nature of the procedure or power concerned, inter alia, include judicial or other independent supervision, grounds justifying application, and limitation of the scope and the duration of such power or procedure.

3. To the extent that it is consistent with the public interest, in particular the sound administration of justice, each Party shall consider the impact of the powers and procedures in this section upon the rights, responsibilities and legitimate interests of third parties.

Title 2—Expedited preservation of stored computer data

Article 16—Expedited preservation of stored computer data

1. Each Party shall adopt such legislative and other measures as may be necessary to enable its competent authorities to order or similarly obtain the expeditious preservation of specified computer data, including traffic data, that has been stored by means of a computer system, in particular where there are grounds to believe that the computer data is particularly vulnerable to loss or modification.

2. Where a Party gives effect to paragraph 1 above by means of an order to a person to preserve specified stored computer data in the person's possession or control, the Party shall adopt such legislative and other measures as may be necessary to oblige that person to preserve and maintain the integrity of that computer data for a period of time as long as necessary, up to a maximum of ninety days, to enable the competent authorities to seek its disclosure. A Party may provide for such an order to be subsequently renewed.

3. Each Party shall adopt such legislative and other measures as may be necessary to oblige the custodian or other person who is to preserve the computer data to keep confidential the undertaking of such procedures for the period of time provided for by its domestic law.

4. The powers and procedures referred to in this article shall be subject to Articles 14 and 15.

Article 17—Expedited preservation and partial disclosure of traffic data

1. Each Party shall adopt, in respect of traffic data that is to be preserved under Article 16, such legislative and other measures as may be necessary to:

   a. ensure that such expeditious preservation of traffic data is available regardless of whether one or more service providers were involved in the transmission of that communication; and

   b. ensure the expeditious disclosure to the Party's competent authority, or a person designated by that authority, of a sufficient amount of traffic data to enable the Party to identify the service providers and the path through which the communication was transmitted.

2. The powers and procedures referred to in this article shall be subject to Articles 14 and 15.

Title 3—Production order

Article 18—Production order

1. Each Party shall adopt such legislative and other measures as may be necessary to empower its competent authorities to order:

   a. a person in its territory to submit specified computer data in that person's possession or control, which is stored in a computer system or a computer-data storage medium; and

b. a service provider offering its services in the territory of the Party to submit subscriber information relating to such services in that service provider's possession or control.

2. The powers and procedures referred to in this article shall be subject to Articles 14 and 15.

3. For the purpose of this article, the term "subscriber information" means any information contained in the form of computer data or any other form that is held by a service provider, relating to subscribers of its services other than traffic or content data and by which can be established:

a. the type of communication service used, the technical provisions taken thereto and the period of service;

b. the subscriber's identity, postal or geographic address, telephone and other access number, billing and payment information, available on the basis of the service agreement or arrangement;

c. any other information on the site of the installation of communication equipment, available on the basis of the service agreement or arrangement.

Title 4—Search and seizure of stored computer data

Article 19—Search and seizure of stored computer data

1. Each Party shall adopt such legislative and other measures as may be necessary to empower its competent authorities to search or similarly access:

a. a computer system or part of it and computer data stored therein; and

b. a computer-data storage medium in which computer data may be stored

in its territory.

2. Each Party shall adopt such legislative and other measures as may be necessary to ensure that where its authorities search or similarly access a specific computer system or part of it, pursuant to paragraph 1.a, and have grounds to believe that the data sought is stored in another computer system or part of it in its territory, and such data is lawfully accessible from or available to the initial system, the authorities shall be able to expeditiously extend the search or similar accessing to the other system.

3. Each Party shall adopt such legislative and other measures as may be necessary to empower its competent authorities to seize or similarly secure computer data accessed according to paragraphs 1 or 2. These measures shall include the power to:

a. seize or similarly secure a computer system or part of it or a computer-data storage medium;

b. make and retain a copy of those computer data;

c. maintain the integrity of the relevant stored computer data;

d. render inaccessible or remove those computer data in the accessed computer system.

4. Each Party shall adopt such legislative and other measures as may be necessary to empower its competent authorities to order any person who has knowledge about the functioning of the

computer system or measures applied to protect the computer data therein to provide, as is reasonable, the necessary information, to enable the undertaking of the measures referred to in paragraphs 1 and 2.

5. The powers and procedures referred to in this article shall be subject to Articles 14 and 15.

Title 5—Real-time collection of computer data

Article 20—Real-time collection of traffic data

1. Each Party shall adopt such legislative and other measures as may be necessary to empower its competent authorities to:

    a. collect or record through the application of technical means on the territory of that Party, and

    b. compel a service provider, within its existing technical capability:

        i.   to collect or record through the application of technical means on the territory of that Party; or

        ii. to co-operate and assist the competent authorities in the collection or recording of,

        traffic data, in real-time, associated with specified communications in its territory transmitted by means of a computer system.

2. Where a Party, due to the established principles of its domestic legal system, cannot adopt the measures referred to in paragraph 1.a, it may instead adopt legislative and other measures as may be necessary to ensure the real-time collection or recording of traffic data associated with specified communications transmitted in its territory, through the application of technical means on that territory.

3. Each Party shall adopt such legislative and other measures as may be necessary to oblige a service provider to keep confidential the fact of the execution of any power provided for in this article and any information relating to it.

4. The powers and procedures referred to in this article shall be subject to Articles 14 and 15.

Article 21—Interception of content data

1. Each Party shall adopt such legislative and other measures as may be necessary, in relation to a range of serious offences to be determined by domestic law, to empower its competent authorities to:

    a. collect or record through the application of technical means on the territory of that Party, and

    b. compel a service provider, within its existing technical capability:

        i.   to collect or record through the application of technical means on the territory of that Party, or

        ii. to co-operate and assist the competent authorities in the collection or recording of,

        content data, in real-time, of specified communications in its territory transmitted by means of a computer system.

2. Where a Party, due to the established principles of its domestic legal system, cannot adopt the measures referred to in paragraph 1.a, it may instead adopt legislative and other measures as may be necessary to ensure the real-time collection or recording of content data on specified communications in its territory through the application of technical means on that territory.

3. Each Party shall adopt such legislative and other measures as may be necessary to oblige a service provider to keep confidential the fact of the execution of any power provided for in this article and any information relating to it.

4. The powers and procedures referred to in this article shall be subject to Articles 14 and 15.

Section 3—Jurisdiction

Article 22—Jurisdiction

1. Each Party shall adopt such legislative and other measures as may be necessary to establish jurisdiction over any offence established in accordance with Articles 2 through 11 of this Convention, when the offence is committed:

   a. in its territory; or

   b. on board a ship flying the flag of that Party; or

   c. on board an aircraft registered under the laws of that Party; or

   d. by one of its nationals, if the offence is punishable under criminal law where it was committed or if the offence is committed outside the territorial jurisdiction of any State.

2. Each Party may reserve the right not to apply or to apply only in specific cases or conditions the jurisdiction rules laid down in paragraphs 1.b through 1.d of this article or any part thereof.

3. Each Party shall adopt such measures as may be necessary to establish jurisdiction over the offences referred to in Article 24, paragraph 1, of this Convention, in cases where an alleged offender is present in its territory and it does not extradite him or her to another Party, solely on the basis of his or her nationality, after a request for extradition.

4. This Convention does not exclude any criminal jurisdiction exercised by a Party in accordance with its domestic law.

5. When more than one Party claims jurisdiction over an alleged offence established in accordance with this Convention, the Parties involved shall, where appropriate, consult with a view to determining the most appropriate jurisdiction for prosecution.

Chapter III—International co-operation

Section 1—General principles

Title 1—General principles relating to international co-operation

Article 23—General principles relating to international co-operation

The Parties shall co-operate with each other, in accordance with the provisions of this chapter, and through the application of relevant international instruments on international co-operation in criminal matters, arrangements agreed on the basis of uniform or reciprocal legislation, and domestic laws, to the widest extent possible for the purposes of investigations or proceedings concerning criminal offences related to computer systems and data, or for the collection of evidence in electronic form of a criminal offence.

Title 2—Principles relating to extradition

Article 24—Extradition

1.   a. This article applies to extradition between Parties for the criminal offences established in accordance with Articles 2 through 11 of this Convention, provided that they are punishable under the laws of both Parties concerned by deprivation of liberty for a maximum period of at least one year, or by a more severe penalty.

     b. Where a different minimum penalty is to be applied under an arrangement agreed on the basis of uniform or reciprocal legislation or an extradition treaty, including the European Convention on Extradition (ETS No. 24), applicable between two or more parties, the minimum penalty provided for under such arrangement or treaty shall apply.

2.   The criminal offences described in paragraph 1 of this article shall be deemed to be included as extraditable offences in any extradition treaty existing between or among the Parties. The Parties undertake to include such offences as extraditable offences in any extradition treaty to be concluded between or among them.

3.   If a Party that makes extradition conditional on the existence of a treaty receives a request for extradition from another Party with which it does not have an extradition treaty, it may consider this Convention as the legal basis for extradition with respect to any criminal offence referred to in paragraph 1 of this article.

4.   Parties that do not make extradition conditional on the existence of a treaty shall recognise the criminal offences referred to in paragraph 1 of this article as extraditable offences between themselves.

5.   Extradition shall be subject to the conditions provided for by the law of the requested Party or by applicable extradition treaties, including the grounds on which the requested Party may refuse extradition.

6.   If extradition for a criminal offence referred to in paragraph 1 of this article is refused solely on the basis of the nationality of the person sought, or because the requested Party deems that it has jurisdiction over the offence, the requested Party shall submit the case at the request of the requesting Party to its competent authorities for the purpose of prosecution and shall report the final outcome to the requesting Party in due course. Those authorities shall take their decision and conduct their investigations and proceedings in the same manner as for any other offence of a comparable nature under the law of that Party.

7.   a. Each Party shall, at the time of signature or when depositing its instrument of ratification, acceptance, approval or accession, communicate to the Secretary General of the Council of Europe the name and address of each authority responsible for making or receiving requests for extradition or provisional arrest in the absence of a treaty.

     b. The Secretary General of the Council of Europe shall set up and keep updated a register of authorities so designated by the Parties. Each Party shall ensure that the details held on the register are correct at all times.

Title 3—General principles relating to mutual assistance

Article 25—General principles relating to mutual assistance

1. The Parties shall afford one another mutual assistance to the widest extent possible for the purpose of investigations or proceedings concerning criminal offences related to computer systems and data, or for the collection of evidence in electronic form of a criminal offence.

2. Each Party shall also adopt such legislative and other measures as may be necessary to carry out the obligations set forth in Articles 27 through 35.

3. Each Party may, in urgent circumstances, make requests for mutual assistance or communications related thereto by expedited means of communication, including fax or e-mail, to the extent that such means provide appropriate levels of security and authentication (including the use of encryption, where necessary), with formal confirmation to follow, where required by the requested Party. The requested Party shall accept and respond to the request by any such expedited means of communication.

4. Except as otherwise specifically provided in articles in this chapter, mutual assistance shall be subject to the conditions provided for by the law of the requested Party or by applicable mutual assistance treaties, including the grounds on which the requested Party may refuse co-operation. The requested Party shall not exercise the right to refuse mutual assistance in relation to the offences referred to in Articles 2 through 11 solely on the ground that the request concerns an offence which it considers a fiscal offence.

5. Where, in accordance with the provisions of this chapter, the requested Party is permitted to make mutual assistance conditional upon the existence of dual criminality, that condition shall be deemed fulfilled, irrespective of whether its laws place the offence within the same category of offence or denominate the offence by the same terminology as the requesting Party, if the conduct underlying the offence for which assistance is sought is a criminal offence under its laws.

Article 26—Spontaneous information

1. A Party may, within the limits of its domestic law and without prior request, forward to another Party information obtained within the framework of its own investigations when it considers that the disclosure of such information might assist the receiving Party in initiating or carrying out investigations or proceedings concerning criminal offences established in accordance with this Convention or might lead to a request for co-operation by that Party under this chapter.

2. Prior to providing such information, the providing Party may request that it be kept confidential or only used subject to conditions. If the receiving Party cannot comply with such request, it shall notify the providing Party, which shall then determine whether the information should nevertheless be provided. If the receiving Party accepts the information subject to the conditions, it shall be bound by them.

Title 4—Procedures pertaining to mutual assistance requests in the absence of applicable international agreements

Article 27—Procedures pertaining to mutual assistance requests in the absence of applicable international agreements

1. Where there is no mutual assistance treaty or arrangement on the basis of uniform or reciprocal legislation in force between the requesting and requested Parties, the provisions of paragraphs 2 through 9 of this article shall apply. The provisions of this article shall not apply where such treaty, arrangement or legislation exists, unless the Parties concerned agree to apply any or all of the remainder of this article in lieu thereof.

2. a. Each Party shall designate a central authority or authorities responsible for sending and answering requests for mutual assistance, the execution of such requests or their transmission to the authorities competent for their execution.

    b. The central authorities shall communicate directly with each other;

    c. Each Party shall, at the time of signature or when depositing its instrument of ratification, acceptance, approval or accession, communicate to the Secretary General of the Council of Europe the names and addresses of the authorities designated in pursuance of this paragraph;

    d. The Secretary General of the Council of Europe shall set up and keep updated a register of central authorities designated by the Parties. Each Party shall ensure that the details held on the register are correct at all times.

3. Mutual assistance requests under this article shall be executed in accordance with the procedures specified by the requesting Party, except where incompatible with the law of the requested Party.

4. The requested Party may, in addition to the grounds for refusal established in Article 25, paragraph 4, refuse assistance if:

    a. the request concerns an offence which the requested Party considers a political offence or an offence connected with a political offence, or

    b. it considers that execution of the request is likely to prejudice its sovereignty, security, *ordre public* or other essential interests.

5. The requested Party may postpone action on a request if such action would prejudice criminal investigations or proceedings conducted by its authorities.

6. Before refusing or postponing assistance, the requested Party shall, where appropriate after having consulted with the requesting Party, consider whether the request may be granted partially or subject to such conditions, as it deems necessary.

7. The requested Party shall promptly inform the requesting Party of the outcome of the execution of a request for assistance. Reasons shall be given for any refusal or postponement of the request. The requested Party shall also inform the requesting Party of any reasons that render impossible the execution of the request or are likely to delay it significantly.

8. The requesting Party may request that the requested Party keep confidential the fact of any request made under this chapter as well as its subject, except to the extent necessary for its execution. If the requested Party cannot comply with the request for confidentiality, it shall promptly inform the requesting Party, which shall then determine whether the request should nevertheless be executed.

9. a. In the event of urgency, requests for mutual assistance or communications related thereto may be sent directly by judicial authorities of the requesting Party to such authorities of the requested Party. In any such cases, a copy shall be sent at the same time to the central authority of the requested Party through the central authority of the requesting Party.

b. Any request or communication under this paragraph may be made through the International Criminal Police Organisation (Interpol).

c. Where a request is made pursuant to sub-paragraph a. of this article and the authority is not competent to deal with the request, it shall refer the request to the competent national authority and inform directly the requesting Party that it has done so.

d. Requests or communications made under this paragraph that do not involve coercive action may be directly transmitted by the competent authorities of the requesting Party to the competent authorities of the requested Party.

e. Each Party may, at the time of signature or when depositing its instrument of ratification, acceptance, approval or accession, inform the Secretary General of the Council of Europe that, for reasons of efficiency, requests made under this paragraph are to be addressed to its central authority.

Article 28—Confidentiality and limitation on use

1. When there is no mutual assistance treaty or arrangement on the basis of uniform or reciprocal legislation in force between the requesting and the requested Parties, the provisions of this article shall apply. The provisions of this article shall not apply where such treaty, arrangement or legislation exists, unless the Parties concerned agree to apply any or all of the remainder of this article in lieu thereof.

2. The requested Party may make the supply of information or material in response to a request dependent on the condition that it is:

    a. kept confidential where the request for mutual legal assistance could not be complied with in the absence of such condition, or

    b. not used for investigations or proceedings other than those stated in the request.

3. If the requesting Party cannot comply with a condition referred to in paragraph 2, it shall promptly inform the other Party, which shall then determine whether the information should nevertheless be provided. When the requesting Party accepts the condition, it shall be bound by it.

4. Any Party that supplies information or material subject to a condition referred to in paragraph 2 may require the other Party to explain, in relation to that condition, the use made of such information or material.

Section 2—Specific provisions

Title 1—Mutual assistance regarding provisional measures

Article 29—Expedited preservation of stored computer data

1. A Party may request another Party to order or otherwise obtain the expeditious preservation of data stored by means of a computer system, located within the territory of that other Party and in

respect of which the requesting Party intends to submit a request for mutual assistance for the search or similar access, seizure or similar securing, or disclosure of the data.

2.   A request for preservation made under paragraph 1 shall specify:

  a.   the authority seeking the preservation;

  b.   the offence that is the subject of a criminal investigation or proceedings and a brief summary of the related facts;

  c.   the stored computer data to be preserved and its relationship to the offence;

  d.   any available information identifying the custodian of the stored computer data or the location of the computer system;

  e.   the necessity of the preservation; and

  f.   that the Party intends to submit a request for mutual assistance for the search or similar access, seizure or similar securing, or disclosure of the stored computer data.

3.   Upon receiving the request from another Party, the requested Party shall take all appropriate measures to preserve expeditiously the specified data in accordance with its domestic law. For the purposes of responding to a request, dual criminality shall not be required as a condition to providing such preservation.

4.   A Party that requires dual criminality as a condition for responding to a request for mutual assistance for the search or similar access, seizure or similar securing, or disclosure of stored data may, in respect of offences other than those established in accordance with Articles 2 through 11 of this Convention, reserve the right to refuse the request for preservation under this article in cases where it has reasons to believe that at the time of disclosure the condition of dual criminality cannot be fulfilled.

5.   In addition, a request for preservation may only be refused if:

  a.   the request concerns an offence which the requested Party considers a political offence or an offence connected with a political offence, or

  b.   the requested Party considers that execution of the request is likely to prejudice its sovereignty, security, *ordre public* or other essential interests.

6.   Where the requested Party believes that preservation will not ensure the future availability of the data or will threaten the confidentiality of or otherwise prejudice the requesting Party's investigation, it shall promptly so inform the requesting Party, which shall then determine whether the request should nevertheless be executed.

7.   Any preservation effected in response to the request referred to in paragraph 1 shall be for a period not less than sixty days, in order to enable the requesting Party to submit a request for the search or similar access, seizure or similar securing, or disclosure of the data. Following the receipt of such a request, the data shall continue to be preserved pending a decision on that request.

Article 30—Expedited disclosure of preserved traffic data

1. Where, in the course of the execution of a request made pursuant to Article 29 to preserve traffic data concerning a specific communication, the requested Party discovers that a service provider in another State was involved in the transmission of the communication, the requested Party shall expeditiously disclose to the requesting Party a sufficient amount of traffic data to identify that service provider and the path through which the communication was transmitted.

2. Disclosure of traffic data under paragraph 1 may only be withheld if:

   a. the request concerns an offence which the requested Party considers a political offence or an offence connected with a political offence; or

   b. the requested Party considers that execution of the request is likely to prejudice its sovereignty, security, *ordre public* or other essential interests.

Title 2—Mutual assistance regarding investigative powers

Article 31—Mutual assistance regarding accessing of stored computer data

1. A Party may request another Party to search or similarly access, seize or similarly secure, and disclose data stored by means of a computer system located within the territory of the requested Party, including data that has been preserved pursuant to Article 29.

2. The requested Party shall respond to the request through the application of international instruments, arrangements and laws referred to in Article 23, and in accordance with other relevant provisions of this chapter.

3. The request shall be responded to on an expedited basis where:

   a. there are grounds to believe that relevant data is particularly vulnerable to loss or modification; or

   b. the instruments, arrangements and laws referred to in paragraph 2 otherwise provide for expedited co-operation.

Article 32—Trans-border access to stored computer data with consent or where publicly available

A Party may, without the authorisation of another Party:

   a. access publicly available (open source) stored computer data, regardless of where the data is located geographically; or

   b. access or receive, through a computer system in its territory, stored computer data located in another Party, if the Party obtains the lawful and voluntary consent of the person who has the lawful authority to disclose the data to the Party through that computer system.

Article 33—Mutual assistance in the real-time collection of traffic data

1. The Parties shall provide mutual assistance to each other in the real-time collection of traffic data associated with specified communications in their territory transmitted by means of a computer system. Subject to the provisions of paragraph 2, this assistance shall be governed by the conditions and procedures provided for under domestic law.

2. Each Party shall provide such assistance at least with respect to criminal offences for which real-time collection of traffic data would be available in a similar domestic case.

Article 34—Mutual assistance regarding the interception of content data

The Parties shall provide mutual assistance to each other in the real-time collection or recording of content data of specified communications transmitted by means of a computer system to the extent permitted under their applicable treaties and domestic laws.

Title 3—24/7 Network

Article 35—24/7 Network

1. Each Party shall designate a point of contact available on a twenty-four hour, seven-day-a-week basis, in order to ensure the provision of immediate assistance for the purpose of investigations or proceedings concerning criminal offences related to computer systems and data, or for the collection of evidence in electronic form of a criminal offence. Such assistance shall include facilitating, or, if permitted by its domestic law and practice, directly carrying out the following measures:

    a. the provision of technical advice;

    b. the preservation of data pursuant to Articles 29 and 30;

    c. the collection of evidence, the provision of legal information, and locating of suspects.

2. a. A Party's point of contact shall have the capacity to carry out communications with the point of contact of another Party on an expedited basis.

    b. If the point of contact designated by a Party is not part of that Party's authority or authorities responsible for international mutual assistance or extradition, the point of contact shall ensure that it is able to co-ordinate with such authority or authorities on an expedited basis.

3. Each Party shall ensure that trained and equipped personnel are available, in order to facilitate the operation of the network.

Chapter IV—Final provisions

Article 36—Signature and entry into force

1. This Convention shall be open for signature by the member States of the Council of Europe and by non-member States which have participated in its elaboration.

2. This Convention is subject to ratification, acceptance or approval. Instruments of ratification, acceptance or approval shall be deposited with the Secretary General of the Council of Europe.

3. This Convention shall enter into force on the first day of the month following the expiration of a period of three months after the date on which five States, including at least three member States of the Council of Europe, have expressed their consent to be bound by the Convention in accordance with the provisions of paragraphs 1 and 2.

4. In respect of any signatory State which subsequently expresses its consent to be bound by it, the Convention shall enter into force on the first day of the month following the expiration of a

period of three months after the date of the expression of its consent to be bound by the Convention in accordance with the provisions of paragraphs 1 and 2.

Article 37—Accession to the Convention

1. After the entry into force of this Convention, the Committee of Ministers of the Council of Europe, after consulting with and obtaining the unanimous consent of the Contracting States to the Convention, may invite any State which is not a member of the Council and which has not participated in its elaboration to accede to this Convention. The decision shall be taken by the majority provided for in Article 20.d. of the Statute of the Council of Europe and by the unanimous vote of the representatives of the Contracting States entitled to sit on the Committee of Ministers.

2. In respect of any State acceding to the Convention under paragraph 1 above, the Convention shall enter into force on the first day of the month following the expiration of a period of three months after the date of deposit of the instrument of accession with the Secretary General of the Council of Europe.

Article 38—Territorial application

1. Any State may, at the time of signature or when depositing its instrument of ratification, acceptance, approval or accession, specify the territory or territories to which this Convention shall apply.

2. Any State may, at any later date, by a declaration addressed to the Secretary General of the Council of Europe, extend the application of this Convention to any other territory specified in the declaration. In respect of such territory the Convention shall enter into force on the first day of the month following the expiration of a period of three months after the date of receipt of the declaration by the Secretary General.

3. Any declaration made under the two preceding paragraphs may, in respect of any territory specified in such declaration, be withdrawn by a notification addressed to the Secretary General of the Council of Europe. The withdrawal shall become effective on the first day of the month following the expiration of a period of three months after the date of receipt of such notification by the Secretary General.

Article 39—Effects of the Convention

1. The purpose of the present Convention is to supplement applicable multilateral or bilateral treaties or arrangements as between the Parties, including the provisions of:

   - the European Convention on Extradition, opened for signature in Paris, on 13 December 1957 (ETS No. 24);

   - the European Convention on Mutual Assistance in Criminal Matters, opened for signature in Strasbourg, on 20 April 1959 (ETS No. 30);

   - the Additional Protocol to the European Convention on Mutual Assistance in Criminal Matters, opened for signature in Strasbourg, on 17 March 1978 (ETS No. 99).

2. If two or more Parties have already concluded an agreement or treaty on the matters dealt with in this Convention or have otherwise established their relations on such matters, or should they in future do so, they shall also be entitled to apply that agreement or treaty or to regulate those

relations accordingly. However, where Parties establish their relations in respect of the matters dealt with in the present Convention other than as regulated therein, they shall do so in a manner that is not inconsistent with the Convention's objectives and principles.

3. Nothing in this Convention shall affect other rights, restrictions, obligations and responsibilities of a Party.

Article 40—Declarations

By a written notification addressed to the Secretary General of the Council of Europe, any State may, at the time of signature or when depositing its instrument of ratification, acceptance, approval or accession, declare that it avails itself of the possibility of requiring additional elements as provided for under Articles 2, 3, 6 paragraph 1.b, 7, 9 paragraph 3, and 27, paragraph 9.e.

Article 41—Federal clause

1. A federal State may reserve the right to assume obligations under Chapter II of this Convention consistent with its fundamental principles governing the relationship between its central government and constituent States or other similar territorial entities provided that it is still able to co-operate under Chapter III.

2. When making a reservation under paragraph 1, a federal State may not apply the terms of such reservation to exclude or substantially diminish its obligations to provide for measures set forth in Chapter II. Overall, it shall provide for a broad and effective law enforcement capability with respect to those measures.

3. With regard to the provisions of this Convention, the application of which comes under the jurisdiction of constituent States or other similar territorial entities, that are not obliged by the constitutional system of the federation to take legislative measures, the federal government shall inform the competent authorities of such States of the said provisions with its favourable opinion, encouraging them to take appropriate action to give them effect.

Article 42—Reservations

By a written notification addressed to the Secretary General of the Council of Europe, any State may, at the time of signature or when depositing its instrument of ratification, acceptance, approval or accession, declare that it avails itself of the reservation(s) provided for in Article 4, paragraph 2, Article 6, paragraph 3, Article 9, paragraph 4, Article 10, paragraph 3, Article 11, paragraph 3, Article 14, paragraph 3, Article 22, paragraph 2, Article 29, paragraph 4, and Article 41, paragraph 1. No other reservation may be made.

Article 43—Status and withdrawal of reservations

1. A Party that has made a reservation in accordance with Article 42 may wholly or partially withdraw it by means of a notification addressed to the Secretary General of the Council of Europe. Such withdrawal shall take effect on the date of receipt of such notification by the Secretary General. If the notification states that the withdrawal of a reservation is to take effect on a date specified therein, and such date is later than the date on which the notification is received by the Secretary General, the withdrawal shall take effect on such a later date.

2. A Party that has made a reservation as referred to in Article 42 shall withdraw such reservation, in whole or in part, as soon as circumstances so permit.

3. The Secretary General of the Council of Europe may periodically enquire with Parties that have made one or more reservations as referred to in Article 42 as to the prospects for withdrawing such reservation(s).

Article 44—Amendments

1. Amendments to this Convention may be proposed by any Party, and shall be communicated by the Secretary General of the Council of Europe to the member States of the Council of Europe, to the non-member States which have participated in the elaboration of this Convention as well as to any State which has acceded to, or has been invited to accede to, this Convention in accordance with the provisions of Article 37.

2. Any amendment proposed by a Party shall be communicated to the European Committee on Crime Problems (CDPC), which shall submit to the Committee of Ministers its opinion on that proposed amendment.

3. The Committee of Ministers shall consider the proposed amendment and the opinion submitted by the CDPC and, following consultation with the non-member States Parties to this Convention, may adopt the amendment.

4. The text of any amendment adopted by the Committee of Ministers in accordance with paragraph 3 of this article shall be forwarded to the Parties for acceptance.

5. Any amendment adopted in accordance with paragraph 3 of this article shall come into force on the thirtieth day after all Parties have informed the Secretary General of their acceptance thereof.

Article 45—Settlement of disputes

1. The European Committee on Crime Problems (CDPC) shall be kept informed regarding the interpretation and application of this Convention.

2. In case of a dispute between Parties as to the interpretation or application of this Convention, they shall seek a settlement of the dispute through negotiation or any other peaceful means of their choice, including submission of the dispute to the CDPC, to an arbitral tribunal whose decisions shall be binding upon the Parties, or to the International Court of Justice, as agreed upon by the Parties concerned.

Article 46—Consultations of the Parties

1. The Parties shall, as appropriate, consult periodically with a view to facilitating:

   a. the effective use and implementation of this Convention, including the identification of any problems thereof, as well as the effects of any declaration or reservation made under this Convention;

   b. the exchange of information on significant legal, policy or technological developments pertaining to cybercrime and the collection of evidence in electronic form;

   c. consideration of possible supplementation or amendment of the Convention.

2. The European Committee on Crime Problems (CDPC) shall be kept periodically informed regarding the result of consultations referred to in paragraph 1.

3. The CDPC shall, as appropriate, facilitate the consultations referred to in paragraph 1 and take the measures necessary to assist the Parties in their efforts to supplement or amend the Convention. At the latest three years after the present Convention enters into force, the European Committee on Crime Problems (CDPC) shall, in co-operation with the Parties, conduct a review of all of the Convention's provisions and, if necessary, recommend any appropriate amendments.

4. Except where assumed by the Council of Europe, expenses incurred in carrying out the provisions of paragraph 1 shall be borne by the Parties in the manner to be determined by them.

5. The Parties shall be assisted by the Secretariat of the Council of Europe in carrying out their functions pursuant to this article.

Article 47—Denunciation

1. Any Party may, at any time, denounce this Convention by means of a notification addressed to the Secretary General of the Council of Europe.

2. Such denunciation shall become effective on the first day of the month following the expiration of a period of three months after the date of receipt of the notification by the Secretary General.

Article 48—Notification

The Secretary General of the Council of Europe shall notify the member States of the Council of Europe, the non-member States which have participated in the elaboration of this Convention as well as any State which has acceded to, or has been invited to accede to, this Convention of:

  a. any signature;

  b. the deposit of any instrument of ratification, acceptance, approval or accession;

  c. any date of entry into force of this Convention in accordance with Articles 36 and 37;

  d. any declaration made under Article 40 or reservation made in accordance with Article 42;

  e. any other act, notification or communication relating to this Convention.

In witness whereof the undersigned, being duly authorised thereto, have signed this Convention.

Done at Budapest, this 23rd day of November 2001, in English and in French, both texts being equally authentic, in a single copy which shall be deposited in the archives of the Council of Europe. The Secretary General of the Council of Europe shall transmit certified copies to each member of the State of the Council of Europe, to the non-member States which have participated in the elaboration of this Convention, and to any State invited to accede to it.

CHILD ONLINE
PROTECTION ACT OF 1998

United State Code Title 15, Chapter 91

Sec. 6501. Definitions

In this chapter:

(1)   Child. The term "child" means an individual under the age of 13.

Section 6502. Regulation of unfair and deceptive acts and practices in connection with collection and use of personal information from and about children on the Internet.

(a)   Acts prohibited

(1) In general. It is unlawful for an operator of a website or online service directed to children, or any operator that has actual knowledge that is collecting personal information from a child, to collect personal information from a child in a manner that violates the regulations prescribed under subsection (b) of this section.

(2) Disclosure to parent protected. Notwithstanding paragraph (1), neither an operator of such a website or online service nor the operator's agent shall be held to be liable under any Federal or State law for any disclosure made in good faith and following reasonable procedures in responding to a request for disclosure of personal information under subsection (b)(1)(B)(iii) of this section to the parent of a child.

(b)   Regulations

(1) In general. Not later than one year after October 21, 1998, the Commission shall promulgate under section 553 of title 5 regulations that—

(A) require the operator of any website or online service directed to children that collects personal information from children or the operator of a website or online service that has actual knowledge that it is collecting personal information from a child—

(i)   to provide notice on the website of what information is collected from children by the operator, how the operator uses such information, and the operator's disclosure practices for such information; and

(ii)   to obtain verifiable parental consent for the collection, use, or disclosure of personal information from children.

(B) require the operator to provide, upon request of a parent under this subparagraph whose child has provided personal information to that website or online service, upon proper identification of that parent, to such parent—

(i)   a description of the specific types of personal information collected from the child by that operator;

(ii)   the opportunity at any time to refuse to permit the operator's further use or maintenance in retrievable form, or future online collection, of personal information from that child; and

(iii)   notwithstanding any other provision of law, a means that is reasonable under the circumstances for the parent to obtain any personal information collected from that child;

(C) prohibit conditioning a child's participation in a game, the offering of a prize, or another activity on the child disclosing more personal information than is reasonably necessary to participate in such activity; and

(D) require the operator of such a website or online service to establish and maintain reasonable procedures to protect the confidentiality, security, and integrity of personal information collected from children.

(2) When consent not required. The regulations shall provide that verifiable parental consent under paragraph (1)(A)(i) is not required in the case of—

(A) online contact information collected from a child that is used only to respond directly on a one-time basis to a specific request from the child and is not used to recontact the child and is not maintained in retrievable form by the operator;

(B) a request for the name or online contact information of a parent or child that is used for the sole purpose of obtaining parental consent or providing notice under this section and where such information is not maintained in retrievable form by the operator if parental consent is not obtained after a reasonable time;

(C) online contact information collection from a child that is used only to respond more than once directly to a specific request from the child and is not used to recontact the child beyond the scope of that request—

(i)   if, before any additional response after the initial response to the child, the operator uses reasonable efforts to provide a parent notice of the online contact information collected from the child, the purposes for which it is to be used, and an opportunity for the parent to request that the operator make no further use of the information and that it not be maintained in retrievable form; or

(ii) without notice to the parent in such circumstances as the Commission may determine are appropriate, taking into consideration the benefits to the child of access to information and services, and risks to the security and privacy of the child, in regulations promulgated under this subsection.

(D) the name of the child and online contact information (to the extent reasonable necessary to protect the safety of a child participant on the site)—

(i)   used only for the purpose of protecting such safety;

(ii)   not used to recontact the child or for any other purpose; and

(iii)   not disclosed on the site, if the operator uses reasonable effectors to provide a parent notice of the name and online contact information collected from the child, the purposes for which it is to be used, and an opportunity for the parent to request that the operator make no further use of the information and that it not be maintained in retrievable form; or

(E) the collection, use, or dissemination of such information by the operator of such a website or online service necessary—

(i)   to protect the security of integrity of its website;
(ii)   to take precautions against liability;
(iii)   to respond to judicial process; or
(iv)   to the extent permitted under other provision of law, to provide information to law enforcement agencies or an investigation on a matter related to public safety.

WORLD INTELLECTUAL PROPERTY ORGANIZATION COPYRIGHT TREATY

CRNR/DC/95
ORIGINAL: English
DATE: December 23, 1996

WORLD INTELLECTUAL PROPERTY ORGANIZATION
GENEVA

DIPLOMATIC CONFERENCE ON CERTAIN COPYRIGHT AND NEIGHBORING RIGHTS QUESTIONS
Geneva, December 2 to 20, 1996

WIPO PERFORMANCES AND PHONOGRAMS TREATY
adopted by the Diplomatic Conference on December 20, 1996

The agreed statements of the Diplomatic Conference (that adopted the Treaty) concerning certain provisions of the WPPT are reproduced in the original text of the Treaty as footnotes under the provisions concerned. These footnotes do not appear in the present text, but are replaced by bracketed references to the corresponding agreed statements.

Contents

Chapter IV: Common Provisions
Article 15: Right to Remuneration for Broadcasting and Communication to the Public
Article 16: Limitations and Exceptions
Article 17: Term of Protection
Article 18: Obligations concerning Technological Measures
Article 19: Obligations concerning Rights Management Information
Article 20: Formalities
Article 21: Reservations
Article 22: Application in Time
Article 23: Provisions on Enforcement of Rights

Chapter V: Administrative and Final Clauses
Article 24: Assembly
Article 25: International Bureau
Article 26: Eligibility for Becoming Party to the Treaty
Article 27: Rights and Obligations under the Treaty
Article 28: Signature of the Treaty
Article 29: Entry into Force of the Treaty
Article 30: Effective Date of Becoming Party to the Treaty
Article 31: Denunciation of the Treaty
Article 32: Languages of the Treaty
Article 33: Depositary

Preamble

The Contracting Parties,

Desiring to develop and maintain the protection of the rights of performers and producers of phonograms in a manner as effective and uniform as possible,

Recognizing the need to introduce new international rules in order to provide adequate solutions to the questions raised by economic, social, cultural and technological developments,

Recognizing the profound impact of the development and convergence of information and communication technologies on the production and use of performances and phonograms,

Recognizing the need to maintain a balance between the rights of performers and producers of phonograms and the larger public interest, particularly education, research and access to information,

Have agreed as follows:

Chapter I: General Provisions

Article 1: Relation to Other Conventions

(1) Nothing in this Treaty shall derogate from existing obligations that Contracting Parties have to each other under the International Convention for the Protection of Performers, Producers of Phonograms and Broadcasting Organizations done in Rome, October 26, 1961 (hereinafter the "Rome Convention").

(2) Protection granted under this Treaty shall leave intact and shall in no way affect the protection of copyright in literary and artistic works. Consequently, no provision of this Treaty may be interpreted as prejudicing such protection. [*See the agreed statement concerning Article 1(2)*]

(3) This Treaty shall not have any connection with, nor shall it prejudice any rights and obligations under, any other treaties.

Article 2: Definitions

For the purposes of this Treaty:

(a) "performers" are actors, singers, musicians, dancers, and other persons who act, sing, deliver, declaim, play in, interpret, or otherwise perform literary or artistic works or expressions of folklore;

(b) "phonogram" means the fixation of the sounds of a performance or of other sounds, or of a representation of sounds, other than in the form of a fixation incorporated in a cinematographic or other audiovisual work; [*See the agreed statement concerning Article 2(b)*]

(c) "fixation" means the embodiment of sounds, or of the representations thereof, from which they can be perceived, reproduced or communicated through a device;

(d) "producer of a phonogram" means the person, or the legal entity, who or which takes the initiative and has the responsibility for the first fixation of the sounds of a performance or other sounds, or the representations of sounds;

(e) "publication" of a fixed performance or a phonogram means the offering of copies of the fixed performance or the phonogram to the public, with the consent of the rightholder, and provided that copies are offered to the public in reasonable quantity; [*See the agreed statement concerning Article 2(e), 8, 9, 12, and 13*]

(f) "broadcasting" means the transmission by wireless means for public reception of sounds or of images and sounds or of the representations thereof; such transmission by satellite is also "broadcasting"; transmission of encrypted signals is "broadcasting" where the means for decrypting are provided to the public by the broadcasting organization or with its consent;

(g) "communication to the public" of a performance or a phonogram means the transmission to the public by any medium, otherwise than by broadcasting, of sounds of a performance or the sounds or the representations of sounds fixed in a phonogram. For the purposes of Article 15, "communication to the public" includes making the sounds or representations of sounds fixed in a phonogram audible to the public.

Article 3: Beneficiaries of Protection under this Treaty
[See the agreed statement concerning Article 3]

(1) Contracting Parties shall accord the protection provided under this Treaty to the performers and producers of phonograms who are nationals of other Contracting Parties.

(2) The nationals of other Contracting Parties shall be understood to be those performers or producers of phonograms who would meet the criteria for eligibility for protection provided under the Rome Convention, were all the Contracting Parties to this Treaty Contracting States of that Convention. In respect of these criteria of eligibility, Contracting Parties shall apply the relevant definitions in Article 2 of this Treaty. [*See the agreed statement concerning Article 3(2)*]

(3) Any Contracting Party availing itself of the possibilities provided in Article 5(3) of the Rome Convention or, for the purposes of Article 5 of the same Convention, Article 17 thereof shall make a notification as foreseen in those provisions to the Director General of the World Intellectual Property Organization (WIPO).

Article 4: National Treatment

(1) Each Contracting Party shall accord to nationals of other Contracting Parties, as defined in Article 3(2), the treatment it accords to its own nationals with regard to the exclusive rights specifically granted in this Treaty, and to the right to equitable remuneration provided for in Article 15 of this Treaty.

(2) The obligation provided for in paragraph (1) does not apply to the extent that another Contracting Party makes use of the reservations permitted by Article 15(3) of this Treaty.

Chapter II: Rights of Performers

Article 5: Moral Rights of Performers

(1) Independently of a performer's economic rights, and even after the transfer of those rights, the performer shall, as regards his live aural performances or performances fixed in phonograms, have the right to claim to be identified as the performer of his performances, except where omission is dictated by the manner of the use of the performance, and to object to any distortion, mutilation or other modification of his performances that would be prejudicial to his reputation.

(2) The rights granted to a performer in accordance with paragraph (1) shall, after his death, be maintained, at least until the expiry of the economic rights, and shall be exercisable by the persons or institutions authorized by the legislation of the Contracting Party where protection is claimed. However, those Contracting Parties whose legislation, at the moment of their ratification of or accession to this Treaty, does not provide for protection after the death of the performer of all rights set out in the preceding paragraph may provide that some of these rights will, after his death, cease to be maintained.

(3) The means of redress for safeguarding the rights granted under this Article shall be governed by the legislation of the Contracting Party where protection is claimed.

Article 6: Economic Rights of Performers in their Unfixed Performances

Performers shall enjoy the exclusive right of authorizing, as regards their performances:

(i) the broadcasting and communication to the public of their unfixed performances except where the performance is already a broadcast performance; and

(ii) the fixation of their unfixed performances.

Article 7: Right of Reproduction

Performers shall enjoy the exclusive right of authorizing the direct or indirect reproduction of their performances fixed in phonograms, in any manner or form. *[See the agreed statement concerning Articles 7, 11 and 16]*

Article 8: Right of Distribution

(1) Performers shall enjoy the exclusive right of authorizing the making available to the public of the original and copies of their performances fixed in phonograms through sale or other transfer of ownership.

(2) Nothing in this Treaty shall affect the freedom of Contracting Parties to determine the conditions, if any, under which the exhaustion of the right in paragraph (1) applies after the first sale or other transfer of ownership of the original or a copy of the fixed performance with the authorization of the performer. [*See the agreed statement concerning Articles 2(e), 8, 9, 12 and 13*]

Article 9: Right of Rental

(1) Performers shall enjoy the exclusive right of authorizing the commercial rental to the public of the original and copies of their performances fixed in phonograms as determined in the national law of Contracting Parties, even after distribution of them by, or pursuant to, authorization by the performer.

(2) Notwithstanding the provisions of paragraph (1), a Contracting Party that, on April 15, 1994, had and continues to have in force a system of equitable remuneration of performers for the rental of copies of their performances fixed in phonograms, may maintain that system provided that the commercial rental of phonograms is not giving rise to the material impairment of the exclusive right of reproduction of performers. [*See the agreed statement concerning Articles 2(e), 8, 9, 12 and 13*]

Article 10: Right of Making Available of Fixed Performances

Performers shall enjoy the exclusive right of authorizing the making available to the public of their performances fixed in phonograms, by wire or wireless means, in such a way that members of the public may access them from a place and at a time individually chosen by them.

Chapter III: Rights of Producers of Phonograms

Article 11: Right of Reproduction

Producers of phonograms shall enjoy the exclusive right of authorizing the direct or indirect reproduction of their phonograms, in any manner or form. [*See the agreed statement concerning Articles 7, 11 and 16*]

Article 12: Right of Distribution

(1) Producers of phonograms shall enjoy the exclusive right of authorizing the making available to the public of the original and copies of their phonograms through sale or other transfer of ownership.

(2) Nothing in this Treaty shall affect the freedom of Contracting Parties to determine the conditions, if any, under which the exhaustion of the right in paragraph (1) applies after the first sale or other transfer of ownership of the original or a copy of the phonogram with the authorization of the producer of the phonogram. [*See the agreed statement concerning Articles 2(e), 8, 9, 12 and 13*]

Article 13: Right of Rental

(1) Producers of phonograms shall enjoy the exclusive right of authorizing the commercial rental to the public of the original and copies of their phonograms, even after distribution of them by or pursuant to authorization by the producer.

(2) Notwithstanding the provisions of paragraph (1), a Contracting Party that, on April 15, 1994, had and continues to have in force a system of equitable remuneration of producers of phonograms for the rental of copies of their phonograms, may maintain that system provided that the commercial rental of phonograms is not giving rise to the material impairment of the exclusive rights of reproduction of producers of phonograms. [*See the agreed statement concerning Articles 2(e), 8, 9, 12 and 13*]

Article 14: Right of Making Available of Phonograms

Producers of phonograms shall enjoy the exclusive right of authorizing the making available to the public of their phonograms, by wire or wireless means, in such a way that members of the public may access them from a place and at a time individually chosen by them.

Chapter IV: Common Provisions

Article 15: Right to Remuneration for Broadcasting and Communication to the Public

(1) Performers and producers of phonograms shall enjoy the right to a single equitable remuneration for the direct or indirect use of phonograms published for commercial purposes for broadcasting or for any communication to the public.

(2) Contracting Parties may establish in their national legislation that the single equitable remuneration shall be claimed from the user by the performer or by the producer of a phonogram or by both. Contracting Parties may enact national legislation that, in the absence of an agreement between the performer and the producer of a phonogram, sets the terms according to which performers and producers of phonograms shall share the single equitable remuneration.

(3) Any Contracting Party may in a notification deposited with the Director General of WIPO, declare that it will apply the provisions of paragraph (1) only in respect of certain uses, or that it will limit their application in some other way, or that it will not apply these provisions at all.

(4) For the purposes of this Article, phonograms made available to the public by wire or wireless means in such a way that members of the public may access them from a place and at a time individually chosen by them shall be considered as if they had been published for commercial purposes. [*See the agreed statement concerning Article 15*]

Article 16: Limitations and Exceptions

(1) Contracting Parties may, in their national legislation, provide for the same kinds of limitations or exceptions with regard to the protection of performers and producers of phonograms as they provide for, in their national legislation, in connection with the protection of copyright in literary and artistic works.

(2) Contracting Parties shall confine any limitations of or exceptions to rights provided for in this Treaty to certain special cases which do not conflict with a normal exploitation of the performance or phonogram and do not unreasonably prejudice the legitimate interests of the performer or of the producer of the phonogram. [*See the agreed statement concerning Articles 7, 11 and 16, and the agreed statement concerning Article 16*]

Article 17: Term of Protection

(1) The term of protection to be granted to performers under this Treaty shall last, at least, until the end of a period of 50 years computed from the end of the year in which the performance was fixed in a phonogram.

(2) The term of protection to be granted to producers of phonograms under this Treaty shall last, at least, until the end of a period of 50 years computed from the end of the year in which the phonogram was published, or failing such publication within 50 years from fixation of the phonogram, 50 years from the end of the year in which the fixation was made.

Article 18: Obligations concerning Technological Measures

Contracting Parties shall provide adequate legal protection and effective legal remedies against the circumvention of effective technological measures that are used by performers or producers of phonograms in connection with the exercise of their rights under this Treaty and that restrict acts, in respect of their performances or phonograms, which are not authorized by the performers or the producers of phonograms concerned or permitted by law.

Article 19: Obligations concerning Rights Management Information

(1) Contracting Parties shall provide adequate and effective legal remedies against any person knowingly performing any of the following acts knowing, or with respect to civil remedies having reasonable grounds to know, that it will induce, enable, facilitate or conceal an infringement of any right covered by this Treaty:

(i) to remove or alter any electronic rights management information without authority;

(ii) to distribute, import for distribution, broadcast, communicate or make available to the public, without authority, performances, copies of fixed performances or phonograms knowing that electronic rights management information has been removed or altered without authority.

(2) As used in this Article, "rights management information" means information which identifies the performer, the performance of the performer, the producer of the phonogram, the phonogram, the owner of any right in the performance or phonogram, or information about the terms and conditions of use of the performance or phonogram, and any numbers or codes that represent such information, when any of these items of information is attached to a copy of a fixed performance or a phonogram or appears in connection with the communication or making available of a fixed performance or a phonogram to the public. [*See the agreed statement concerning Article 19*]

Article 20: Formalities

The enjoyment and exercise of the rights provided for in this Treaty shall not be subject to any formality.

Article 21: Reservations

Subject to the provisions of Article 15(3), no reservations to this Treaty shall be permitted.

Article 22: Application in Time

(1) Contracting Parties shall apply the provisions of Article 18 of the Berne Convention, *mutatis mutandis*, to the rights of performers and producers of phonograms provided for in this Treaty.

(2) Notwithstanding paragraph (1), a Contracting Party may limit the application of Article 5 of this Treaty to performances which occurred after the entry into force of this Treaty for that Party.

Article 23: Provisions on Enforcement of Rights

(1) Contracting Parties undertake to adopt, in accordance with their legal systems, the measures necessary to ensure the application of this Treaty.

(2) Contracting Parties shall ensure that enforcement procedures are available under their law so as to permit effective action against any act of infringement of rights covered by this Treaty, including expeditious remedies to prevent infringements and remedies which constitute a deterrent to further infringements.

Chapter V: Administrative and Final Clauses

Article 24: Assembly

(1)   (a) The Contracting Parties shall have an Assembly.

(b) Each Contracting Party shall be represented by one delegate who may be assisted by alternate delegates, advisors and experts.

(c) The expenses of each delegation shall be borne by the Contracting Party that has appointed the delegation. The Assembly may ask WIPO to grant financial assistance to facilitate the participation of delegations of Contracting Parties that are regarded as developing countries in conformity with the established practice of the General Assembly of the United Nations or that are countries in transition to a market economy.

(2)   (a) The Assembly shall deal with matters concerning the maintenance and development of this Treaty and the application and operation of this Treaty.

(b) The Assembly shall perform the function allocated to it under Article 26(2) in respect of the admission of certain intergovernmental organizations to become party to this Treaty.

(c) The Assembly shall decide the convocation of any diplomatic conference for the revision of this Treaty and give the necessary instructions to the Director General of WIPO for the preparation of such diplomatic conference.

(3)   (a) Each Contracting Party that is a State shall have one vote and shall vote only in its own name.

(b) Any Contracting Party that is an intergovernmental organization may participate in the vote, in place of its Member States, with a number of votes equal to the number of its Member States which are party to this Treaty. No such intergovernmental organization shall participate in the vote if any one of its Member States exercises its right to vote and vice versa.

(4) The Assembly shall meet in ordinary session once every two years upon convocation by the Director General of WIPO.

(5) The Assembly shall establish its own rules of procedure, including the convocation of extraordinary sessions, the requirements of a quorum and, subject to the provisions of this Treaty, the required majority for various kinds of decisions.

Article 25: International Bureau

The International Bureau of WIPO shall perform the administrative tasks concerning the Treaty.

Article 26: Eligibility for Becoming Party to the Treaty

(1) Any Member State of WIPO may become party to this Treaty.

(2) The Assembly may decide to admit any intergovernmental organization to become party to this Treaty which declares that it is competent in respect of, and has its own legislation binding on all its Member States on, matters covered by this Treaty and that it has been duly authorized, in accordance with its internal procedures, to become party to this Treaty.

(3) The European Community, having made the declaration referred to in the preceding paragraph in the Diplomatic Conference that has adopted this Treaty, may become party to this Treaty.

Article 27: Rights and Obligations under the Treaty

Subject to any specific provisions to the contrary in this Treaty, each Contracting Party shall enjoy all of the rights and assume all of the obligations under this Treaty.

Article 28: Signature of the Treaty

This Treaty shall be open for signature until December 31, 1997, by any Member State of WIPO and by the European Community.

Article 29: Entry into Force of the Treaty

This Treaty shall enter into force three months after 30 instruments of ratification or accession by States have been deposited with the Director General of WIPO.

Article 30: Effective Date of Becoming Party to the Treaty

This Treaty shall bind

(i) the 30 States referred to in Article 29, from the date on which this Treaty has entered into force;

(ii) each other State from the expiration of three months from the date on which the State has deposited its instrument with the Director General of WIPO;

(iii) the European Community, from the expiration of three months after the deposit of its instrument of ratification or accession if such instrument has been deposited after the entry into force of this Treaty according to Article 29, or, three months after the entry into force of this Treaty if such instrument has been deposited before the entry into force of this Treaty;

(iv) any other intergovernmental organization that is admitted to become party to this Treaty, from the expiration of three months after the deposit of its instrument of accession.

Article 31: Denunciation of the Treaty

This Treaty may be denounced by any Contracting Party by notification addressed to the Director General of WIPO. Any denunciation shall take effect one year from the date on which the Director General of WIPO received the notification.

Article 32: Languages of the Treaty

(1) This Treaty is signed in a single original in English, Arabic, Chinese, French, Russian and Spanish languages, the versions in all these languages being equally authentic.

(2) An official text in any language other than those referred to in paragraph (1) shall be established by the Director General of WIPO on the request of an interested party, after consultation with all the interested parties. For the purposes of this paragraph, "interested party" means any Member State of WIPO whose official language, or one of whose official languages, is involved and the European Community, and any other intergovernmental organization that may become party to this Treaty, if one of its official languages is involved.

Article 33: Depositary

The Director General of WIPO is the depositary of this Treaty.

[End]

Public Law 107-56 (excerpts)

Title II—Enhanced Surveillance Procedures

Sec. 201. Authority to Intercept Wire, Oral, and Electronic Communications relating to Terrorism.

Section 2516(1) of title 18, United States Code, is amended—

(1) by redesignating paragraph (p), as so redesignated by section 434(2) of the Antiterrorism and Effective Death Penalty Act of 1996 (Public Law 104 -132; 110 Stat. 1274), as paragraph (r); and

(2) by inserting after paragraph (p), as so redesignated by section 201(3) of the Illegal Immigration Reform and Immigrant Responsibility Act of 1996 (division C of Public Law 104-208; 110 Stat. 3009-565), the following new paragraph:

(q) any criminal violation of section 229 (relating to chemical weapons); or sections 2332, 2332a, 2332b, 2332d, 2339A, or 2339B of this title (relating to terrorism); or

Sec. 202. Authority to Intercept Wire, Oral, and Electronic Communications relating to Computer Fraud and Abuse Offenses.

Section 2516(1)(c) of title 18, United States Code, is amended by striking "and section 1341 (relating to mail fraud)," and inserting "section 1341 (relating to mail fraud), a felony violation of section 1030 (relating to computer fraud and abuse)."

Sec. 203. Authority to Share Criminal Investigative Information.

(a) Authority to Share Grand Jury Information:

(1) In general—Rule 6(e)(3)(C) of the Federal Rules of Criminal Procedure is amended to read as follows:

(C)(i) Disclosure otherwise prohibited by this rule of matters occurring before the grand jury may also be made—

(I) when so directed by a court preliminarily to or in connection with a judicial proceeding;

(II) when permitted by a court at the request of the defendant, upon a showing that grounds may exist for a motion to dismiss the indictment because of matters occurring before the grand jury;

(III) when the disclosure is made by an attorney for the government to another Federal grand jury;

(IV) when permitted by a court at the request of an attorney for the government, upon a showing that such matters may disclose a violation of state criminal law, to an appropriate official of a state or subdivision of a state for the purpose of enforcing such law; or

(V) when the matters involve foreign intelligence or counterintelligence (as defined in section 3 of the National Security Act of 1947 (50 U.S.C. 401a)), or foreign intelligence information (as defined in clause (iv) of this subparagraph), to any Federal law enforcement, intelligence, protective, immigration, national defense, or national security official in order to assist the official receiving that information in the performance of his official duties.

(ii) If the court orders disclosure of matters occurring before the grand jury, the disclosure shall be made in such manner, at such time, and under such conditions as the court may direct.

(iii) Any Federal official to whom information is disclosed pursuant to clause (i)(V) of this subparagraph may use that information only as necessary in the conduct of that person's official duties subject to any limitations on the unauthorized disclosure of such information. Within a reasonable time after such disclosure, an attorney for the government shall file under seal a notice with the court stating the fact that such information was disclosed and the departments, agencies, or entities to which the disclosure was made.

(iv) In clause (i)(V) of this subparagraph, the term "foreign intelligence information" means—

(I) information, whether or not concerning a United States person, that relates to the ability of the United States to protect against—

(aa) actual or potential attack or other grave hostile acts of a foreign power or an agent of a foreign power;

(bb) sabotage or international terrorism by a foreign power or an agent of a foreign power; or

(cc) clandestine intelligence activities by an intelligence service or network of a foreign power or by an agent of foreign power; or

(II) information, whether or not concerning a United States person, with respect to a foreign power or foreign territory that relates to—

(aa) the national defense or the security of the United States; or
(bb) the conduct of the foreign affairs of the United States.

(2) Conforming amendment. Rule 6(e)(3)(D) of the Federal Rules of Criminal Procedure is amended by striking "(e)(3)(C)(i)" and inserting "(e)(3)(C)(i)(I)".

(b) Authority to Share Electronic, Wire, and Oral Interception Information.

(1) Law enforcement. Section 2517 of title 18, United States Code, is amended by inserting at the end the following:

"(6) Any investigative or law enforcement officer, or attorney for the Government, who by any means authorized by this chapter, has obtained knowledge of the contents of any wire, oral, or electronic communication, or evidence derived there from, may disclose such contents to any other Federal law enforcement, intelligence, protective, immigration, national defense, or national security official to the extent that such contents include foreign intelligence or counterintelligence (as defined in section 3 of the National Security Act of 1947 (50 U.S.C. 401a)), or foreign intelligence information (as defined in subsection (19) of section 2510 of this title), to assist the official who is to receive that information in the performance of his official duties. Any Federal official who receives information pursuant to this provision may use that information only as necessary in the conduct of that person's official duties subject to any limitations on the unauthorized disclosure of such information."

(2) Definition. Section 2510 of title 18, United States Code, is amended by—

(A)   in paragraph (17), by striking "and" after the semicolon;
(B)   in paragraph (18), by striking the period and inserting "; and "; and
(C)   by inserting at the end the following:

(19) "foreign intelligence information" means—

(A) information, whether or not concerning a United States person, that relates to the ability of the United States to protect against—

(i) actual or potential attack or other grave hostile acts of a foreign power or an agent of a foreign power;

(ii) sabotage or international terrorism by a foreign power or an agent of a foreign power; or

(iii) clandestine intelligence activities by an intelligence service or network of a foreign power or by an agent of a foreign power; or

(B) information, whether or not concerning a United States person, with respect to a foreign power or foreign territory that relates to—

(i) the national defense or the security of the United States; or

(ii) the conduct of the foreign affairs of the United States.

(c) Procedures. The Attorney General shall establish procedures for the disclosure of information pursuant to section 2517(6) and Rule 6(e)(3)(C)(i)(V) of the Federal Rules of Criminal Procedure that identifies a United States person, as defined in section 101 of the Foreign Intelligence Surveillance Act of 1978 (50 U.S.C. 1801).

(d) Foreign Intelligence Information.

(1) In general. Notwithstanding any other provision of law, it shall be lawful for foreign intelligence or counterintelligence (as defined in section 3 of the National Security Act of 1947 (50 U.S.C. 401a)) or foreign intelligence information obtained as part of a criminal investigation to be disclosed to any Federal law enforcement, intelligence, protective, immigration, national defense, or national security official in order to assist the official receiving that information in the performance of his official duties. Any Federal official who receives information pursuant to this provision may use that information only as necessary in the conduct of that person's official duties subject to any limitations on the unauthorized disclosure of such information.

(2) Definition. In this subsection, the term "foreign intelligence information" means—

(A) information, whether or not concerning a United States person, that relates to the ability of the United States to protect against—

(i) actual or potential attack or other grave hostile acts of a foreign power or an agent of a foreign power;

(ii) sabotage or international terrorism by a foreign power or an agent of a foreign power; or

(iii) clandestine intelligence activities by an intelligence service or network of a foreign power or by an agent of a foreign power; or

(B) information, whether or not concerning a United States person, with respect to a foreign power or foreign territory that relates to—

(i) the national defense or the security of the United States; or

(ii) the conduct of the foreign affairs of the United States.

Sec. 204. Clarification of Intelligence Exceptions from Limitations on Interception and Disclosure of Wire, Oral, and Electronic Communications.

Section 2511(2)(f) of title 18, United States Code, is amended—

> (1) by striking "this chapter or chapter 121" and inserting "this chapter or chapter 121 or 206 of this title"; and
> (2) by striking "wire and oral" and inserting "wire, oral, and electronic."

Sec. 205. Employment of Translators by the Federal Bureau of Investigation.

(a) Authority. The Director of the Federal Bureau of Investigation is authorized to expedite the employment of personnel as translators to support counter terrorism investigations and operations without regard to applicable Federal personnel requirements and limitations.

(b) Security Requirements. The Director of the Federal Bureau of Investigation shall establish such security requirements as are necessary for the personnel employed as translators under subsection (a).

(c) Report. The Attorney General shall report to the Committees on the Judiciary of the House of Representatives and the Senate on—

(1) the number of translators employed by the FBI and other components of the Department of Justice;

(2) any legal or practical impediments to using translators employed by other Federal, State, or local agencies, on a full, part-time, or shared basis; and

(3) the needs of the FBI for specific translation services in certain languages, and recommendations for meeting those needs.

Sec. 206. Roving Surveillance Authority under the Foreign Intelligence Surveillance Act of 1978.

Section 105(c)(2)(B) of the Foreign Intelligence Surveillance Act of 1978 (50 U.S.C. 1805(c)(2)(B)) is amended by inserting ", or in circumstances where the Court finds that the actions of the target of the application may have the effect of thwarting the identification of a specified person, such other persons," after "specified person."

Sec. 207. Duration of FISA Surveillance of Non-United States Persons Who are Agents of a Foreign Power.

(a) Duration.

 (1) Surveillance. Section 105(e)(1) of the Foreign Intelligence Surveillance Act of 1978 (50 U.S.C. 1805(e)(1)) is amended by—

 (A) inserting "(A)" after "except that," and

 (B) inserting before the period the following: ", and (B) an order under this Act for a surveillance targeted against an agent of a foreign power, as defined in section 101(b)(1)(A) may be for the period specified in the application or for 120 days, whichever is less."

 (2) Physical Search. Section 304(d)(1) of the Foreign Intelligence Surveillance Act of 1978 (50 U.S.C. 1824(d)(1)) is amended by—

 (A) striking "forty-five" and inserting "90";

 (B) inserting "(A)" after "except that," and

 (C) inserting before the period the following: ", and (B) an order under this section for a physical search targeted against an agent of a foreign power as defined in section 101(b)(1)(A) may be for the period specified in the application or for 120 days, whichever is less."

(b) Extension.

 (1) In general. Section 105(d)(2) of the Foreign Intelligence Surveillance Act of 1978 (50 U.S.C. 1805(d)(2)) is amended by—

 (A) inserting "(A)" after "except that," and

 (B) inserting before the period the following: ", and (B) an extension of an order under this Act for a surveillance targeted against an agent of a foreign power as defined in section 101(b)(1)(A) may be for a period not to exceed 1 year."

 (2) Defined term. Section 304(d)(2) of the Foreign Intelligence Surveillance Act of 1978 (50 U.S.C. 1824(d)(2) is amended by inserting after "not a United States person," the following: "or against an agent of a foreign power as defined in section 101(b)(1)(A)."

Sec. 208. Designation of Judges.

Section 103(a) of the Foreign Intelligence Surveillance Act of 1978 (50 U.S.C. 1803(a)) is amended by

(1) striking "seven district court judges" and inserting "11 district court judges," and

(2) inserting "of whom no fewer than 3 shall reside within 20 miles of the District of Columbia" after "circuits."

Sec. 209. Seizure of Voice-Mail Messages Pursuant to Warrants.

Title 18, United States Code, is amended—

(1) in section 2510

    (A) in paragraph (1), by striking beginning with "and such" and all that follows through "communication," and

    (B) in paragraph (14), by inserting "wire or" after "transmission of," and

        (2) in subsections (a) and (b) of section 2703

        (A) by striking "Contents of electronic" and inserting "Contents of wire or electronic" each place it appears;

        (B) by striking "contents of an electronic" and inserting "contents of a wire or electronic" each place it appears; and

        (C) by striking "any electronic" and inserting "any wire or electronic" each place it appears.

Sec. 210. Scope of Subpoenas for Records of Electronic Communications.

Section 2703(c)(2) of title 18, United States Code, as redesignated by section 212, is amended—

(1) by striking "entity the name, address, local and long distance telephone toll billing records, telephone number or other subscriber number or identity, and length of service of a subscriber" and inserting the following: "entity the—

"(A) name;

"(B) address;

"(C) local and long distance telephone connection records, or records of session times and durations;

"(D) length of service (including start date) and types of service utilized;

"(E) telephone or instrument number or other subscriber number or identity, including any temporarily assigned network address; and

"(F) means and source of payment for such service (including any credit card or bank account number) of a subscriber;" and

(2) by striking "and the types of services the subscriber or customer utilized."

Sec. 211. Clarification of Scope.

Section 631 of the Communications Act of 1934 (47 U.S.C. 551) is amended—

(1) in subsection (c)(2)

(A) in subparagraph (B), by striking "or";

(B) in subparagraph (C), by striking the period at the end and inserting "; or"; and

(C) by inserting at the end the following:

(D) to a government entity as authorized under chapters 119, 121, or 206 of title 18, United States Code, except that such disclosure shall not include records revealing cable subscriber selection of video programming from a cable operator; and

(2) in subsection (h), by striking "A governmental entity" and inserting "Except as provided in subsection (c)(2)(D), a governmental entity.

Sec. 212. Emergency Disclosure of Electronic Communications to Protect Life and Limb.

(a) Disclosure of Contents.

(1) In general. Section 2702 of title 18, United States Code, is amended—

(A) by striking the section heading and inserting the following:

"Sec. 2702. Voluntary disclosure of customer communications or records;"

(B) in subsection (a)—

(i) in paragraph (2)(A), by striking "and" at the end;

(ii) in paragraph (2)(B), by striking the period and inserting "; and"; and

(iii) by inserting after paragraph (2) the following:

"(3) a provider of remote computing service or electronic communication service to the public shall not knowingly divulge a record or other information pertaining to a subscriber to or customer of such service (not including the contents of communications covered by paragraph (1) or (2)) to any governmental entity.";

(C) in subsection (b), by striking "Exceptions. A person or entity" and inserting "Exceptions for disclosure of communications. A provider described in subsection (a)";

(D) in subsection (b)(6)—

(i) in subparagraph (A)(ii), by striking "or";

(ii) in subparagraph (B), by striking the period and inserting "; or"; and

(iii) by adding after subparagraph (B) the following:

"(C) if the provider reasonably believes that an emergency involving immediate danger of death or serious physical injury to any person requires disclosure of the information without delay."; and

(E) by inserting after subsection (b) the following:

(c) Exceptions for Disclosure of Customer Records. A provider described in subsection (a) may divulge a record or other information pertaining to a subscriber to or customer of such service (not including the contents of communications covered by subsection (a)(1) or (a)(2))—

(1) as otherwise authorized in section 2703;

(2) with the lawful consent of the customer or subscriber;

(3) as may be necessarily incident to the rendition of the service or to the protection of the rights or property of the provider of that service;

(4) to a governmental entity, if the provider reasonably believes that an emergency involving immediate danger of death or serious physical injury to any person justifies disclosure of the information; or

(5) to any person other than a governmental entity.

(2) Technical and conforming amendment. The table of sections for chapter 121 of title 18, United States Code, is amended by striking the item relating to section 2702 and inserting the following:

"2702. Voluntary disclosure of customer communications or records."

(b) Requirements for Government Access.

(1) In general. Section 2703 of title 18, United States Code, is amended

(A) by striking the section heading and inserting the following:

"Sec. 2703. Required disclosure of customer communications or records";

(B) in subsection (c) by redesignating paragraph (2) as paragraph (3);

(C) in subsection (c)(1)—

(i) by striking "(A) Except as provided in subparagraph (B), a provider of electronic communication service or remote computing service may" and inserting "A governmental entity may require a provider of electronic communication service or remote computing service to";

(ii) by striking "covered by subsection (a) or (b) of this section" to any person other than a governmental entity.

"(B) A provider of electronic communication service or remote computing service shall disclose a record or other information pertaining to a subscriber to or customer of such service (not including the contents of communications covered by subsection (a) or (b) of this section) to a governmental entity" and inserting ")";

(iii) by redesignating subparagraph (C) as paragraph (2);

(iv) by redesignating clauses (i), (ii), (iii), and (iv) as subparagraphs (A), (B), (C), and (D), respectively;

(v) in subparagraph (D) (as redesignated) by striking the period and inserting "; or"; and

(vi) by inserting after subparagraph (D) (as redesignated) the following:

"(E) seeks information under paragraph (2)."; and

(D) in paragraph (2) (as redesignated) by striking "subparagraph (B)"and insert "paragraph (1)."

(2) Technical and conforming amendment. The table of sections for chapter 121 of title 18, United States Code, is amended by striking the item relating to section 2703 and inserting the following:

"2703. Required disclosure of customer communications or records."

Sec. 213. Authority for Delaying Notice of the Execution of a Warrant.

Section 3103a of title 18, United States Code, is amended—

(1) by inserting "(a) In General." before "In addition"; and

(2) by adding at the end the following:

(b) Delay. With respect to the issuance of any warrant or court order under this section, or any other rule of law, to search for and seize any property or material that constitutes evidence of a criminal offense in violation of the laws of the United States, any notice required, or that may be required, to be given may be delayed if

(1) the court finds reasonable cause to believe that providing immediate notification of the execution of the warrant may have an adverse result (as defined in section 2705);

(2) the warrant prohibits the seizure of any tangible property, any wire or electronic communication (as defined in section 2510), or, except as expressly provided in chapter 121, any stored wire or electronic information, except where the court finds reasonable necessity for the seizure; and

(3) the warrant provides for the giving of such notice within a reasonable period of its execution, which period may thereafter be extended by the court for good cause shown.

Sec. 214. Pen Register and Trap and Trace Authority under FISA.

(a) Applications and Orders. Section 402 of the Foreign Intelligence Surveillance Act of 1978 (50 U.S.C. 1842) is amended—

(1) in subsection (a)(1), by striking "for any investigation to gather foreign intelligence information or information concerning international terrorism" and inserting "for any investigation to obtain foreign intelligence information not concerning a United States person or to protect against international terrorism or clandestine intelligence activities, provided that such investigation of a United States person is not conducted solely upon the basis of activities protected by the first amendment to the Constitution";

(2) by amending subsection (c)(2) to read as follows:

"(2) a certification by the applicant that the information likely to be obtained is foreign intelligence information not concerning a United States person or is relevant to an ongoing investigation to protect against international terrorism or clandestine intelligence activities, provided that such investigation of a United States person is not conducted solely upon the basis of activities protected by the first amendment to the Constitution."

(3) by striking subsection (c)(3); and

(4) by amending subsection (d)(2)(A) to read as follows:

(A) shall specify

(i) the identity, if known, of the person who is the subject of the investigation;

(ii) the identity, if known, of the person to whom is leased or in whose name is listed the telephone line or other facility to which the pen register or trap and trace device is to be attached or applied;

(iii) the attributes of the communications to which the order applies, such as the number or other identifier, and, if known, the location of the telephone line or other facility to which the pen register or trap and trace device is to be attached or applied and, in the case of a trap and trace device, the geographic limits of the trap and trace order.

(b) Authorization During Emergencies. Section 403 of the Foreign Intelligence Surveillance Act of 1978 (50 U.S.C. 1843) is amended—

(1) in subsection (a), by striking "foreign intelligence information or information concerning international terrorism" and inserting "foreign intelligence information not concerning a United States person or information to protect against international terrorism or clandestine intelligence activities, provided that such investigation of a United States person is not conducted solely upon the basis of activities protected by the first amendment to the Constitution"; and

(2) in subsection (b)(1), by striking "foreign intelligence information or information concerning international terrorism" and inserting "foreign intelligence information not concerning a United States person or information to protect against international terrorism or clandestine intelligence activities, provided that such investigation of a United States person is not conducted solely upon the basis of activities protected by the first amendment to the Constitution."

Sec. 215. Access to Records and other Items under the Foreign Intelligence Surveillance Act.

Title V of the Foreign Intelligence Surveillance Act of 1978 (50 U.S.C. 1861 et seq.) is amended by striking sections 501 through 503 and inserting the following:

Sec. 501. Access to Certain Business Records for Foreign Intelligence and International Terrorism Investigations.

(a)(1) The Director of the Federal Bureau of Investigation or a designee of the Director (whose rank shall be no lower than Assistant Special Agent in Charge) may make an application for an order requiring the production of any tangible things (including books, records, papers, documents, and other items) for an investigation to protect against international terrorism or clandestine intelligence activities, provided that such investigation of a United States person is not conducted solely upon the basis of activities protected by the first amendment to the Constitution.

(2) An investigation conducted under this section shall—

(A) be conducted under guidelines approved by the Attorney General under Executive Order 12333 (or a successor order); and

(B) not be conducted of a United States person solely upon the basis of activities protected by the first amendment to the Constitution of the United States.

(b) Each application under this section—

(1) shall be made to—

(A) a judge of the court established by section 103(a); or

(B) a United States Magistrate Judge under chapter 43 of title 28, United States Code, who is publicly designated by the Chief Justice of the United States to have the power to hear applications and grant orders for the production of tangible things under this section on behalf of a judge of that court; and

(2) shall specify that the records concerned are sought for an authorized investigation conducted in accordance with subsection (a)(2) to protect against international terrorism or clandestine intelligence activities.

(c)(1) Upon an application made pursuant to this section, the judge shall enter an ex parte order as requested, or as modified, approving the release of records if the judge finds that the application meets the requirements of this section.

(2) An order under this subsection shall not disclose that it is issued for purposes of an investigation described in subsection (a).

(d) No person shall disclose to any other person (other than those persons necessary to produce the tangible things under this section) that the Federal Bureau of Investigation has sought or obtained tangible things under this section.

(e) A person who, in good faith, produces tangible things under an order pursuant to this section shall not be liable to any other person for such production. Such production shall not be deemed to constitute a waiver of any privilege in any other proceeding or context.

Sec. 502. Congressional Oversight.

(a) On a semiannual basis, the Attorney General shall fully inform the Permanent Select Committee on Intelligence of the House of Representatives and the Select Committee on Intelligence of the Senate concerning all requests for the production of tangible things under section 402.

(b) On a semiannual basis, the Attorney General shall provide to the Committees on the Judiciary of the House of Representatives and the Senate a report setting forth with respect to the preceding 6-month period—

(1) the total number of applications made for orders approving requests for the production of tangible things under section 402; and

(2) the total number of such orders either granted, modified, or denied.

Sec. 216. Modification of Authorities Relating to use of Pen Registers and Trap and Trace Devices.

(a) General Limitations. Section 3121(c) of title 18, United States Code, is amended—

(1) by inserting "or trap and trace device" after "pen register";

(2) by inserting ", routing, addressing," after "dialing"; and

(3) by striking "call processing" and inserting "the processing and transmitting of wire or electronic communications so as not to include the contents of any wire or electronic communications."

(b) Issuance of Orders.

(1) In general. Section 3123(a) of title 18, United States Code, is amended to read as follows:

(a) In General.

(1) Attorney for the government. Upon an application made under section 3122(a)(1), the court shall enter an ex parte order authorizing the installation and use of a pen register or trap and trace device anywhere within the United States, if the court finds that the attorney for the Government has certified to the court that the information likely to be obtained by such installation and use is relevant to an ongoing criminal investigation. The order, upon service of that order, shall apply to any person or entity providing wire or electronic communication service in the United States whose assistance may facilitate the execution of the order. Whenever such an order is served on any person or entity not specifically named in the order, upon request of such person or entity, the attorney for the Government or law enforcement or investigative officer that is serving the order shall provide written or electronic certification that the order applies to the person or entity being served.

(2) State investigative or law enforcement officer. Upon an application made under section 3122(a)(2), the court shall enter an ex parte order authorizing the installation and us of a pen register or trap and trace device within the jurisdiction of the court, if the court finds that the State law enforcement or investigative officer has certified to the court that the information likely to be obtained by such installation and use is relevant to an ongoing criminal investigation.

(3)(A) Where the law enforcement agency implementing an ex parte order under this subsection seeks to do so by installing and using its own pen register or trap and trace device on a packet-switched data network of a provider of electronic communication service to the public, the agency shall ensure that a record will be maintained which will identify—

(i) any officer or officers who installed the device and any officer or officers who accessed the device to obtain information from the network;

(ii) the date and time the device was installed, the date and time the device was uninstalled, and the date, time, and duration of each time the device is accessed to obtain information;

(iii) the configuration of the device at the time of its installation and any subsequent modification thereof; and

(iv) any information which has been collected by the device.

To the extent that the pen register or trap and trace device can be set automatically to record this information electronically, the record shall be maintained electronically throughout the installation and use of such device.

"(B) The record maintained under subparagraph (A) shall be provided ex parte and under seal to the court which entered the ex parte order authorizing the installation and use of the device within 30 days after termination of the order (including any extensions thereof)."

(2) Contents of order. Section 3123(b)(1) of title 18, United States Code, is amended—

(A) in subparagraph (A)—

(i) by inserting "or other facility" after "telephone line"; and

(ii) by inserting before the semicolon at the end "or applied"; and

(B) by striking subparagraph (C) and inserting the following:

"(C) the attributes of the communications to which the order applies, including the number or other identifier and, if known, the location of the telephone line or other facility to which the pen register or trap and trace device is to be attached or applied, and, in the case of an order authorizing installation and use of a trap and trace device under subsection (a)(2), the geographic limits of the order; and."

(3) Nondisclosure requirements. Section 3123(d)(2) of title 18, United States Code, is amended—

(A) by inserting "or other facility" after "the line"; and

(B) by striking ", or who has been ordered by the court" and inserting "or applied, or who is obligated by the order."

(c) Definitions.

(1) Court of competent jurisdiction. Section 3127(2) of title 18, United States Code, is amended by striking subparagraph (A) and inserting the following:

"(A) any district court of the United States (including a magistrate judge of such a court) or any United States court of appeals having jurisdiction over the offense being investigated; or."

(2) Pen register. Section 3127(3) of title 18, United States Code, is amended—

(A) by striking "electronic or other impulses" and all that follows through "is attached" and inserting "dialing, routing, addressing, or signaling information transmitted by an instrument or facility from which a wire or electronic communication is transmitted, provided, however, that such information shall not include the contents of any communication"; and

(B) by inserting "or process" after "device" each place it appears.

(3) Trap and trace device. Section 3127(4) of title 18, United States Code, is amended—

(A) by striking "of an instrument" and all that follows through the semicolon and inserting "or other dialing, routing, addressing, and signaling information reasonably likely to identify the source of a wire or electronic communication, provided, however, that such information shall not include the contents of any communication"; and

(B) by inserting "or process" after "a device."

> (4) Conforming amendment Section 3127(1) of title 18, United States Code, is amended—

(A) by striking "and"; and

(B) by inserting ", and 'contents' Sec." after "electronic communication service."

> (5) Technical amendment. Section 3124(d) of title 18, United States Code, is amended by striking "the terms of."

> (6) Conforming amendment. Section 3124(b) of title 18, United States Code, is amended by inserting "or other facility" after "the appropriate line."

Sec. 217. Interception of Computer Trespasser Communications.

Chapter 119 of title 18, United States Code, is amended—

(1) in section 2510—

(A) in paragraph (18), by striking "and" at the end;

(B) in paragraph (19), by striking the period and inserting a semicolon; and

(C) by inserting after paragraph (19) the following:

> (20) 'protected computer' has the meaning set forth in section 1030; and
> (21) 'computer trespasser'

(A) means a person who accesses a protected computer without authorization and thus has no reasonable expectation of privacy in any communication transmitted to, through, or from the protected computer; and

(B) does not include a person known by the owner or operator of the protected computer to have an existing contractual relationship with the owner or operator of the protected computer for access to all or part of the protected computer; and

(2) in section 2511(2), by inserting at the end the following:

(i) It shall not be unlawful under this chapter for a person acting under color of law to intercept the wire or electronic communications of a computer trespasser transmitted to, through, or from the protected computer, if—

> (I) the owner or operator of the protected computer authorizes the interception of the computer trespasser's communications on the protected computer;

(II) the person acting under color of law is lawfully engaged in an investigation;

(III) the person acting under color of law has reasonable grounds to believe that the contents of the computer trespasser's communications will be relevant to the investigation; and

(IV) such interception does not acquire communications other than those transmitted to or from the computer trespasser."

Sec. 218. Foreign Intelligence Information.

Sections 104(a)(7)(B) and section 303(a)(7)(B) (50 U.S.C. 1804(a)(7)(B) and 1823(a)(7)(B)) of the Foreign Intelligence Surveillance Act of 1978 are each amended by striking "the purpose" and inserting "a significant purpose."

Sec. 219. Single-Jurisdiction Search Warrants for Terrorism.

Rule 41(a) of the Federal Rules of Criminal Procedure is mended by inserting after "executed" the following: "and (3) in an investigation of domestic terrorism or international terrorism (as defined in section 2331 of title 18, United States Code), by a Federal magistrate judge in any district in which activities related to the terrorism may have occurred, for a search of property or for a person within or outside the district."

Sec. 220. Nationwide Service of Search Warrants for Electronic Evidence.

(a) In General. Chapter 121 of title 18, United States Code, is amended—

(1) in section 2703, by striking "under the Federal Rules of Criminal Procedure" every place it appears and inserting "using the procedures described in the Federal Rules of Criminal Procedure by a court with jurisdiction over the offense under investigation"; and

(2) in section 2711—

(A) in paragraph (1), by striking "and";

(B) in paragraph (2), by striking the period and inserting "; and"; and

(C) by inserting at the end the following:

"(3) the term 'court of competent jurisdiction' has the meaning assigned by section 3127, and includes any Federal court within that definition, without geographic limitation."

(b) Conforming Amendment. Section 2703(d) of title 18, United States Code, is amended by striking "described in section 3127(2)(A)."

Sec. 221. Trade Sanctions.

(a) In general. The Trade Sanctions Reform and Export Enhancement Act of 2000 (Public Law 106-387; 114 Stat. 1549A- 67) is amended—

(1) by amending section 904(2)(C) to read as follows:

"(C) used to facilitate the design, development, or production of chemical or biological weapons, missiles, or weapons of mass destruction."

(2) in section 906(a)(1)—

(A) by inserting ", the Taliban or the territory of Afghanistan controlled by the Taliban," after "Cuba"; and

(B) by inserting ", or in the territory of Afghanistan controlled by the Taliban," after "within such country"; and

(3) in section 906(a)(2), by inserting ", or to any other entity in Syria or North Korea" after "Korea."

(b) Application of the Trade Sanctions Reform and Export Enhancement Act. Nothing in the Trade Sanctions Reform and Export Enhancement Act of 2000 shall limit the application or scope of any law establishing criminal or civil penalties, including any executive order or regulation promulgated pursuant to such laws (or similar or successor laws), for the unlawful export of any agricultural commodity, medicine, or medical device to——

(1) a foreign organization, group, or person designated pursuant to Executive Order 12947 of January 23, 1995, as amended;

(2) a Foreign Terrorist Organization pursuant to the Antiterrorism and Effective Death Penalty Act of 1996 (Public Law 104-132);

(3) a foreign organization, group, or person designated pursuant to Executive Order 13224 (September 23, 2001);

(4) any narcotics trafficking entity designated pursuant to Executive Order 12978 (October 21, 1995) or the Foreign Narcotics Kingpin Designation Act (Public Law 106-120); or

(5) any foreign organization, group, or persons subject to any restriction for its involvement in weapons of mass destruction or missile proliferation.

Sec. 222. Assistance to Law Enforcement Agencies.

Nothing in this Act shall impose any additional technical obligation or requirement on a provider of a wire or electronic communication service or other person to furnish facilities or technical assistance. A provider of a wire or electronic communication service, landlord, custodian, or other person who furnishes facilities or technical assistance pursuant to section 216 shall be reasonably compensated for such reasonable expenditures incurred in providing such facilities or assistance.

Sec. 223. Civil Liability for Certain Unauthorized Disclosures.

(a) Section 2520 of title 18, United States Code, is amended—

(1) in subsection (a), after "entity," by inserting, "other than the United States,";

(2) by adding at the end the following:

"(f) Administrative Discipline. If a court or appropriate department or agency determines that the United States or any of its departments or agencies has violated any provision of this chapter, and the court or appropriate department or agency finds that the circumstances surrounding the violation raise serious questions about whether or not an officer or employee of the United States acted willfully or intentionally with respect to the violation, the department or agency shall, upon receipt of a true and correct copy of the decision and findings of the court or appropriate department or agency promptly initiate a proceeding to determine whether disciplinary action against the officer or employee is warranted. If the head of the department or agency involved determines that disciplinary action is not warranted, he or she shall notify the Inspector General with jurisdiction over the department or agency concerned and shall provide the Inspector General with the reasons for such determination"; and

(3) by adding a new subsection (g), as follows:

"(g) Improper Disclosure Is Violation. Any willful disclosure or use by an investigative or law enforcement officer or governmental entity of information beyond the extent permitted by section 2517 is a violation of this chapter for purposes of section 2520(a)."

(b) Section 2707 of title 18, United States Code, is amended—

(1) in subsection (a), after "entity," by inserting, " other than the United States";

(2) by striking subsection (d) and inserting the following:

"(d) Administrative Discipline. If a court or appropriate department or agency determines that the United States or any of its departments or agencies has violated any provision of this chapter, and the court or appropriate department or agency finds that the circumstances surrounding the violation raise serious questions about whether or not an officer or employee of the United States acted willfully or intentionally with respect to the violation, the department or agency shall, upon receipt of a true and correct copy of the decision and findings of the court or appropriate department or agency promptly initiate a proceeding to determine whether disciplinary action against the officer or employee is warranted. If the head of the department or agency involved determines that disciplinary action is not warranted, he or she shall notify the Inspector General with jurisdiction over the department or agency concerned and shall provide the Inspector General with the reasons for such determination." and

(3) by adding a new subsection (g), as follows:

"(g) Improper Disclosure. Any willful disclosure of a "record," as that term is defined in section 552a(a) of title 5, United States Code, obtained by an investigative or law enforcement officer, or a governmental entity, pursuant to section 2703 of this title, or from a device installed pursuant to section 3123 or 3125 of this title, that is not a disclosure made in the proper performance of the official functions of the officer or governmental entity making the disclosure, is a violation of this chapter. This provision shall not apply to information previously lawfully disclosed (prior to the commencement of any civil or administrative proceeding under this chapter) to the public by a Federal, State, or local governmental entity or by the plaintiff in a civil action under this chapter."

(c)(1) Chapter 121 of title 18, United States Code, is amended by adding at the end the following:

Sec. 2712. Civil Actions Against the United States.

(a) In General. Any person who is aggrieved by any willful violation of this chapter or of chapter 119 of this title or of sections 106(a), 305(a), or 405(a) of the Foreign Intelligence Surveillance Act of 1978 (50 U.S.C. 1801 et seq.) may commence an action in United States District Court against the United States to recover money damages. In any such action, if a person who is aggrieved successfully establishes such a violation of this chapter or of chapter 119 of this title or of the above specific provisions of title 50, the Court may assess as damages—

(1) actual damages, but not less than $10,000, whichever amount is greater; and

(2) litigation costs, reasonably incurred.

(b) Procedures. (1) Any action against the United States under this section may be commenced only after a claim is presented to the appropriate department or agency under the procedures of the Federal Tort Claims Act, as set forth in title 28, United States Code.

(2) Any action against the United States under this section shall be forever barred unless it is presented in writing to the appropriate Federal agency within 2 years after such claim accrues or unless action is begun within 6 months after the date of mailing, by certified or registered mail, of notice of final denial of the claim by the agency to which it was presented. The claim shall accrue on the date upon which the claimant first has a reasonable opportunity to discover the violation.

(3) Any action under this section shall be tried to the court without a jury.

(4) Notwithstanding any other provision of law, the procedures set forth in section 106(f), 305(g), or 405(f) of the Foreign Intelligence Surveillance Act of 1978 (50 U.S.C. 1801 et seq.) shall be the exclusive means by which materials governed by those sections may be reviewed.

(5) An amount equal to any award against the United States under this section shall be reimbursed by the department or agency concerned to the fund described in section 1304 of title 31, United States Code, out of any appropriation, fund, or other account (excluding any part of such appropriation, fund, or account that is available for the enforcement of any Federal law) that is available for the operating expenses of the department or agency concerned.

(c) Administrative Discipline. If a court or appropriate department or agency determines that the United States or any of its departments or agencies has violated any provision of this chapter, and the court or appropriate department or agency finds that the circumstances surrounding the violation raise serious questions about whether or not an officer or employee of the United States acted willfully or intentionally with respect to the possible violation, the department or agency shall, upon receipt of a true and correct copy of the decision and findings of the court or appropriate department or agency promptly initiate a proceeding to determine whether disciplinary action against the officer or employee is warranted. If the head of the department or agency involved determines that disciplinary action is not warranted, he or she shall notify the Inspector General with jurisdiction over the department or agency concerned and shall provide the Inspector General with the reasons for such determination.

(d) Exclusive Remedy. Any action against the United States under this subsection shall be the exclusive remedy against the United States for any claims within the purview of this section.

(e) Stay of Proceedings. (1) Upon the motion of the United States, the court shall stay any action commenced under this section if the court determines that civil discovery will adversely affect the ability of the Government to conduct a related investigation or the prosecution of a related criminal case. Such a stay shall toll the limitations periods of paragraph (2) of subsection (b).

(2) In this subsection, the terms "related criminal case" and "related investigation" mean an actual prosecution or investigation in progress at the time at which the request for the stay or

any subsequent motion to lift the stay is made. In determining whether an investigation or a criminal case is related to an action commenced under this section, the court shall consider the degree of similarity between the parties, witnesses, facts, and circumstances involved in the two proceedings, without requiring that any one or more factors be identical.

(3) In requesting a stay under paragraph (1), the Government may, in appropriate cases, submit evidence ex parte in order to avoid disclosing any matter that may adversely affect a related investigation or a related criminal case. If the Government makes such an ex parte submission, the plaintiff shall be given an opportunity to make a submission to the court, not ex parte, and the court may, in its discretion, request further information from either party.

(2) The table of sections at the beginning of chapter 121 is amended to read as follows:

"2712. Civil Action against the United States."

Sec. 224. Sunset.

(a) In General. Except as provided in subsection (b), this title and the amendments made by this title (other than sections 203(a), 203(c), 205, 208, 210, 211, 213, 216, 219, 21, and 222, and the amendments made by those sections) shall cease to have effect on December 31, 2005.

(b) Exception. With respect to any particular foreign intelligence investigation that began before the date on which the provisions referred to in subsection (a) cease to have effect, or with respect to any particular offense or potential offense that began or occurred before the date on which such provisions cease to have effect, such provisions shall continue in effect.

Sec. 225. Immunity for Compliance with FISA Wiretap.

Section 105 of the Foreign Intelligence Surveillance Act of 1978 (50 U.S.C. 1805) is amended by inserting after subsection (g) the following:

"(h) No cause of action shall lie in any court against any provider of a wire or electronic communication service, landlord, custodian, or other person (including any officer, employee, agent, or other specified person thereof) that furnishes any information, facilities, or technical assistance in accordance with a court order or request for emergency assistance under this Act."

INDEX

1